Advance Praise for
The World as It Could Be

"A leading expert on the Church's social teachings, Father Williams writes with verve and clarity on the development of doctrine in fields as diverse as the legitimate use of force, global governance, our duties to our neighbors, and the challenge of scientific advances that have run ahead of moral reflection."

—Mary Ann Glendon,
Professor of Law, Harvard University

"This is an important book—a richly sourced, intelligent and engaging overview of the roots and current state of Catholic social thought. Grounded in excellent scholarship and written with admirable clarity and balance, this text will be an invaluable resource for Catholics serious about understanding the social implications of their faith for years to come."

— + Charles J. Chaput,
O.F.M. Cap., Archbishop of Philadelphia

"This volume not only explores the riches of Catholic social teaching, but clarifies and develops important aspects of that teaching. It is essential reading for anyone interested in Catholic social thought."

—Kenneth L. Grasso,
Texas State University

"Someone who knew nothing of the tradition of Catholic thought about morality and social life would find in *The World As It Could Be* a lucid and compelling introduction to the subject. But Fr. Williams' book is far more than that. It is a philosophically sophisticated engagement with that great and challenging tradition by a scholar who recognizes that, for all its virtues, it is and will always be a work in progress."

—Robert P. George, McCormick
Professor of Jurisprudence, Princeton University

THE WORLD AS
IT COULD BE

THE WORLD AS IT COULD BE

CATHOLIC SOCIAL THOUGHT FOR A NEW GENERATION

THOMAS D. WILLIAMS

A HERDER & HERDER BOOK
THE CROSSROAD PUBLISHING COMPANY

The Crossroad Publishing Company
www.CrossroadPublishing.com

Printed in the United States of America.
The text of this book is set in Adobe Garamond
The display face is Mrs. Eaves

Project Management by
The Crossroad Publishing Company
John Jones

For this edition numerous people have shared their talents and ideas, and we gratefully acknowledge Fr. Thomas D. Williams, who has been most gracious during the course of our cooperation.

We thank especially:

Cover design: George Foster   Text design: Web Fusion
Development: Claudia Volkman and John Jones   Printing: Versa Press

Message development, text development, package, and market positioning by
The Crossroad Publishing Company

Cataloging-in-Publication Data is available from the Library of Congress
Books published by The Crossroad Publishing Company may be purchased at special quantity discount rates for classes and institutional use. For information, please e-mail info@CrossroadPublishing.com
ISBN 13: 978-0-8245-2666-5

14 13 12 11

Table of Contents

Abbreviations of Magisterial Documents cited (in alphabetical order)[1]

CA—Pope John Paul II, encyclical letter *Centesimus Annus* (1991).

CCC—*Catechism of the Catholic Church* (1992).

CL—Pope John Paul II, post-synodal apostolic exhortation *Christifideles Laici* (1988).

CSD—Pontifical Council for Justice and Peace, *Compendium of the Social Doctrine of the Church* (2004).

CV—Pope Benedict XVI, encyclical letter *Caritas in Veritate* (2009).

DCE—Pope Benedict XVI, encyclical letter *Deus Caritas Est* (2005).

DF—First Vatican Council, Dogmatic Constitution on the Catholic Faith, *Dei Filius* (1870).

DH—Second Vatican Council, Declaration on Religious Freedom, *Dignitatis Humanae* (1965).

DI—Congregation for the Doctrine of the Faith, Declaration on the Unicity and Salvific Universality of Jesus Christ and the Church, *Dominus Iesus* (2000).

DIU—Pope Leo XIII, encyclical letter *Diuturnum* (1881).

DS—H. Denzinger and A. Schönmetzer, eds., *Enchiridion Symbolorum,* 33rd ed. (Freiburg, 1965).

DV—Congregation for the Doctrine of the Faith, Instruction on Respect for Human Life in its Origin and on the Dignity of Procreation, *Donum Vitæ* (1987).

EV—Pope John Paul II, encyclical letter *Evangelium Vitae* (1995).

FC—Pope John Paul II, post-synodal apostolic exhortation *Familiaris Consortio* (1981).

FR—Pope John Paul II, encyclical letter *Fides et Ratio* (1998).

GS—Second Vatican Council, Pastoral Constitution on the Church in the Modern World, *Gaudium et Spes* (1965).

HG—Pope Pius XII, encyclical letter *Humani Generis* (1950).

HV—Pope Paul VI, encyclical letter *Humanae Vitae* (1968).

ID—Pope Leo XIII, encyclical letter *Immortale Dei* (1885).

LE—Pope John Paul II, encyclical letter *Laborem Exercens* (1981).

LC—Congregation for the Doctrine of the Faith, Instruction on Christian Freedom and Liberation, *Libertatis Conscientia* (1986).

LG—Second Vatican Council, Dogmatic Constitution on the Church, *Lumen Gentium* (1965).

LF—Pope John Paul II, Letter to Families, *Gratissimam Sane* (1994).

LN—Congregation for the Doctrine of the Faith, Instruction on Certain Aspects of the "Theology of Liberation," *Libertatis Nuntius* (1984).

LP—Pope Leo XIII, encyclical letter *Libertas* (1888).

LW—Pope John Paul II, Letter to Women (1995).

MM—Pope John XXIII, encyclical letter *Mater et Magistra* (1961).

OA—Pope Paul VI, apostolic letter *Octogesima Adveniens* (1971).

OT—Second Vatican Council, Decree on Priestly Formation, *Optatam Totius* (1965).

PO—Pope Leo XIII, encyclical letter *Pastoralis Officii* (1891).

PP—Pope Paul VI, encyclical letter *Populorum Progressio* (1967).

PRM—Pope Pius XII, Pentecost Radio Message of 1941.

PT—Pope John XXIII, encyclical letter *Pacem in Terris* (1963).

QA—Pope Pius XI, encyclical letter *Quadragesimo Anno* (1931).

RM—Pope John Paul II, encyclical letter *Redemptoris Missio* (1990).

RN—Pope Leo XIII, encyclical letter *Rerum Novarum* (1891).

SRS—Pope John Paul II, encyclical letter *Sollicitudo Rei Socialis* (1987).

SS—Pope Benedict XVI, encyclical letter *Spe Salvi* (2007).

VS—Pope John Paul II, encyclical letter *Veritatis Splendor* (1993).

Introduction

The Need for Development

The "development of doctrine" debates of the nineteenth century culminated in the now-classic "Essay on the Development of Christian Doctrine," first published by Blessed John Henry Newman in 1845. Drawing on the writings of the Church Fathers, Newman sought to lay out stable guidelines to distinguish between the authentic development of doctrine and its corruption. For Newman, such arguments held more than academic interest. They provided assurance that the Roman Catholic Church (into which he was in the process of incorporating) with its centuries-old structures and doctrines was indeed the same Church founded by Jesus Christ upon the Apostles.

Newman set out to explain certain difficulties and apparent historical inconsistencies in Catholic belief and practice, but in so doing he also produced an *apologia* for the necessity of the development of doctrine. Development is not only a historical fact but also an existential necessity. In the first place, this development burgeons, as Newman realized, as an essential fruit of theological study. Theology, in its classical sense as *fides quaerens intellectum*, seeks an ever deeper understanding of those truths embraced through faith and thus offers the Church new ways of understanding and formulating her beliefs. As Newman wrote, these truths "from their very depth and richness cannot be fully understood at once, but are more and more clearly expressed and taught the longer they last."[1] Secondly, the emergence of variant theological opinions and heterodox beliefs also stimulates the development of doctrine by prodding the Church's Magisterium to clarify the Church's stand on questions heretofore undefined. Although not a good in itself (*pace* contemporary proponents of "faithful dissent"), heresy yields the positive byproduct of more precise expressions of the Church's beliefs. Finally, from a more pastoral angle, the development of doctrine also issues from efforts to make the deposit of faith intelligible to people of different historical and cultural milieus, through the adaptation of its language and explanations to changing situations.

The doctrines considered by Newman in his "Essay" dealt principally with articles of faith and sacramental discipline. Among these figured topics such as the Canon of the New Testament, the consubstantiality of the Father and the Son, the Eucharist, original sin, and infant baptism, all of which form part of what we would now call dogmatic or systematic theology. Yet a case can certainly be made that where doctrine in the area of *dogmatics* inevitably develops to accommodate new historical situations, the Church's *moral* doctrine necessarily develops at a faster pace still.[2] Advances in the biomedical and genetic sciences, for example, necessitate a permanently updated response from the Church to guide and form the consciences of the faithful. Complex ethical issues of recent vintage, such as cloning or stem cell research, have arisen because of scientific progress that opens up whole new arenas of moral concern. As the medical sciences acquire the technical ability to *do* more, moral theology must furnish guidelines regarding the associated ethical issues that such progress creates.

Nowhere is the need for ongoing development more acutely felt, however, than in the area of the Church's social teaching—that branch of moral theology that deals with the ordering of social, political, economic, and cultural realities according to the exigencies of the Gospel.[3] If one might be permitted to say so, this continuous evolution and open-ended *aggiornamento* make Catholic social thought one of the most exciting areas of theology in which to be engaged. The pace with which society itself evolves necessitates a corresponding effort on the part of the Church to comprehend, analyze, and evaluate these changes and their relationship to the common good. More than any other theological discipline, Catholic social thought bears an inherent dynamism and elasticity that allow it to effectively respond to the ethical concerns of each successive generation. It taps the imagination and engages the conscience of every new generation of men and women to envision *the world as it could be*, if all temporal realities were imbued with the spirit of the Gospel of Jesus Christ.

The foundational principles underlying Catholic social doctrine, based as they are on human nature and Christian revelation, do not change.

Therefore, the centrality of the human person and his inviolable dignity, concerns for justice and charity, and attention to the common good will always form the base of the Church's social thought. Yet many other corollary judgments require an ongoing adaptation.

A recent case-in-point is Catholic just war theory. Originally articulated by St. Augustine and restructured by Thomas Aquinas, Catholic understanding of conditions for declaring and waging war continues to undergo needed development. The fact that such doctrines develop does not necessarily mean that our predecessors got it wrong or that the Church is simply "changing her mind" on prior teaching, but rather that major shifts in geo-political structures and military practice have radically altered the character and moral makeup of human warfare. Reacting to the emergence of weapons of mass destruction and the horrors of World War II, the Vatican II Constitution on the Church in the Modern World, *Gaudium et Spes*, called for a reevaluation of the conditions for war. Recent development of more precise, guided weaponry and the emergence of new forms of terrorism have led to further study, debate, and re-elaboration of ethical conditions for engaging in warfare, and this discussion will surely continue in the years to come.

What is true for just war theory is equally true of a plethora of similar social questions. Rapid changes in world economic markets, with attendant growth in economic interdependence as well as financial speculation, have given birth to a broad gamut of moral questions unknown to ethicists a mere generation ago. The social and cultural dimensions of bioethical advances highlight the cross-pollination between Catholic social thought and other areas of special moral theology, occasioned by a world of instant communication and online information. Unprecedented contact with other cultures and systems of thought underscores the need to revisit questions of religious and ethical pluralism, religious liberty, and freedom of conscience.

This book intends to offer a modest contribution to this ongoing ethical discussion. Without the slightest pretense of offering a comprehensive analysis of contemporary social justice issues, I will present a number of ethical reflections that seem particularly relevant in these first decades of the twenty-first century, especially in the light of the pontificates of John Paul II and Benedict XVI. Having taught Catholic social doctrine for a number of years in the setting of a Roman pontifical university, I have been able to follow some of the ebb and flow of Catholic social thought both in Rome and abroad, and to benefit from discussions with eminent thinkers in this area. Some of the chapters of this book originally were presented as papers for academic conferences or appeared as articles in theological journals, while others have been written specifically for this publication. All have been reworked to produce what I hope is a fluid, organic treatment of a connected group of pressing issues for Catholic social thought.

I will begin by looking at the question of multiculturalism in its manifold expressions, reconsidering the relationship of public to private, the one and the many, and particular and common good. From there, I will move to an exploration of dignity as the foundational concept undergirding human rights, especially as it is presently challenged in its universality and human exclusivity. After these broader considerations I will devote three consecutive chapters to areas where life ethics intersects with social ethics, namely the abortion question, human violence, and the death penalty. Our discussion will then shift to a more traditional aspect of Catholic social teaching concerning economic society, which will also occupy three chapters. Here I will first consider the legacy of Pope Paul VI's landmark encyclical *Populorum Progressio*, especially through the lens of the social Magisterium of Popes John Paul II and Benedict XVI. I will then proceed to question the suitability of "distribution" as a central point of reference for discussions on economic development. Finally, I will examine the much debated question of global governance, drawing inspiration from Benedict XVI's social encyclical, *Caritas in Veritate*. The next two chapters explore the question of religious liberty—first as it distinguishes itself from the contemporary "virtue" of tolerance, and second, in regard to the discernment necessary among religions themselves. I will close the book with two chapters on Benedict XVI's specific contribution to Catholic social thought as expressed in his first encyclical, *Deus Caritas Est*, and in his 2009 social encyclical, *Caritas in Veritate*.

We must also make an important distinction between the theological discipline called "Catholic social doctrine" (or "Catholic social teaching") and the broader area of Catholic social thought. Unlike other areas of theological study, such as sexual ethics or Christology, the content of Catholic social doctrine is defined by a corpus of magisterial teaching.[4] Although it makes use of auxiliary texts and materials, the proper matter of the discipline and therefore its content is determined principally by these papal texts. Being first a "doctrine," rather than a field of study, it makes sense that these papal documents have a defining character. Thus, university and seminary courses of Catholic social doctrine usually explain and discuss the development and content of this growing corpus of doctrine, often making use of collections of the social encyclicals as their point of reference or textbook. Catholic social thought, on the other hand, refers to the broader discussion among Catholic scholars that takes this doctrine as its inspiration and permanent reference point.

I hasten to repeat that this book in no way attempts to be comprehensive in its scope. It is heuristic in its nature and aims only to stoke the fires of public debate by bringing up some questions that may be overlooked in many contemporary forums of Catholic social thought. Challenging the status quo of social ethics not only in practice but also in theory forms an essential part of our discipline, and I welcome the corrections and criticisms that must necessarily ensue from such an endeavor. This is all for the general good and serves to enrich all who commit themselves to this discipline. Understanding *the world as it could be* is an ever developing and never finalized endeavor, one that demands a cooperative effort on the part of all Christian scholars, and indeed, of all people of good will.

Chapter 1

Unity, Diversity, and the Common Good

There is perhaps no older nor more enduring philosophical problem than that of "the one and the many." Whether we are talking about ancient Milesian speculation regarding first matter—a single sort of stuff from which all else emerges—or about the controversies between Heraclitus' world in flux and Parmenides' unity of all things, problems of change and permanence, diversity and unity, have dominated philosophy in the Western world from the beginning.

Contemporary theologians, too, often struggle with similar themes. In 2001, Cardinals Joseph Ratzinger and Walter Kasper famously faced off in opposing articles in *America* magazine on the question of the relationship between the universal Church and the local churches.[1] The unity of the faith and the plurality of theologies is another area where this strain can be observed and where the Magisterium has felt the need to step in on more than one occasion.[2] Such theological tensions between the one and the many can also be observed in the areas of soteriology (e.g., *Dominus Iesus* or the CDF's response to Jacques Dupuis' *Toward a Christian Theology of Religious Pluralism*[3]), liturgy (e.g., the question of inculturation versus the universality of the one liturgy), and moral theology (e.g., the virulent responses to John Paul's attempt to rein in some heterodox theories in his 1993 encyclical letter *Veritatis Splendor*).

Yet tensions between the one and the many are not restricted to the domain of academic speculation. They are especially evident at the level of socio-political organization and of culture and therefore are of particular interest to Catholic social doctrine. Many of today's most heated controversies swirl around these very tensions. Which is more important, the citizen or the state? Which should take preference, individual freedoms or the common good? Thus, on the one hand, the trend of "political correctness" seeks to rein in cultural heterodoxies by holding up a series of moral axioms to which all members of society are called to adhere. The political correctness movement seeks "unity" and "homogeneity," at least regarding certain cultural sensibilities. This *centripetal* force of political correctness is contrasted by the "multiculturalist" movement, which exerts a contrary *centrifugal* force on society, celebrating diversity in its manifold expressions. Multiculturalism presents variety not only as a fact to be acknowledged but also as a good to be pursued.

In this context, the question facing Catholic social thought becomes:

- How do we achieve social cohesion in the midst of societal multiplicity?
- Which should take precedence?
- By what criteria and on what grounds should one be sacrificed to the other?
- How can harmony be achieved between them, and in what does it consist?

In the pages that follow, I will examine the relationship between the one and the many in the context of the free society, drawing especially on the thought of Pope John Paul II in his 1991 encyclical *Centesimus Annus*. Striking the correct balance between the two, and indeed correctly positing the nature of their relationship, is essential to the right ordering of human society.

Individualism and Collectivism

At the socio-political level, the two extreme positions regarding the one and the many generally go by the names of individualism and collectivism. Individualism would refer to a social theory emphasizing the liberty, rights, and independent action of the individual, whereas collectivism—the socialist principle of control by the people collectively, or the state—sees the good of the social body as paramount. Our generation instinctively rejects attempts at homogenization and recoils from anything that resembles walking in mindless lockstep. Diversity is not only recognized but celebrated and promoted. At the same time, people recognize a need for universal principles or common values that would serve as moral glue to cement a group of individuals into a true human community and protect minorities from the hegemony of majority opinion.[4]

In a 1961 essay, Karol Wojtyla characterized these two extremes in the following way:

> On the one hand, persons may easily place their own individual good above the common good of the collectivity, attempting to subordinate the collectivity to themselves and use it for their individual good. This is the error of individualism, which gave rise to liberalism in modern history and to capitalism in economics. On the other hand, society, in aiming at the alleged good of the whole, may attempt to subordinate persons to itself in such a way that the true good of persons is excluded and they themselves fall prey to the collectivity. This is the error of totalitarianism, which in modern times has borne the worst possible fruit.[5]

Now some would assert that the very nature of a "free society" would favor individualism over collectivism. Where socialist collectivism curbs the freedom of its citizens, liberal individualism would seem to guarantee it. Actually, the solution proposed by Pope John Paul II in *Centesimus Annus* is more subtle and ultimately more satisfying.

In *Centesimus Annus*, Pope John Paul begins the fifth chapter on "State and Culture" with praise of the "rule of law," where the law is sovereign "and not the arbitrary will of individuals."[6] He contrasts an organization of society containing a balance of powers—legislative, executive, and judicial—with different forms of totalitarianism (here he specifically mentions Marxist Leninism), where some arrogate to themselves the exercise of absolute power over the rest. Up to this point, his analysis is fairly standard and would garner a broad consensus. It is the statement that follows that departs from conventional wisdom.

John Paul affirms that the real difference between totalitarianism and democracy based on a rule of law is not so much the concentration of power into a single individual or party versus a system of checks and balances that broadens the base of power, but rather the more fundamental understanding of truth and the common good.[7] Totalitarianism is based on voluntarism, or the supremacy of will over reason, whereas a rule of law places will at the service of reason. A rule of law reflects natural justice—the ethical demands of the truth of the human person that are a requirement of right reason. The reason John Paul speaks of, however, refers not only to technical skill and internal logic but also extends to the fullness of truth and the transcendence of the human person. According to John Paul, "totalitarianism arises out of a denial of truth in the objective sense. If there is no transcendent truth in obedience to which man achieves his full identity, then there is no sure principle for guaranteeing just relations between people" (no. 44).

The rule of political expediency is characteristic of a totalitarian state. The breakdown of moral absolutes is necessary, in fact, to permit such a state the free exercise of statecraft with no accountability to transcendent principles. The will of the ruler becomes the sole criterion of moral good and evil.[8] Thus, John Paul wrote that the state "which sets itself above all values, cannot tolerate the affirmation of an *objective criterion of good and evil* beyond the will of those in power, since such a criterion, in given circumstances, could be used to judge their actions."[9]

The consequent evil of such a political system is its denial of a transcendent point of reference outside of the will of individuals by which to guarantee and indeed understand just relations between people. The denial of objective truth importantly entails "the denial of the transcendent dignity of the human person who, as the visible image of the invisible God, is therefore by his very nature the subject of rights which no one may violate—no individual, group, class, nation or State."[10]

Therefore, the true benefit of a political order based on a rule of law does not stem merely from a balance of powers and the consequent balance of opposing personal interests. The real superiority of such a system is its implicit or explicit recognition that outside the system itself exist objective principles of justice, to which the system is accountable and which it serves to advance. The division of political powers exists not merely to assure a system of checks and balances on personal will and self-interest, but in order to achieve justice and the common good.[11] Here, will is subject to reason and not vice versa.

It is in this light that we can understand John Paul's oft-cited remark in its deepest sense: "A democracy without values easily turns into open or thinly disguised totalitarianism."[12] This is not an exercise in rhetoric for dramatic effect. Although democracy may seem to be the antithesis of totalitarianism, since it distributes political power among the citizenry and their elected representatives, if it fails to recognize objective truth and goodness beyond political expediency, it literally falls into the same error found at the heart of totalitarianism.[13] It denies the role of moral reason in the organization of society and allows the will to reign.

"If one does not acknowledge transcendent truth," John Paul continues, "then the force of power takes over, and each person tends to make full use of the means at his disposal in order to impose his own interests or his own opinion, with no regard for the rights of others. People are then respected only to the extent that they can be exploited for selfish ends."[14] In other words, when the Arthurian "might for right" falls back into the Thucydidean "might makes right," the result is totalitarianism.

In his 1995 encyclical letter, *Evangelium Vitae*, John Paul drew out the practical consequences of such a transition, especially as regards the right to life. He noted that at the level of politics and government, the right to life is often questioned or denied on the basis of executive fiat or the will of the majority.

"This is the sinister result of a relativism which reigns unopposed," he writes, where "the 'right' ceases to be such because it is no longer firmly founded on the inviolable dignity of the person, but is made subject to the will of the stronger part."[15] When this happens, democracy denies itself and "effectively moves towards a form of totalitarianism."[16]

The Common Good: The State's Reason for Being

And here we come to the central social principle of the common good. It is an established principle of Catholic social thought that the state or political authority exists to promote the common good of society.[17] This is its sole *raison d'être*. Yet here differing notions of the common good will yield radically different conclusions regarding the nature and role of the state.

A view of the common good as the good of the abstract collectivity, as manifested in twentieth-century totalitarianisms, is unacceptable on several grounds. The individual is subsumed into the whole and has value only in relation to the state. Even if Marxist Communism had "worked," for example, on a practical level, it would have been a pyrrhic victory. A state that functions as perfectly as a Swiss watch, but whose members are reduced to the role of pieces of that watch, does not yield a truly human society at all. Society has no value apart from its members, and the good of a society must always be evaluated by the good not only of the whole but of the parts as well. A polity that does not protect and promote the freedom and creativity of its members has failed in what is most essential to human society.

If, on the other hand, the common good is viewed through a utilitarian optic as the greatest pleasure (or happiness) for the greatest number, then it is likewise difficult to see how the totalitarianism spoken of by Pope John Paul can be avoided. This is the real danger of modern democracies with an underlying individualistic ethic—a calculus of maximizing happiness where each member of society is assigned a value of 1 permits and even encourages the sacrifice of the minority for the majority. The maximization of happiness often demands this. Where one must be shot in order to save a hundred, a utilitarian ethic doesn't think twice about shooting the one. There are no moral absolutes in utilitarianism, since the "moral" choice will always reflect a cost-benefit analysis and any cost can be justified by proportionate benefits. The flaws of utilitarianism are compounded when the "good" of the greatest number is reduced to personal autonomy rather than a more substantive idea of human flourishing.

The definition of the common good offered by the Second Vatican Council, and subsequently appropriated by the *Catechism of the Catholic Church*, while at first glance lacking conceptual richness, in reality proves exceptionally useful. The Council describes the common good as "the sum total of social conditions which allow people, either as groups or as individuals, to reach their fulfillment more fully and more easily."[18]

Here the bond uniting political authority to the common good emerges. Importantly, the common good tutored by the public authority does not describe a final *outcome* of human flourishing, since this can never be achieved by the State, but rather a culture or social *environment* that propitiates human flourishing. Certain social conditions are necessary for men and women to freely and responsibly achieve their fulfillment in cooperation with others. Human flourishing can never be imposed from without, since by its very nature it must be the result of free and responsible action. As the ultimate guarantor of the opportunity for this free and responsible action, the State is required to assure the conditions necessary for its achievement.

At the same time, this set of social conditions reflects a substantive idea of human nature and the human good and is not a mere expression of consensus or convention. It is human reason that recognizes the requirements of the common good rather than the human will arbitrarily imposing them. The protection of human freedoms, the satisfaction of human needs and rights, and the stability and security of a just social order give the common good a solid foundation of non-negotiable human goods.[19] This vital environment is—or should be—the aim of political structures and policies.

The basic requirements of this moral and cultural environment are within the reach of human reason, and their explicit recognition is necessary for a free and just human society. Again, it was in *Evangelium Vitae* that John Paul articulated this important statement:

> It is therefore urgently necessary, for the future of society and the development of a sound democracy, to rediscover those essential and innate human and moral values which flow from the very truth of the human being and express and safeguard the dignity of the person: values which no individual, no majority and no State can ever create, modify or destroy, but must only acknowledge, respect and promote.[20]

Diversity is an ambiguous word. There is a valid and necessary diversity *within* the common good but also a diversity that *threatens* the foundations of the common good. Diversity is not to be celebrated for its own sake but inasmuch as it contributes to the common good and indeed forms a constitutive component of the common good.[21] Along with diversity, a recognition of a basic core of moral truths is essential for the establishment and permanence of a free society.[22] Justice, equality, and human dignity must be recognized as non-negotiable moral truths, rather than mere expedient conventions, in order for the free society to truly be so. Diversity contributes to the common good only as long as it acknowledges its own limits and respects the basic, unchanging principles and values that make a free society possible.

Personalism: Bridge between Common and Particular

John Paul's theory of Thomistic personalism proves especially illuminating for understanding the problem of the one and the many. It attempts to reconcile the errors of collectivism and individualism through a more robust understanding of the common good. In the first place, following the Thomistic tradition to which it is heir, it posits a hierarchy or ordering of what is particular to what is common. We Americans appreciate that our national motto is *e pluribus unum* (Out of many, one) rather than *ex uno plures*. What unites us stands above what divides or distinguishes us, and the fundamental tendency is toward union rather than division.[23] At the same time, personalism does not allow the individual to be completely subordinated to the whole.[24] On the contrary, through a correct understanding of the dignity and rights of the person, moral absolutes become possible once again when the inviolability of the individual is at stake.

In Wojtyla's words:

> Thomistic personalism maintains that the individual good of persons should be by nature subordinate to the common good at which the collectivity, or society, aims—but this subordination may under no circumstances devalue the persons themselves. There are certain rights that every society must guarantee to persons, for without these rights the life and development of persons is impossible. One of these basic rights is the right to freedom of conscience. This right is always violated by so-called objective totalitarianism, which holds that the human person should be completely subordinate to society in all things. In contrast, Thomistic personalism maintains that the person should be subordinate to society in all that is indispensable for the realization of the common good, but that the true common good never threatens the good of the person, even though it may demand considerable sacrifice of a person.[25]

Personalism's understanding of the common good derives from its understanding of the person himself. The inherent dignity of the person demands that persons always be treated as ends rather than means, loved rather than used. This principle has profound consequences for political ethics and the organization of society, since it prohibits the absolute subordination of the individual to the collectivity and demands respect for the inviolability and hence the radical equality of all persons.

It is a popular misconception that the common good stands in opposition to the particular good of individuals. The common good is not contrary to the particular good of persons but rather comprises it, as well as the good of families and other mediating social institutions and associations. Since it is not identified with the good of the abstract collectivity, the common good is truly the good of *one and all*. As the *Catechism of the Catholic Church* states: "The common good is always oriented towards the progress of persons: the order of things must be subordinate to the order of persons, and not the other way around."[26] The Catechism, in fact, places respect for each and every person at the heart of the content of the common good. It states:

> First, the common good presupposes respect for the person as such. In the name of the common good, public authorities are bound to respect the fundamental and inalienable rights of the human person. Society should permit each of its members to fulfill his vocation. In particular, the common good resides in the conditions for the exercise of the natural freedoms indispensable for the development of the human vocation, such as "the right to act according to a sound norm of conscience and to safeguard . . . privacy, and rightful freedom also in matters of religion."[27]

Looking at the complementarity of the common good and the particular good helps to better understand the social nature of subsidiarity, which is often erroneously seen as a merely individualistic principle. Subsidiarity is a component of the common good and not a counterbalance to it. Although subsidiarity is fundamentally a limiting principle on the interference of a society of a higher order in the life of a society of a lower order, it is not meant to advance individualism over the common good. On the contrary, it is meant to *further* the common good, since the common good itself entails the good of persons and societies of all levels. In order to achieve the rich soil necessary for human flourishing, societies of a higher order *must* respect societies of a lower order and allow them the necessary autonomy for the responsible exercise of their proper competencies. Again, this is an important ingredient of the common good, rather than a limitation of it.

At the same time, personalism also remedies the excesses of individualism. It offers a deeper explanation of the relationship between the particular good of individuals and the common good. Although the ordering of what is particular to what is common may seem to place the person on an inferior status *vis-à-vis* the community, this is not true. Attention to the common good, far from destroying the particular good of persons, is essential to it. Just as the common good comprises the particular good of persons, so the particular good necessarily is achieved through attention to the common good. Herein lies the logic of the Second Vatican Council in saying that man is in fact "the only creature on earth which God willed for itself," and at the same time, he cannot "fully find himself except through a sincere gift of himself."[28]

In the words of Pope John Paul, these two aspects—self-affirmation and the sincere gift of self—"not only do not exclude each other, they mutually confirm and complete each other. *Man affirms himself most completely by giving of himself.*"[29] In other words, the true good of the human person is found not in self-interest but in self-giving. By attending responsibly to the common good, the human subject effectively advances his particular good as well. This is why the Christian virtue of solidarity, described by Pope John Paul as "a firm and persevering determination to commit oneself to the common good," is necessary for human flourishing.[30] In the end, the human person realizes his full potential only by going beyond himself and by giving himself to others. By asking human beings to look to the common good above personal self-interest, society elevates its members and indicates to them the path to authentic fulfillment.

Above all, the proposal offered by Christian personalism is a Trinitarian solution. It understands the mutual self-giving manifested in the inner life of the Father, Son, and Holy Spirit as a paradigm for human society.[31] Made in the image and likeness of the Trinitarian Godhead, man is called to communion and self-giving.

At the same time, the more lofty theological truths underlying a Christian notion of the common good do not obviate the need for a realism based on another theological truth—that of original sin. Man's tendency to selfishness must be curbed by social and political structures that both educate in virtue and restrain vice. This anthropological realism helps explain the Church's insistence on human rights.

The Role of Human Rights

As an ethical category, human rights prove uniquely useful in addressing the problem of the one and the many, in that they lay claim to a universality that unites the human race, while simultaneously according a moral absoluteness and inviolability to the individual. Moreover, the *Catechism of the Catholic Church* places the defense of rights at the core of the common good.[32]

Despite a fair amount of opposition (and alongside a frank acknowledgment of some of the limitations of the U.N. language), the Church has consistently supported the United Nations in its articulation of universal human rights. As we have seen above, rights make a statement about objective human goods, and thus counter the voluntarism present in totalitarianism. When the United Nations endeavors to spread the idea that every human person possesses an inherent dignity, that women possess the same fundamental rights as men, that certain ways of treating children are always and everywhere wrong, it is proclaiming the existence of universal moral truths. Where these human rights are violated, contemporary society rightly denounces them as contrary to morality. The moral realism implicit in human rights language stands in contrast to the moral or cultural relativism that threatens democracies today.

In 1947, on the occasion of the United Nations debate about universal human rights, the Executive Board of the American Anthropological Association issued a statement expressing opposition to the United Nations' attempt to formulate a universal declaration of human rights. Written by leading members of the AAA, the Statement argued that individual cultures and societies must be evaluated on their own terms and not by universal standards. "How can the proposed Declaration be applicable to all human beings," the authors asked, "and not be a statement of rights conceived only in terms of the values prevalent in the countries of Western Europe and America?"[33] The Statement added that "standards and values are relative to the culture from which they derive," and "what is held to be a human right in one society may be regarded as anti-social by another people."[34]

For those who see morality as a question of cultural convention, one moral code is no better than another, any more than driving on the right side of the road in America or Italy is better than driving on the left side of the road in Australia or the United Kingdom. We may prefer one way over another, but it is not morally superior to the other. When rights are deemed to be partisan, or simple cultural constructs, the possibility of a rule of moral reason becomes impossible, and the only remaining option is the balance of individual wills and the exercise of an ultimately unreasonable power. In its more radical forms, multiculturalism undermines the conditions necessary for the common good, since it—like totalitarianism—denies the existence of universal moral truths.

Thus, contemporary public debates around such topics as abortion, which we examine in greater detail in Chapter 3, suppose that no binding moral norms may be applied. You may choose not to engage in behavior you deem morally unacceptable, but you may not limit another's license to do so. Moral principles are seen to flow from personal opinion or religious convictions but not from reason. When one wishes to extend opposition to abortion to others, such attempts are immediately construed as an imposition of personal values on others.

Yet the fact that a given moral principle is simultaneously accessible to human reason and also taught by a given religious body or held as a personal moral conviction does not reduce the principle to a matter of religion or individual values. Larceny is prohibited both by the fifth commandment of the Decalogue and the state penal codes everywhere. Homicide is likewise forbidden both by moral and civil law. The positivism proclaimed by the Enlightenment, which reduces authority to power and divorces civil law from moral law, can only end in a "thinly veiled totalitarianism." This is not to deny the real, often enormous difficulties involved in balancing conflicting rights claims or arriving at an agreement concerning universal moral norms. Cultural (and religious) differences are indeed often the biggest contributors to these difficulties. Yet just because this enterprise is difficult does not mean that it is futile. Given the alternatives, it is imperative.

Catholic social doctrine, and *Centesimus Annus* in particular, offers a refreshing and satisfying alternative to Enlightenment theories regarding public authority and the common good. For a free society to remain so, a voluntaristic understanding of the common good must give way to a rediscovery and acknowledgement of the objective moral truth that lies at its base. Yet understanding this objective moral truth entails understanding who the human person is, and the dignity that sets him apart from the rest of the universe of created things. A sound notion of the common good rests on the foundation of a sound Christian anthropology. In recent years the notion of human dignity itself has become something of a battle zone, with opposing theories vying to win enduring public approval. The results of this contest will have far-reaching consequences not only for our understanding of the common good, but for the future of society.

Chapter 2

Dignity and Its Discontents

The idea of human dignity stands at the very core of Catholic social doctrine. The Church's social concern revolves around the human person, and the focus of this concern is man's dignity and the rights that issue from it. It is the human person's innate, God-given dignity that sets him above the rest of creation, as the only creature on earth that God willed for its own sake. (See GS, no. 24). Moreover, it is this dignity that undergirds our understanding of the rights of man. If human rights are to lay claim to universality, they must be rooted in something other than social convention or fluctuating sensibilities; they must be objectively *true*. When applied to the area of human rights the question of foundations is more than academic—it cuts to the heart of what rights really are and how we can distinguish true rights from special interests or specious pretensions. It also allows a reasoned discussion as to why some beings are rights-bearers and others are not. Here both reason and faith have important contributions to make.

Both ecclesial and secular statements on human rights have tended to posit this foundation in "human dignity."[1] This catch-all phrase usually seems to be understood as a self-evident anthropological principle that needs no explanation. Even if this were once true (which is doubtful), it is certainly not true now. "Dignity" as a concept has grown so amorphous and malleable as to justify nearly anything, and can even be employed to bolster contradictory claims. Catholic social thought needs to clearly distinguish its understanding of human dignity from other notions of the term. The two essential questions that have emerged in discussions of dignity regard its *universality* and its *exclusivity*. That is, what matters most is whether dignity is uniformly and universally possessed by all human beings and whether it is exclusive to humans or also shared with other beings. The answer to these questions has a direct bearing on human rights, which are understood to proceed from dignity. Thus, whither dignity, thither rights.

News stories furnish simple but eloquent examples of this. On October 10, 2008, for instance, the *Wall Street Journal* reported on a newly instated rule requiring scientists in Switzerland to take into account the inherent dignity of flora in conducting their field tests.[2] Of particular note is the terminology with which they chose to frame their arguments. The new Swiss ruling came as a result of an interpretive report on the meaning of a 1992 amendment to the Swiss national constitution requiring "account to be taken of the dignity of creation when handling animals, plants and other organisms." The amendment was subsequently turned into a law known as the Gene Technology Act, but said nothing specific about plants. In 2008, the Swiss government asked the Swiss Federal Ethics Committee on Non-Human Biotechnology to analyze the implications of the amendment for plants as well. The result was a 22-page report entitled "The Dignity of Living Beings with Regard to Plants,"[3] which was subsequently dubbed a Bill of Rights for Plants.

A majority of the ethics panel adopted what it called a "biocentric" moral view, and concluded that "living organisms should be considered morally for their own sake because they are alive." The panel also determined that humans cannot claim "absolute ownership" over plants and, moreover, that "individual plants have an inherent worth." The document's wording pulls no punches. The drafters declared that because of their dignity, "we may not use [plants] just as we please, even if the plant community is not in danger, or if our actions do not endanger the species, or if we are not acting arbitrarily."

Though such provisions can seem humorous to us, they are very real and already affect the lives of many people. Nor is this newest form of rights extension limited to the Swiss. Contemporaneously a new national constitution was approved in Ecuador, containing the world's first bill of rights for nature. On September 28, 2008, voters ratified the new Constitution, replacing the Constitution of 1998.

Title One, Chapter Seven of the Constitution is titled "Derechos de la naturaleza," or "The Rights of Nature." Article 71 of the Constitution reads:

Art. 71. Nature or *Pachamama*, where life is reproduced and exists, has the right to integral respect of its existence, and of the conservation and regeneration of its vital cycles, structure, functions and evolutionary processes.

Every person, community, people, or nationality will be able to demand the recognitions of rights of nature before the public organisms. The application and interpretation of these rights will follow the related principles established in the Constitution.

Article 72 similarly states:

Art. 72. Nature has the right to restoration. This integral restoration is independent of the obligation on natural and juridical persons or the State to indemnify the people and the collectives that depend on the natural systems.[4]

As strange as this new legislation may seem to us, it represents a logical progression of a trend that first relativized human rights, then sought recognition of animal rights, and finally has arrived at plant rights and even the rights of inanimate nature. Since in secular legal texts such as these, no foundation for human rights has been acknowledged other than the elastic concept of "dignity," there is no objective criterion to which to appeal to stem this inexorable spread of rights. Wherever dignity can be attributed, rights necessarily follow.

Here Jacques Maritain's famous statement, referring to the drafting of the Universal Declaration of Human Rights, that "men mutually opposed in their theoretical conceptions can come to a merely practical agreement regarding a list of human rights"[5] no longer holds true. The lack of recognized foundations leaves rights agreements up to an ever shifting public opinion, expressed in momentary majorities.

Not only can opinions and sensibilities *theoretically* change over time; they have *de facto* changed in radical ways in the past 60 years. Where rights have historically been appealed to as recourse of the weak against the strong and of minorities against majorities, the absence of acknowledged rational foundations has often turned them into just another instrument of power and the exercise of raw will. Rights need rational foundations. If rights are truly rooted in "dignity," then dignity itself calls for both a precise definition and a cogent justification.

The Universal Declaration of Human Rights places the adjective "universal" before "declaration," but it could have just as easily, and perhaps more accurately, been called the UN Declaration of *Universal* Human Rights. If human rights aren't attributed universally to every human being, they wind up being power plays of interest groups. The real value of rights language, in fact, is its appeal to objective moral norms rooted in human nature.

Yet the ambiguity plaguing the idea of dignity threatens the two key dimensions of human rights mentioned earlier, namely their *universality* and *exclusivity*. These two aspects of human dignity, and hence human rights, cry out for rational grounding. In brief, universality means a recognition of rights for *all* human beings and exclusivity means a recognition of rights *only* for human beings. In point of fact, these two principles are inextricably linked and mutually implicational. Rights can only be universal if they are exclusive and can only be exclusive if they are universal.

Both of these dimensions are widely contested today but nonetheless stand at the heart of the Universal Declaration's understanding of human rights. The preamble of the Declaration begins with the stated premise that "recognition of the inherent dignity and of the equal and inalienable rights of all members of the human family is the foundation of freedom, justice, and peace in the world."[6]

Universality and exclusivity are really two sides of a coin that philosophers refer to nowadays—often pejoratively—as "human exceptionalism." As a theory, human exceptionalism holds that human beings are unique among all other earthly beings and should be treated in an essentially different way than other beings. It is closely allied to an anthropocentric worldview that places human beings at the center of the cosmos, and attributes to them a singular importance.

As we have seen, the Universal Declaration appeals to dignity as the foundation of human rights, yet it offers no grounding or definition for dignity itself. If rights depend on dignity, the fate of rights is inextricably linked to the fate of dignity. Where dignity is attributed to plants and animals, rights must necessarily follow. The root cause of doubt concerning the universality and exclusivity of rights stems from ambiguity concerning the universality and exclusivity of human dignity. If rights proceed from dignity, only a universal human dignity can ground universal human rights.

The Two Notions of Dignity

There are essentially two different schools for viewing dignity and its application to beings. The first sees dignity as a binary function that admits of no degrees—a toggle switch that is either on or off. According to this first school, some beings possess dignity and others do not, and those who do so possess it fully. This way of seeing dignity explains human equality as the equal possession of an ontological dignity that merits equal respect.[7] The idea of human equality would immediately vanish if men and women were seen to possess dignity in unequal measure. Although we recognize that persons vary in many important ways—in their intelligence, athletic abilities, aesthetic sensibilities, temperament, degree of empathy, and so forth—we traditionally have accorded these differences no grounds for ontological inequality among humans.

The second school sees dignity as an infinitely variegated quality, possessed by different beings in different measures. This variegation is found not only among species but also necessarily among members of the same species. As the Australian ethicist, Peter Singer, would say, an underdeveloped human being could easily possess a lower dignity than a highly developed chimpanzee. This school, which has grown in popularity in recent years, reveals no justification for human equality other than pragmatic considerations. At the practical level (the theory goes), while we know that each being possesses a dignity that is differentiable from others, we accept the useful fiction of human equality to preserve public order. While we know that your dignity is, in fact, different from mine because of differences in our native intelligence, moral sensitivity, psychological soundness, etc., we will pretend that we share an equal dignity.

Such arguments often come to the fore in disputes over abortion, since the unborn child's personhood or lack thereof frequently determines whether the individual is eligible for protection as a subject of constitutional and moral rights, and particularly, the right to life. In his book *Rethinking Life and Death*, Peter Singer cites recent discussions in bioethics and concludes that a person is "a being with certain characteristics such as rationality and self-awareness."[8] Personhood, Singer claims, should not be attributed to every member of the human species but only to those members who display such characteristics. Likewise, members of other species should not be randomly excluded from the category of personhood. "There are other persons on this planet. The evidence for personhood is at present most conclusive for the great apes, but whales, dolphins, elephants, monkeys, dogs, pigs, and other animals may eventually also be shown to be aware of their own existence over time and capable of reasoning."[9] And since Singer judges these characteristics by their exercise and not their possession, he can query: "Why should we treat the life of an anencephalic human child as sacrosanct, and feel free to kill healthy baboons in order to take their organs?"[10]

Though in a more nuanced way, similar arguments appear in John Rawls's *A Theory of Justice*, first published in 1971.[11] Equality among persons despite evident differences in natural attributes stands at the heart of Rawls's theory, and Rawls presents the minimal criterion of "moral personality" as the basis of this equality. Moral personality would constitute an essential dividing line between those deserving of justice and those who fall outside the protection of both law and morality. He states that "it is precisely the moral persons who are entitled to equal justice."[12] Moral persons, Rawls writes, are distinguishable by two traits: "first they are capable of having (and are assumed to have) a conception of their good (as expressed by a rational plan of life); and second they are capable of having (and are assumed to acquire) a sense of justice."[13]

Unlike Christian anthropology, which recognizes in human persons an equal dignity by reason of their common human nature, Rawls separates human beings into two categories: "moral persons," capable of having a conception of their good and a sense of justice, and others. Rawls dismisses the problematic nature of moral personality as the necessary attribute for the possession of rights. "I assume," he writes, "that the capacity for the sense of justice is possessed by the overwhelming majority of mankind, and therefore this question does not raise a serious practical problem."[14]

Yet it can and often does present real problems. Rawls himself had to backpedal and acknowledge that a distinction may be made between capacity and exercise.[15] In fact, only by recognizing personhood's roots in human nature and by distinguishing the possession of certain attributes from their exercise can this hurdle by cleared. In this regard, John Finnis helpfully posits the basis of human equality and equal rights on the fact that

> each living human being possesses, *actually and not merely potentially*, the *radical capacity* to reason, laugh, love, repent, and choose *as this unique, personal individual*, a capacity that is not some

abstract characteristic of a species but rather consists in the unique, individual, organic functioning of the organism that comes into existence as a new substance at the conception of that human being and subsists until his or her death, whether ninety minutes, ninety days, or ninety years later; a capacity, individuality, and personhood that subsists as real and precious even while its operations come and go with many changing factors such as immaturity, injury, sleep, and senility.[16]

Though the Church's Magisterium offers no philosophical definition of person, it makes clear that a distinction between human beings and persons is foreign to a Christian understanding of humanity, and regardless of the label applied, all human beings are equal in dignity and must be treated as persons.[17] In the 1987 declaration *Donum Vitae* of the Congregation for the Doctrine of the Faith, the topic is broached in the form of a rhetorical question: "How could a human individual not be a human person?"[18] The document goes on to conclude that the "human being is to be respected and treated as a person from the moment of conception" which in turn carries with it the corollary that "from that same moment his rights as a person must be recognized, among which in the first place is the inviolable right of every innocent human being to life."[19]

In certain hard cases, however, such as those of severely handicapped children, the unborn, or terminally ill persons, the fiction of equality is easily replaced with the more logically consistent category of "quality of life" as the yardstick for differentiated human dignity and its accompanying differences in regard. Certain severely handicapped children will never achieve the capacity for the "sense of justice" that Rawls holds up as a necessary attribute of moral personhood.

Why Equality Presupposes Dignity

If, as the Universal Declaration claims, "recognition of the inherent dignity and of the equal and inalienable rights of all members of the human family is the foundation of freedom, justice, and peace in the world," it can only be a dignity of the first sort. It can only be an ontological dignity found in equal measure in all human beings, not one that permits of gradation.

Yet how is such a dignity to be rationally explained? The year 2009 celebrated the 200th anniversary of Charles Darwin's birth and 150th anniversary of the publication of *The Origin of Species*. In a world that has embraced the neo-Darwinian axiom that human beings differ from other animals only in degree and not in kind, and that all beings exist on an unbroken continuum, we may speak of humans beings as superior to other animals, or more highly evolved, but only as part of this continuum and not as a qualitative jump. Moreover, the very idea of species becomes fluid, since one member of the species could be more highly evolved than another.

As Mortimer Adler wrote some years ago, "if all the possible forms of life were to coexist simultaneously on earth, that is, if every possible organism that could be bred were to exist at the same time, there would be no species at all. There would just be individual differences, one individual and another differing in degree."[20] He goes on to write:

> If man differed from ape as ape differed from horse or horse from bird or bird from frog, then the evolutionist's hypothesis would be as applicable to the origin of the human species as it is plainly applicable to the origin of all other species of animal life. But if man differs from all other animals by a marked discontinuity, a marked discontinuity in the hierarchy of nature, then I'd say that the evolutionist's hypothesis is not applicable to man.[21]

Adler showed the inherent problem with one of the implications of materialist theories of evolution. Without a solidly grounded idea of human dignity, based in human exceptionalism, it is impossible to show the universality and exclusivity of human rights. Human equality and the democratic system itself similarly find themselves bereft of any rational grounding, since "equality" implies that all members of the species possess the same fundamental dignity. If, on the other hand, man's specific difference from other animals is merely one of degree and not of kind, then the difference in dignity between one human being and another could be as significant as the differences between man and another sort of animal.

We are all familiar with the opening line of the second paragraph of the United States Declaration of Independence: "We hold these truths to be self-evident, that all men are created equal, that they are endowed by their Creator with certain unalienable Rights, that among these are Life, Liberty and the pursuit of Happiness." Is this really so? Are these truths self-evident, or are they simply self-evident to a person with a Christian worldview? Did Plato and Aristotle think that all men were *created*, much less created *equal*? Do the Hutus and the Tutsis agree that all men are created equal? Would Confucianists, Hindus, and Muslims all agree that all men and women are created equal, endowed by their Creator with certain inalienable rights? Clearly, they would not.

This famous line of the Declaration was originally: "We hold these truths to be *sacred* and *undeniable*;" Jefferson changed *sacred* and *undeniable* to "self-evident" during the writing of his rough draft of the Declaration. Perhaps we would have been better off if he had left "sacred and undeniable" rather than the less plausible "self-evident." In the end, these truths upon which all of western democracy are posited stand extremely precariously in the balance. As Joseph Ratzinger sagely observed, "this slender remnant of rational basic moral certainty is not the product of reason alone but is based on surviving remnants of insights from the Jewish-Christian tradition."[22]

Ratzinger noted furthermore: "The basic moral insights revealed by Christianity were so obvious to all and so incontrovertible that even in the conflict between confessions they could be regarded as insights that every rational man took for granted."[23] For a clear example of this, one could look to John Locke, who had considerable influence on the American founders. In his *Letter Concerning Toleration*, he writes that "no opinions contrary to human society, or to those moral rules which are necessary to the preservation of civil society, are to be tolerated by the magistrate." Yet he immediately adds that examples of such divergence from common morality "are rare." No sect, he asserts, "can easily arrive to such a degree of madness as that it should think fit to teach, for doctrines of religion, such things as manifestly undermine the foundations of society and are, therefore, condemned by the judgement of all mankind."[24] Even if this was formerly the case, it is clearly no longer so, because of both the continuing evolution of western society and its increasing exchange with individuals and ideas coming from a radically different cultural and religious matrix. And so Ratzinger concludes: "But what seemed a compelling, God-given insight of reason retained its evidential character only for so long as the entire culture, the entire existential context, bore the imprint of Christian tradition."[25]

Theology's Service to Philosophy:
Why All Human Beings Are Equal

Over time, I have understood increasingly why Pope John Paul II and Pope Benedict XVI have insisted so strongly on the recognition of the Christian roots of Europe. It clearly was not just for the sake of the historical record, giving credit where credit is due. It was rather to shore up key European values for the long haul, especially in the face of competing world views and views of the human person. If we forget *why* we believe all human beings are equal (which may not be self-evident outside of a Christian worldview), then we may easily cease to believe *that* they are equal at all.[26]

This idea was driven home especially strongly by certain non-Christian European thinkers, such as Marcello Pera, who joined John Paul and Benedict in asking for the inclusion of the Christian roots of Europe in the European Constitutional Treaty. Their support expressed a growing concern that without a grounding in a Christian worldview Europe may not be able to preserve its ethical patrimony when confronted with radically different conceptions of the human person and society. Another "methodological atheist," German philosopher Jürgen Habermas, wrote in 2004: "Christianity, and nothing else, is the ultimate foundation of liberty, conscience, human rights, and democracy, the benchmarks of Western civilization. To this day, we have no other options. We continue to nourish ourselves from this source. Everything else is postmodern chatter."[27]

If we look, in fact, at the language used by the Church when speaking of human dignity, we find that nearly all of it is theological in nature. The dignity of the human person is rooted in his creation in the image and likeness of God, in the universal vocation to divine filiation and communion with God, and in the redemption achieved by Jesus Christ on the cross. As the Second Vatican Council declares, without the assistance of revelation, "man remains a question to himself, one that is dimly perceived and left unanswered."[28] "Only divine revelation—by simultaneously throwing 'a new light on all things' (GS 11), and opening up 'new horizons closed to human reason' (GS 24)—can enable us to perceive 'his dignity ... and vocation ... in their true light' (GS 12)."[29]

And Pope John Paul, in his 1994 book-length interview *Crossing the Threshold of Hope*, wrote:

The Gospel is the fullest confirmation of all of human rights. Without it we can easily find ourselves far from the truth about man. The Gospel, in fact, confirms the divine rule which upholds the moral order of the universe and confirms it, particularly through the Incarnation itself... *The Redeemer confirms human rights* simply by restoring the fullness of the dignity man received when God created him in His image and likeness.[30]

Divine revelation is useful for *knowing* the truth, but far less so for *communicating* it convincingly in the public square, where only arguments from reason are admitted. Yet neither should we be too dismissive of the importance of these theological arguments. As Ratzinger has noted: "A culture and a nation that cuts itself off from the great ethical and religious forces of its own history commits suicide."[31]

Sacred Scripture reveals many truths which the unaided light of reason alone can also attain, but this neither makes Scripture superfluous nor invalidates the knowledge acquired by reason.[32] As the First Vatican Council taught, the truth attained by philosophy and the truth of revelation are neither identical nor mutually exclusive. There exists, rather, "a twofold order of knowledge," one order being that of natural reason, the other divine faith.[33] Since, however, original sin weakened man's intelligence—so that only with difficulty does he arrive at certain truths—theology provides an invaluable assistance to philosophical research and political science.

In a well-known text, Saint Thomas Aquinas considers whether it is fitting that truths accessible to reason should be proposed to man as an object of belief.[34] Aquinas enumerates three disadvantages that would result if certain truths were left solely to the inquiry of human intelligence. First, few people would arrive at these truths, either because of a natural indisposition to speculative thought, or laziness, or a lack of time to devote to such pursuits. Second, these truths would be reached only after a long time because of their complexity and depth, the need for previous knowledge of many things, and the fact that youth do not possess the calm and prudence needed to reach the knowledge of sublime truths. Third, much falsehood is mingled into the knowledge acquired by human reason, especially on more difficult topics, and given that many people who are considered "wise" teach contrary opinions regarding these issues. These same arguments, which Aquinas adduces regarding the revelation of divine truths like the existence of God, apply equally well to principles of natural law.[35]

Revelation provides an especially useful service by shoring up natural ethics with certain principles regarding the nature of the human person and what he deserves in justice. "Numerous are the philosophical errors concerning the nature of justice and rights," writes Benedict Ashley, "which require to be corrected in the light of God's Word. For example, the materialists deny the difference between human beings and brute animals, and hence either deny both any rights, or (more recently) claim that animals have the same rights as humans."[36] Thus, for example, though human reason is capable of discerning the essential difference between persons and non-persons, many do not arrive at this truth, so Scripture's attestations concerning the uniqueness of the human person made in God's image and likeness and redeemed by Christ play a vital role in bringing it to light or confirming it.

This doesn't mean that we should abandon philosophical argument in favor of theological discourse. It does mean that we often arrive at rational truths through revelation, and are then obliged to retrace our steps to explain rationally why things are so. In other words, as John Paul wrote in *Fides et ratio*, the *intellego ut credam* goes hand in hand with *credo ut intellegam*—"I believe in order that I may understand." "Sacred Scripture indicates with remarkably clear cues how deeply related are the knowledge conferred by faith and the knowledge conferred by reason."[37]

Pope John Paul himself left us a splendid example of a Christian philosopher who strove to translate truths of faith into philosophical argument. Again, in *Crossing the Threshold of Hope* we see how John Paul's Thomistic personalism stemmed from his desire to understand and make accessible the truths of the Gospel:

> And it is precisely from a pastoral point of view that, in *Love and Responsibility*, I formulated the concept of a *personalistic principle*. This principle is an attempt to translate the commandment of love into the language of philosophical ethics. *The person is a being for whom the only suitable dimension is love.* We are just to a person if we love him. This is as true for God as it is for man. Love for a person *excludes the possibility of treating him as an object of pleasure*. This is a principle of Kantian ethics and constitutes his so-called second

imperative. This imperative, however, does not exhaust the entire content of the commandment of love… It requires more; it requires the affirmation of the person as a person.[38]

The Thomistic personalism of Karol Wojtyla may still today offer the best philosophical grounding for the dignity and rights of the person. Wojtyla's insistence on the radical difference between persons and non-persons, his embrace and reformulation of the Kantian principle by which persons must always be treated as ends rather than mere means, his anthropological and ethical realism—all of these offer a coherent system to explain and defend human rights and the universal dignity that undergirds them.

Christians are uniquely positioned to make the arguments that society desperately needs to hear regarding the foundations of human dignity and human rights. Given the real aberrations that human rights theories suffer on an international scale, aberrations that grow more acute month by month and year by year, this is a task that can no longer be delayed. Old arguments must be dusted off and reproposed. New arguments must be formulated and promulgated. As Pope John Paul wrote two decades ago:

A new state of affairs today both in the Church and in social, economic, political and cultural life, calls with a particular urgency for the action of the lay faithful. If lack of commitment is always unacceptable, the present time renders it even more so. *It is not permissible for anyone to remain idle.*[39]

The idleness that John Paul denounced has many names, one of which is apathy in the face of new social injustices and threats to human dignity. Christians are enjoined to stay awake, to be attentive to the signs of the times, and to actively engage and shape the culture in which they live. One of the key social issues of our time where human dignity is ignored or even trampled upon goes under the broad title of "the culture of death."[40] To this issue we now turn.

Chapter 3

Abortion as a Social Justice Issue

Debates regarding human dignity are not hypothetical constructions of the academy.[1] They have real-life consequences. One class of human beings that has already been legally denied the attribute of dignity and its attendant human and civil rights is the class of the unborn. For some bizarre reason, however, Catholic social thought has traditionally excluded abortion from its considerations. Thankfully, this omission is being corrected in decisive ways.

When the 2004 *Compendium of the Social Doctrine of the Church* first fell into my hands some months before its promulgation, one of the pleasant "surprises" was the text's specific treatment and forthright condemnation of abortion, both in the context of human rights and in that of the family as the sanctuary of life. Pleasant though it was, it was still a surprise. In a letter dated March 2006, Cardinal Renato Martino, president of the Pontifical Council for Justice and Peace, stated bluntly: "The social doctrine of the Church, to date, has not placed due emphasis on the defense of life from conception to its natural end." This unusually frank admission was actually an understatement. Social doctrine textbooks are virtually silent on the topic of abortion, and rarely do seminary or university courses on social doctrine deal with this issue except tangentially. The disconcerting fact is that for all intents and purposes the topic of abortion falls outside of Catholic social doctrine as it is presently taught and understood.

The absence of abortion in academic discussions of Catholic social doctrine may come as a shock to some, as it is certainly counter-intuitive. For many in the pro-life movement, for instance, the abortion question stands out as the foremost social justice issue of our time. As well, in the popular mindset, Catholic teaching is especially (indeed, it is supposed, unhealthily) focused on abortion. Moreover, in his groundbreaking 1995 encyclical on life issues, *Evangelium Vitae*, Pope John Paul II practically declared that Catholic social doctrine should shift its attention toward life issues. On beginning his discussion of the gravity of attacks against life in our day, particularly abortion, he explicitly invoked the memory of Leo XIII's encyclical *Rerum Novarum* and compared the life issues of today with the worker question of Leo's time:

> Just as a century ago it was the working classes which were oppressed in their fundamental rights, and the Church very courageously came to their defense by proclaiming the sacrosanct rights of the worker as a person, so now, when another category of persons is being oppressed in the fundamental right to life, the Church feels in duty bound to speak out with the same courage on behalf of those who have no voice. Hers is always the evangelical cry in defense of the world's poor, those who are threatened and despised and whose human rights are violated.[2]

This text, drawn from the beginning of the encyclical letter *Evangelium Vitae*, frames the entire question of abortion specifically in terms of the Church's social teaching. If Leo's 1891 encyclical concentrated its attention on the plight of the working class as the social group most in need of courageous defense at the time, the attention of the social Magisterium should now swing toward the new class of oppressed. John Paul II went on to say: "Today there exists a great multitude of weak and defenseless human beings, unborn children in particular, whose fundamental right to life is being trampled upon."[3] If, John Paul reasoned, at the end of the last century the Church could not be silent about the injustices of those times, *still less* can she be silent today. Yet despite John Paul's appeal, abortion is no more present in Catholic social doctrine today than it was in 1995. Why is this so, and what can be done about it?

In this chapter I mean to address four closely related questions. First, I will briefly establish my assertion that *de facto* abortion is excluded presently from the realm of Catholic social teaching. Second, I wish to examine possible reasons behind this absence. Third, I will consider why abortion and its related problems fall within the proper competence of Catholic social thought and should be accorded greater attention within this field. Fourth, I will explore the singular contribution that Catholic social thought is called to make to the abortion problem and other related life issues.

The Neglect of Abortion in Catholic Social Teaching

Before all else, we must establish that abortion is indeed left out of Catholic social doctrine—understood, as we mentioned in the introduction, as define by a corpus of magisterial teaching. It was Pope Pius XII who coined the expression "social encyclical" in his radio message of June 1, 1941, referring to Leo XIII's *Rerum Novarum*.[4] Pope John XXIII, in his 1961 encyclical *Mater et Magistra*, again employed the term in reference to the same encyclical,[5] and from there the term found its way into the common vocabulary of the Church's Magisterium. Later, Pope John Paul II would similarly refer to Paul VI's *Populorum Progressio* as a social encyclical in his 1987 commemorative encyclical *Sollicitudo Rei Socialis*.[6]

Although the Magisterium offers no definition of "social encyclical," one understands that the expression refers to those encyclicals (and related documents, like Paul VI's apostolic letter *Octogesima Adveniens*) that deal specifically and often exclusively with the just organization of society. Roughly speaking, the collection of social encyclicals combine to make up the corpus of the social Magisterium of the Church, with the notable addition of Pope Pius XII's radio message of Pentecost 1941 commemorating the fiftieth anniversary of *Rerum Novarum*. While obviously not an encyclical at all, the text of his address is usually considered part of the body of Catholic social doctrine as well. Though elements of social teaching found in other papal texts could also be considered part of Catholic social doctrine, they are rarely included in courses on the subject.

Nearly all the social encyclicals begin by retracing the legacy of social encyclicals that have come before them. These ever-growing lists furnish us with an informal "canon" of social encyclicals; there are slight discrepancies from list to list, however, which could also suggest some flexibility.[7] Most recently, Pope Benedict XVI set forth his own catalog of such encyclicals in his first teaching document, *Deus Caritas Est.* There, after enumerating the milestones in the development of the Catholic social Magisterium, Benedict writes: "My great predecessor John Paul II left us a trilogy of social Encyclicals: *Laborem Exercens* (1981), *Sollicitudo Rei Socialis* (1987) and finally *Centesimus Annus* (1991)."[8] Conspicuous by its absence, of course, is any mention of *Evangelium Vitae* as a social encyclical.

A quick review of the content of the social encyclicals reveals a great silence surrounding the topic of abortion. Of all nine recognized social encyclicals,[9] the word "abortion" appears a scant four times, and none treats it in any depth. *Rerum Novarum, Quadragesimo Anno, Mater et Magistra, Pacem in Terris, Populorum Progressio* and *Laborem Exercens* never cite abortion at all, though in *Mater et Magistra*, John XXIII opposes solutions to population growth that "attack human life at its very source" (no. 189) and reminds us that "[h]uman life is sacred" and "[f]rom its very inception it reveals the creating hand of God" (no. 194). In *Octogesima Adveniens*, Paul VI mentions abortion in the context of Malthusian solutions to the unemployment problem (no. 18). Pope John Paul mentions abortion in passing in *Sollicitudo Rei Socialis* as a counterexample to a growing appreciation for life and human dignity (no. 26), as well as speaking against "systematic campaigns against birth" as a "new form of oppression" (no. 25). In *Centesimus Annus* he directly adverts to abortion twice, first in reference to widespread anti-childbearing campaigns employed to stem the supposed demographic problem (no. 39), and second in the context of human rights as the necessary foundation for the democratic system (no. 47). Further on, the same encyclical mentions "respect for life from the moment of conception until death" amongst the concerns of the Church's social teaching (no. 54).

I hasten to add that the generalized omission of abortion from the *social* Magisterium in no way implies that popes have been silent on the topic. On numerous occasions, Pope John Paul II spoke out forcefully on the question, and his encyclical *Evangelium Vitae* addresses the matter of abortion in great length. Yet according to current thinking, *Evangelium Vitae* is not a social encyclical. Thus, while the popes have indeed vigorously condemned abortion, they have not chosen to do so in the context of Catholic social doctrine. Why is this? What factors have contributed to the neglect of abortion in the social Magisterium?

Reasons for the Silence of CST on Abortion

In part, this silence stems from the relatively recent advent of abortion as a large-scale ethical problem. With the development of medicine's ability to kill as well as to heal, the number of abortions has multiplied exponentially in the past four decades. Moreover, abortion only became legal in many countries in recent decades as well. Therefore the first mention of abortion in the social Magisterium appears only in 1971, in Paul VI's apostolic letter *Octogesima Adveniens* (no. 18). Yet this fact only partly explains the separation of life issues from social doctrine. While it certainly justifies the absence of abortion from early texts, it doesn't account for the continued exclusion of abortion from the discipline of Catholic social doctrine. By my reckoning, the silence reflects the widespread understanding of social doctrine as primarily *economic* in character, and of abortion as a *bioethical* problem rather than an issue of social justice.

This question can be addressed from different angles. I propose to do so first from a historical perspective and second from a taxonomic perspective.

The Prototypical Function of Rerum Novarum *in Catholic Social Doctrine*

Until Benedict XVI's publication of *Caritas in Veritate*, Leo XIII's 1891 encyclical *Rerum Novarum* was considered the touchstone for all Catholic social doctrine. The vast majority of the social encyclicals make direct reference to *Rerum Novarum* and its content and were often promulgated to commemorate important anniversaries of the encyclical.[10]

The papal Magisterium has referred more than once to *Rerum Novarum* as the "Magna Charta" of Catholic social thought. On the fortieth anniversary of this document, Pope Pius XI wrote that "Leo's Encyclical has proved itself the Magna Charta upon which all Christian activity in the social field ought to be based, as on a foundation."[11] More recently, Pope John Paul II wrote: "In this way, Pope Leo XIII, in the footsteps of his Predecessors, created a lasting paradigm for the Church."[12]

Taking *Rerum Novarum* as their point of departure, these letters update the ethical analysis of the social question in the light of new realities but generally following the categories set out by Leo's text. As a result, the initial focus on the worker question has endured, and economics have never relinquished center stage in Catholic social thought.[13] Though the Church's understanding of what constitutes her social teaching slowly broadened, it still remained strongly wedded to *Rerum Novarum*.

While the importance and originality of *Rerum Novarum* cannot be denied, the conferral of a normative character to a text of this nature could not but have a limiting effect on subsequent expositions of Catholic social ethics. Whereas *Rerum Novarum* ably addressed the worker problem, analyzing the socialist solution and reaffirming the Catholic belief in a natural right to private property, it did not deal with a host of other essential questions of social justice. Leo, in fact, had no intention of penning a comprehensive treatise on Christian social ethics. *Rerum Novarum* was a thoughtful response to a pressing pastoral concern, but to expect to find in it the pattern for Church teaching on every social issue is to ask more from the document than it can possibly give.

A case could be made that the ecclesial document truly deserving the title of "Magna Carta," a foundational document for all later Catholic social thought, would be the 1965 Conciliar Constitution of the Church in the Modern World, *Gaudium et Spes*. The text was probably the single most important development of Catholic social doctrine in the twentieth century. Whereas *Rerum Novarum* offered a perceptive analysis of the worker problem, *Gaudium et Spes* tackled the whole gamut of social justice issues. In systematic fashion it laid out first the foundations of Catholic social ethics in the dignity and vocation of the human person, and then proceeded to explore the interdependence of person and society, the meaning of man's activity in the world, the social nature of marriage, the importance of culture, economic development, the political community, international relations, and the project of peace.

The Taxonomy of Moral Theology

A second cause of the absence of abortion from Catholic social teaching can be found in the taxonomy of moral theology, of which Catholic social doctrine is a branch.[14] Moral theology is traditionally broken down into fundamental and special, with the latter being further subdivided into three subcategories: (a) sexual-marital ethics, (b) life ethics, and (c) social ethics—the area of Catholic social thought. As we saw earlier, Catholic social doctrine is more limited than social ethics in that it refers specifically to the content of the corpus of Magisterial teaching contained in the social encyclicals.

These categories determine the structure of theological studies in the moral field and the differentiation carries out an important pedagogical function. Specific moral questions generally fall into one or another of these categories, and to avoid useless repetition are not treated over and over in different disciplines. Since at its heart abortion is a sin against the fifth commandment and consists essentially in the taking of an innocent unborn human life, it pertains in its moral species to the realm of bioethics. To avoid redundancy, since abortion is treated in depth in courses of life ethics, it is generally excluded from courses on social doctrine.

In What Sense Abortion Properly Falls within the Realm of Catholic Social Thought

Does the discipline of Catholic social teaching properly include abortion and other life-related moral issues? More fundamentally perhaps, what are the breadth, proper scope, and limits of Catholic social teaching? It obviously does not intend to embrace the whole of Christian morality, and has a specificity all its own. Does this specificity extend to abortion?

The Necessary Overlap Between the Areas of Moral Theology

The academic distinctions that articulate moral theology into diverse branches, while useful for focusing our attention and delineating disciplines, may also contribute to an unhealthy, modular approach to learning. In his 1998 encyclical *Fides et Ratio*, Pope John Paul II warned against an overspecialization that threatens the unity of knowledge. "The segmentation of knowledge," he wrote, "with its splintered approach to truth and consequent fragmentation of meaning, keeps people today from coming to an interior unity."[15] The fact is that the lines drawn between the different branches of moral theology are not nearly as clear and neat as they may first appear. Both sexual ethics and life ethics intersect and overlap with social ethics in significant ways.

In the proper sense, sexual ethics examines the correct use of human freedom in the area of sexual activity, with special emphasis on the virtue of chastity as the right ordering and integration of human sexuality. The nature of the human person as a sexual being, the purpose of the reproductive faculty, the morality of sexual conduct between spouses, between unmarried persons, between persons of the same sex, and with oneself all constitute the proper matter of this area of study.

At the same time, however, sexual and marital ethics also enter into the realm of Catholic social thought. Intrinsic to sexual morality is its public, social dimension. The family as the primordial human community and basic cell of society, the place of the institution of marriage in the social fabric, marriage and divorce laws, the status of civil unions between persons of the same sex, and the adoption of children, constitute several of the many questions of sexual and marital ethics that properly fall within the competence of Catholic social thought.

A similar analysis can be applied to the second sector of special moral theology, that of life morality or bioethics. While this area specifically explores (1) the morality of human activity touching on the beginning of human life, (2) medical and biological activity aimed at the preservation and betterment of human health, and (3) end-of-life ethics, it also has an important social dimension.[16]

Properly bioethical issues become social questions when they are addressed in a legal or juridical context and insofar as they impinge on the common good and social justice. Healthcare systems with their socio-political dynamics, medical malpractice, publicly funded experimentation on embryos, laws regarding euthanasia, cloning, and assisted suicide—to name but a few—all enter into this sphere.[17] Abortion is no exception. Abortion refers to the deliberate termination of an unborn human being, and therefore, by its moral species, it belongs to the field of bioethics. Yet in the matter of abortion the job of the bioethicist is relatively simple. For those who accept the status of an unborn child as a human being, the moral judgment involved is eminently straightforward and requires little discussion. Direct abortion is morally repugnant and merits universal condemnation.

The numerous moral issues surrounding abortion at the social and political level, however, are far-ranging and complex, and demand attentive study and careful exposition. The place of the right to life in a broader theory of human rights, the role of natural law in jurisprudence, the moral (in)admissibility of supporting imperfect laws as part of a long-term pro-life strategy, the question of conscientious objection for medical personnel—these questions form but the tip of the iceberg requiring answers from Catholic social thought. Given the nature of the social, juridical, economic, and political debates that swirl around abortion in the world today, it presents a much more daunting task for social ethics than for bioethics.

Analysis from the Perspective of Social Justice and the Common Good

Along with charity, "social justice" is the central and specific virtue of Catholic social thought, and determines the proper scope of this discipline. It extends to a number of areas, generally grouped around the socio-cultural, political, familial, and economic spheres. Whereas the interpersonal nature of justice means that all justice is, in a sense, social, the Papal Magisterium has consistently employed the terminology of "social justice" and "social charity" to refer to the right ordering of those structures and institutions that most directly affect the common good.[18] Pope Pius XI, for his part, treated "social justice" and the common good as virtual synonyms.[19] The *Catechism of the Catholic Church* likewise says that "society ensures social justice by providing the conditions that allow associations and individuals to obtain their due,"[20] a description very similar to that of the common good.

From this perspective, the question becomes: To what degree and in what manner is abortion today a question of social justice? Abortion is, in fact, an emblematic and singular socio-ethical problem. To illustrate the uniqueness of abortion, it suffices to exhibit six characteristics that distinguish it from related socio-ethical phenomena:

1.   Abortion deals specifically with the destruction of *innocent* life. This differentiates discussion of abortion from many other related social justice issues. We are not discussing the killing of aggressive enemies, as in war, or potentially "guilty life," as in capital punishment, with all the moral considerations that must be brought to bear on these cases. This is why then-Cardinal Joseph Ratzinger in June 2004 wrote: "There may be a legitimate diversity of opinion even among Catholics about waging war and

applying the death penalty, but not however with regard to abortion and euthanasia."[21] Though all life is precious, moral theology has always differentiated the destruction of "innocent life" as particularly heinous and always and everywhere worthy of condemnation.[22] No one can "in any circumstance, claim for himself the right to destroy directly an *innocent* human being."[23] No one is more innocent and defenseless than an unborn child.

2.   A second distinguishing factor of abortion as a quintessentially *social* phenomenon is the sheer *magnitude of the problem*. Even though completely reliable statistics are unavailable, conservative estimates place the number of legal abortions performed worldwide each year at 25-30 million, a figure that alone makes abortion a social problem of staggering proportions. "Humanity today offers us a truly alarming spectacle," wrote Pope John Paul, "if we consider not only how extensively attacks on life are spreading but also their unheard-of numerical proportion."[24] An isolated murder would be a social problem, but one of reduced proportions. A serial killer would pose a more serious social problem still. But yearly killings in the millions cry out for immediate and decisive action. The volume of abortions underscores the social nature of the problem and makes abortion one of the most serious social justice issues not only of the present day but of all time.

3.   Unlike other instances of massive killing of human life, like terrorism or serial killing, which stand clearly outside of the law, abortion widely enjoys *legal sanction*. Abortion involves the systematic, ostensibly hygienic, legal elimination of innocent human life. Pope John Paul wrote of the novelty of this menace, due to its institutional nature. "They are not only threats coming from the outside," he wrote, "from the forces of nature or the 'Cains' who kill the 'Abels'; no, they are *scientifically and systematically programmed threats*."[25]

     Later, he remarked on the peculiarity of abortion as a legal "right." After listing a series of terrible threats to human life, such as poverty, malnutrition, war, and the arms trade, he then contrasts them with a new class of threats on life. Not only are these attacks on life no longer considered as crimes, he writes, "paradoxically they assume the nature of 'rights,' to the point that the State is called upon to give them *legal recognition and to make them available through the free services of health care personnel.*"[26] Especially in societies that prize their legal structures and where legality and morality are often conflated, legalized homicide assumes a particularly heinous social quality.

4.   A fourth distinguishing aspect of abortion is its arbitrary division of human beings into those worthy of life and those unworthy. Abortion deals not with the random killing of unrelated individuals, but the *circumscription of an entire class* of human beings (the unborn) as non-citizens and non-persons, excluded from the basic rights and protections accorded to all other human beings. In this way abortion mimics the great moral tragedies of all time, which always began with the denigration of an entire class of people as unworthy of life or freedom.

Historically the greatest social evils perpetrated on humanity—genocide, racism, anti-Semitism, sexism, slavery—have always violated the principle of equality, relegating an entire sector of the human family to an inferior status with a dignity lower than the rest. Abortion is no different. Since human rights flow from human dignity, once dignity is called into question equal rights cannot but share in the same fate. If human dignity depends on anything other than simple membership in the human race—be it intelligence, athletic ability, social status, race, age, or health—we immediately find ourselves in the situation of having to distinguish between persons. As John Paul wrote: "How is it still possible to speak of the dignity of every human person when the killing of the weakest and most innocent is permitted? In the name of what justice is the most unjust of discriminations practised: some individuals are held to be deserving of defence and others are denied that dignity?"[27]

5.   Abortion even distinguishes itself from related bioethical questions such as euthanasia and assisted suicide because of the absence of the possibility of *informed consent*. The status of the unborn as voiceless and the most vulnerable adds a further dimension to the discussion of the morality and gravity of abortion. Here the bioethical category of "autonomy" cannot be applied, since unborn children have no way of speaking for themselves.

6. Finally, abortion differs from other major social ills such as unemployment and divorce because of its relative *invisibility*. Not only are the victims themselves voiceless, but those who perpetrate abortion have no interest in speaking publicly about it, and neither do the women and girls who abort. It takes place behind closed doors and relies on persons and institutions uninvolved in the process to speak out. Yet even legislators are squeamish about frank discussions of the phenomenon of abortion, and pro-life advertising is often banned from network television. Though legal, the grim reality of abortion is considered taboo in public discourse. As in the case of slavery, the social injustice of abortion relies on the courage of persons and institutions uninvolved in the process to speak out.

The Specific Contribution of Catholic Social Doctrine to the Abortion Question

The fourth and final question to be treated could read like this: If the scope of Catholic social teaching ought indeed to embrace the abortion problem, what is its distinctive contribution to the debate? What does it bring to the table that wasn't there already?

Catholic social thought furnishes two distinctive elements to the abortion debate. First, it lays a bridge between moral theology and public discourse. In its long experience dealing with social questions, the Church has sought not only to set forth the Christian truth in all its richness but also to influence Christians and all people of good will in building a civilization of justice and love. To this end, Catholic social doctrine often employs a natural-law vocabulary friendly to all persons of good will and frames its arguments using accessible concepts and constructions that can be brought to bear on moral discourse in a non-confessional environment.[28]

Second, perhaps more than any institution in the world, the Church in its social teaching has developed a series of principles to address the complex moral questions in the social order. As new situations have arisen as a result of the rapidly changing socio-political landscape, the Church has shown admirable elasticity in accommodating new states of affairs while ever defending the essential dignity of the person and the family. With its moral and intellectual tradition the Catholic Church is uniquely qualified to offer cogent solutions to ethical problems that touch on the right ordering of the *res publica*. It is this second contribution—at the level of content—that I would like to briefly comment on now.

The Common Good

A key element of the patrimony of Catholic social doctrine is the concept of the common good, not only as a general principle but also in its specific content. As we have seen, *Gaudium et Spes* defined the common good as "the sum of those conditions of social life which allow social groups and their individual members relatively thorough and ready access to their own fulfillment."[29] The Catechism separates these "conditions of social life" into three groups, the first of which comprises respect for the human person, and consequently respect for his "fundamental and inalienable rights."[30]

Pope John Paul developed this point still further by stating: "It is impossible to further the common good without acknowledging and defending the right to life, upon which all the other inalienable rights of individuals are founded and from which they develop."[31] In other words, not only is the right to life included in the notion of the common good—which is the finality of the social order—it constitutes a foundational pillar of that order. Therefore John Paul could add: "Disregard for the right to life, precisely because it leads to the killing of the person whom society exists to serve, is what most directly conflicts with the possibility of achieving the common good."[32]

The Principle of Equality

The democratic system as it is understood today is based on the principle of equality—the radical ontological and civic equality of all citizens. The doctrine of universal human equality comes down to our generation as a specifically Christian contribution to political science. The idea that every human being is a child of God, created in his image and called to divine sonship and eternal beatitude, grounded the understanding that all human beings are brothers and sisters and share an equal human dignity. Even those who reject the Church and Christianity itself—such as the architects of the French Revolution—owe an enormous debt to Christianity, without which the motto "*Liberté, Egalité, Fraternité*" would have never materialized.[33] In a democratic system, even non-citizens merit the same human treatment and possess the same human rights, even if they do not enjoy all the civil rights (work, vote, participation in the public life, etc.) of citizenship.

Equality of persons corresponds to the impartiality of justice. Portrayals of the goddess Justice as of the sixteenth century depict her blindfolded, with a balance in her left hand and a sword in her right. The blindfold represents impartiality, the indistinct and equitable treatment given to all, without discrimination of persons. What is important is not who I have before me, but the simple fact that I have some*one* before me. The exclusion of unborn persons from the principle of equality constitutes an assault against the foundations of democracy itself. If one group is denied its basic human rights, who is to say which group will be next? The artificial separation of human beings into classes of worthy and unworthy, useful and unuseful, wanted and unwanted, apes history's gravest crimes against humanity.

The Preferential Option for the Poor

The Church's preferential option for the poor, an evangelical principle, refers to a deliberate emphasis on and attention to those most in need. Pope John Paul II called it "a special form of primacy in the exercise of Christian charity" that should affect the life of every Christian.[34] On numerous occasions the Magisterium has clarified that the "poor" in question does not refer to a social class, or merely to those who suffer material need, but to the entire sphere of human misery and indigence. "This misery," we read in the Catechism, "elicited the compassion of Christ the Savior, who willingly took it upon himself and identified himself with the least of his brethren."[35]

Just as a mother or father dedicates a disproportionate amount of time and energy to a child who is sick, without for that reason loving the other children any less, Christians are called to focus their efforts preferentially toward the most defenseless and needy among us. Applying this principle to contemporary society, the social injustice that most cries out to Christian conscience, for the reasons we saw earlier, is the deliberate and massive attack on the most vulnerable members of society, the unborn. If any human group merits special care and solidarity from the general populace, it is the unborn.

The Church's Teaching on the Rule of Law

Catholic social doctrine reaffirms the Pauline doctrine of respect for and obedience to civil law.[36] Yet it also insists that to be legitimate, human law must mirror God's eternal law. Human laws can go beyond the requirements of the natural moral law, but cannot contravene it without losing their legitimacy. Citing Saint Thomas Aquinas, the *Catechism* states: "A human law has the character of law to the extent that it accords with right reason, and thus derives from the eternal law. Insofar as it falls short of right reason it is said to be an unjust law, and thus has not so much the nature of law as of a kind of violence."[37]

The important distinction between just and unjust laws, posited on a rejection of a positivistic understanding of civil law and a necessary connection between law and morality, provides the philosophical grounding for the concept of *conscientious objection*, whereby citizens rightly disobey laws or commands that enjoin immoral action.[38] Laws that contradict the common good by failing to uphold basic human rights fall into the category of unjust laws, that not only fail to bind in conscience, but also require resistance.[39] Such is the case of laws permitting abortion.[40]

The Church's understanding of the scope and limits of human law sheds light on the contemporary situation where abortion is given legal protection in most countries. It also leads to a series of questions, to which it furnishes the necessary principles to derive answers:

- What does it mean for society to grant legal approval to the systematic elimination of unborn children?
- What is the proper response to an unjust law in a democratic polity?
- Since law has a pedagogical function in forming the moral consciences of citizenry, especially given the modern tendency to conflate the legal and moral spheres, how can the deforming influence of unjust abortion laws be deflected and redressed?
- What is the proper role of civil law in the protection of life?
- When are civil disobedience and conscientious objection permitted or even required and what form should they take?
- If a given law permits evil without imposing it, how does the moral obligation of citizens change as a result?
- What is the essential difference between imposing religious doctrine *and* defense of the common good that coincides with religiously informed moral judgment?

These questions—just a selection from the many possibilities—reveal the importance of Catholic social doctrine in dealing with the immense social fallout of abortion in the legal and social realms.

Church Teaching on Politics in General and the Role of Catholic Legislators in Particular

As in the case of human laws, the Church has amassed a body of social teaching regarding the nature and role of public authority. Central to this teaching is the understanding that public authority exists for the sole purpose of achieving and protecting the common good.[41] John Paul referred to the common good as "the end and criterion regulating political life,"[42] and thus, when politicians fail in their duty to the common good, they lose their reason for being. Moreover, "[i]t is impossible to further the common good without acknowledging and defending the right to life, upon which all the other inalienable rights of individuals are founded and from which they develop."[43]

As in the closely related case of abortion as unjust law, the situation of politicians who support abortion legislation gives rise to numerous questions for Catholic social teaching. Given the number of such questions, I will limit myself to offering a representative sample, rather than attempt to be exhaustive or to expound the corresponding teaching to answer each query.

- In what way does a pro-abortion politician "formally cooperate" with evil?
- Since a legislator has the power to make something licit or illicit, at least in a conventional sense, is this worse than actually performing abortions?
- In what cases is so-called "single-issue politics" legitimate or obligatory? Can and should one issue trump the rest, and under what conditions? Does abortion constitute one of those cases?
- How is a Catholic politician's relationship with the Church affected by his promotion of abortion legislation? Are there circumstances under which he should be refused Holy Communion?[44]
- What moral legitimacy does the "seamless garment" approach to life issues hold? How is abortion similar and dissimilar to other life issues such as capital punishment, immigration and welfare reform, etc.?

- Is it morally permissible to be "personally opposed but publicly favorable" to abortion, as Catholic Governor Mario Cuomo articulated his position?[45]
- In what way do the distinct and complementary roles of the legislature and the judiciary affect a proper response to the abortion problem?
- What are the conditions and limits of the democratic process? Is everything up for debate and subject to the fluid will of the majority?

Once again, while not exhaustive, this brief list of questions effectively illustrates the complexity of the politico-ethical problems engendered by the abortion issue and the importance of the contribution of Catholic social teaching in providing guidance for their resolution.

Conclusions: Paths to a Solution

If, as has been argued, the teaching furnished by the Catholic social Magisterium is essential for a thoroughgoing response to the abortion problem and ought to be formally included in our understanding of its scope, what can be done to bring this about? I see two possible courses of action.

The first would be to induct *Evangelium Vitae* into the roster of social encyclicals. As we have seen, Pope John Paul in that encyclical offered a good justification for doing just that. *Evangelium Vitae* expounds a series of principles undergirding the just society, which are not treated with equal depth elsewhere in the Church's social Magisterium. In *Evangelium Vitae*, John Paul examined the role and purpose of the rule of law, as well as its limitations. He spoke about cooperation in evil, the legitimacy of imperfect laws, principles regarding conscientious objection, and a series of other related issues, elucidating the moral nuances relating to life issues. He analyzed the democratic system and the importance of moral truth as an enduring point of reference for the attainment of the common good. Much more of the encyclical, in fact, deals with the social and juridical ramifications of life issues than with the straightforward fundamental moral principles at their base.

A second approach would be to extend our understanding of what constitutes the corpus of Catholic social teaching beyond the monographic social encyclicals to include *all* Magisterial teaching on social matters. This would require much more work on the part of those who teach and write on this discipline, since it involves parsing Magisterial texts and gleaning the teachings offered on issues of social justice.

Thankfully, an important step has already been taken in this direction with the promulgation of the *Compendium of the Social Doctrine of the Church*. This important text has advanced the development of the discipline of Catholic social doctrine in two significant ways. First, it draws not only from the canon of social encyclicals but also from other Magisterial texts that touch on social justice issues. In citing everything from Leo XIII's *Immortale Dei* to Pius XI's *Casti Connubii* to John Paul II's *Dives in Misericordia*, the *Compendium* underscores the breadth of the Catholic social Magisterium far beyond the confines of the so-called social encyclicals. It should be noted that the Compendium also references *Evangelium Vitae* in numerous instances. Second, in adopting an organic structure more similar to *Gaudium et Spes* than *Rerum Novarum*, the *Compendium* systematically lays out the foundational principles of Catholic social thought and draws from them their practical applications in the social, political, cultural and economic realms. This methodological option encourages thinking of Catholic social doctrine in a more thematic way, relativizing the place of the economy in the whole of social ethics, and making room for other central social justice issues—such as life issues.

These changes will take place gradually but are already in motion. Pope Benedict XVI gave a decisive push to this movement by including "life issues" among the core requirements for integral human development in his social encyclical *Caritas in Veritate*. As we will see in the final chapter of this book, *Caritas in Veritate*, more than any other social encyclical to date, underscores the importance of life issues for Catholic social teaching. Taking up John Paul's call, Benedict insists that openness to life stands at the center of true development and calls respect for life one of the most striking aspects of development in the present day.[46] For those truly concerned with justice and peace in the world, there is no better place to start.

Promoting a culture of life means imbuing society with a greater respect for the human person as a child of God. It means creating a heightened awareness of the inherent rights of the person, and a renewed Christian sense of how human beings are to be treated—as persons to be loved, and not as instruments to be used or discarded. This Christian understanding of the person also bears directly on our moral evaluation of physical violence in its many forms, another area of Catholic social thought for a new generation.

Chapter 4

A Presumption Against Violence?

A key area of social ethics that has come to the fore in recent years is the spiny issue of "violence," in its manifold expressions ranging from wife- (or husband-) beating, war, and torture to child abuse, media violence, and corporal punishment.[1] Pope Benedict has noted, for instance, that violence "puts the brakes on authentic development and impedes the evolution of peoples towards greater socio-economic and spiritual well-being."[2] Despite constant popular references to violence in modern culture, the topic of violence as a moral category has received remarkably little serious study. A hundred years ago, Georges Sorel noted that "[t]he problems of violence still remain very obscure."[3] In 1969, Hannah Arendt observed that despite the enormous role that violence has always played in human affairs, it surprisingly "has been singled out so seldom for special consideration," and hadn't at the time even rated an entry in the *Encyclopedia of the Social Sciences*.[4] Unfortunately, despite the numerous psychological studies done on "aggression" in recent decades,[5] and the research done on more specific subjects such as violence in the media,[6] this lacuna has yet to be filled. This is true of Catholic social teaching as well.

We must however note with satisfaction that despite the daily violence one witnesses on the six o'clock news or reads about in the morning paper, there seems to be compelling evidence that violence has in fact been steadily *declining* throughout the world in recent centuries. In a 2007 *New*

Republic article, Harvard professor Steven Pinker noted that "[v]iolence has been in decline over long stretches of history, and today we are probably living in the most peaceful moment of our species' time on earth."[7] As one would expect, the absolute decline of violent acts has marched hand in hand with a shift in people's sensibilities and moral judgments regarding violence. Thus Pinker goes on to say (not without a little hyperbole):

> Cruelty as entertainment, human sacrifice to indulge superstition, slavery as a labor-saving device, conquest as the mission statement of government, genocide as a means of acquiring real estate, torture and mutilation as routine punishment, the death penalty for misdemeanors and differences of opinion, assassination as the mechanism of political succession, rape as the spoils of war, pogroms as outlets for frustration, homicide as the major form of conflict resolution—all were unexceptionable features of life for most of human history. But, today, they are rare to nonexistent in the West, far less common elsewhere than they used to be, concealed when they do occur, and widely condemned when they are brought to light.

Moreover, many barbaric practices once common in the past—such as slavery, amputation, blinding, branding, flaying, disembowelment, burning at the stake, and breaking on the wheel—have become all but obsolete in the last five centuries. People in the West now view with abhorrence what were ordinary features of past societies from which we emerged.

Yet for the moral analysis that concerns us here, these sociological data, though consoling, tell us relatively little about what violence is and how one ought to approach it from the perspective of Catholic social thought. And here we run into our most formidable hurdle in attempting to evaluate violence as a moral category in its own right. The short list of violent actions listed above—ranging from slavery to homicide— illustrates the breadth of human acts that can be grouped under the capacious umbrella of "violence." A moral analysis of slavery differs substantially from that of war or the application of thumb screws to extract confessions, and each of these acts pertains to a moral species not shared by the others.

James Gilligan has written that "[h]uman violence is much more complicated, ambiguous and, most of all, tragic, than is commonly realized or acknowledged."[8] This ambiguity goes beyond the psychological, economic, and social components of the phenomenon and touches its very nature. It is hard to pin down just what violence is. Perhaps the dearth of research on the topic can at least be partially explained by the ambiguity of the term itself. Like many other words in our day, "violence" carries with it a plethora of the most varied connotations, some of which are mutually exclusive.

Terms like aggression, assault, bullying, and battery are frequently used as synonyms of violence. Yet especially when considered in its moral dimension, the word *violence* is most often used as a synonym for "war," and discussions about the ethical issues surrounding violence easily stray to the more familiar terrain of just war theory. Thus Hannah Arendt's important essay cited above, although broadly titled, "On Violence," devolves into a discussion of civil strife, revolution and especially the Vietnam War. This is understandable but regrettable, for where armed conflict between states provides one ready example of violence, the two are far from the same thing, and the ethical questions pertaining to each similarly vary.

Since our present analysis is socio-ethical, we are particularly interested in violence as an identifiable form of human behavior. We can therefore rule out other legitimate definitions of violence. More abstract or figurative usages of the word, such as the violence of a storm or the violence done to grammar in email communication, will obviously fall outside our interest here. We will not concern ourselves with the emotional, psychological, chemical, media-related, or hormonal causes of violent behavior, nor with its effects on society at large. We will not address meanings of violence whose very definitions already contain a negative moral judgment, such as the Random House Webster's definition of violence as "an *unjust* or *unwarranted* exertion of force or power," since the adjectives "unjust" and "unwarranted" already qualify such actions as morally censurable. We will limit ourselves rather to exploring violence as human action, consciously chosen by a free moral agent.

Yet here we immediately encounter a nearly insurmountable obstacle, for the simple reason that violence does not, in fact, exist as a specifiable human act. It would seem, rather, almost to be a *mode* of action or a *way* that other acts are carried out. This may help to explain why it does not exist as a verb but only as a noun, adjective, or adverb (to "violate" corresponds to "violation" rather than "violence"). Rather than committing violence per se, it seems that we perform some other action in a more or less violent way.

In order to proceed, therefore, and to engage in a meaningful examination of the morality of violence, we will have to offer a necessarily restrictive and debatable definition of the same. It must include physical aggression and must also entail vehemence. In referring to violence as a human act, then, the definition we will work with is "*the use of physical force with the intent to cause physical harm to another human being.*"

Our central moral question then becomes: Is there such a thing as rationally chosen violence? Or in terms of Catholic social thought, is violence ever compatible with "charity in truth"? Philosophical ethics tells us that morally good behavior is reasonable, and that prudence—the *auriga virtutum*—is itself *recta ratio agibilium*, right reason in what ought to be done, or "rightly ordered conduct." Is violence ever of this sort? Is it always of this sort? Or if it is sometimes of this sort but not always, what accompanying factors determine its reasonableness or unreasonableness? This is the task before us.

A necessary first step in this process will involve an analysis of human acts and their moral taxonomy. We must establish what sort of acts are possible, how they are categorized, and into which category violence falls. Here I will venture to modify a more traditional analysis of moral acts, hoping to achieve greater precision in defining key terms.

Four Moral Categories of Human Actions

In categorizing types of moral acts, I propose four basic sorts of human actions, which are mutually exclusive and collectively exhaustive: (1) those that by their object are good, (2) those that are indifferent, (3) those that are evil, and (4) those that are generally excluded but not absolutely so. An essential part of our analysis will consist in discerning whether violence falls into the last or second-to-last category.

1. There are certain actions that are morally good by their species. Whether or not they have a character of obligation, they are praiseworthy in themselves. Examples of such morally good actions include the worship of God and the corporal and spiritual works of mercy. To help an elderly woman put her carry-on bag in the overhead bin on an airplane is simply a morally good thing to do. To stand up for a child being picked on at school recess is similarly

a meritorious act in itself. We could say that such acts are *simply good*. By their very object, these actions are not merely compatible with a morally good life, they are laudable in themselves and contribute to making one a good person.

It is true that circumstance and intention could vitiate these moral acts. Helping the elderly woman with her luggage in order to gain the approval of the pretty flight attendant could well eliminate the moral merit of one's action, just as Jesus counseled against praying on street corners in order to be seen. Yet of themselves prayer and assistance of the needy are good and they need no *added moral value* from intention or circumstance to be considered commendable. We could say that, all other things being equal (i.e., where no vitiating circumstance or intention is present), these actions are morally good and praiseworthy.

2.   On the opposite end of the spectrum, there are some acts to always and everywhere be excluded, as ends or as means called *intrinsically evil acts*. In the words of Pope John Paul II,

> there are objects of the human act which are by their nature "incapable of being ordered" to God, because they radically contradict the good of the person made in his image. These are the acts which, in the Church's moral tradition, have been termed "intrinsically evil" (*intrinsece malum*): they are such *always and per se*, in other words, on account of their very object, and quite apart from the ulterior intentions of the one acting and the circumstances.[9]

Such actions cannot be integrated into a morally good life. Regardless of the good consequences that may emerge from these choices, they can never be given a positive moral evaluation, since the acts themselves are iniquitous. Examples here include murder, adultery, torture, genocide, slavery and suicide.[10] Similarly, there are precepts forbidding always and everywhere such actions called moral absolutes or exceptionless moral norms.

In describing moral absolutes, Aristotle distinguishes between two types of actions always to be excluded as objects of choice: those whose definitions already bespeak immoderation, and those whose objects are always and everywhere evil in themselves because of their incompatibility with right reason. In his

Nichomachean Ethics, when discussing passions and emotions in terms of their mean, he states the following:

> But not every action or passion admits of a mean; for some have names that already imply badness, e.g. spite, shamelessness, envy, and in the case of actions adultery, theft, murder.... It is not possible, then, ever to be right with regard to them; one must always be wrong.[11]

Regarding the first type of intrinsically evil acts, we have already noted that, according to some definitions of the term, "violence" carries with it an inherent sense of immorality, which would make its justification a thorny enterprise altogether. For example, *The Concise Oxford Dictionary* offers a definition of violence as "unlawful exercise of physical force." Now if violence is by definition "unlawful," it has already been judged morally reprehensible. Others, such as John Hymers, argue that violence is "disordered force,"[12] and other definitions include the adjective "abusive" or "immoderate" when describing violence. By any of these definitions, violence as a specifiable human act is already morally excluded. Yet violence as we have defined it ("the use of physical force with the intent to cause physical harm to another person") is not this sort of act, since its definition bears no inherent immoderation. Nor is it necessarily an act of the second type of intrinsic moral evil as described by Aristotle, those whose objects are always and everywhere evil in themselves.

3. There are some acts that are, in themselves, morally neutral. According to the opinion of many, morally indifferent human acts are impossible, given the context in which they are chosen.[13] Here, however, I speak not of concretely instantiated human actions but human actions in the abstract, or what Thomas Aquinas called actions that are "indifferent in species."[14] Playing golf, reading a book, going for a walk, or buying groceries could fall into this category. These actions are compatible with human goodness and can be integrated into a program of moral excellence yet do not bespeak such excellence in and of themselves. In these cases, intention and circumstances grow in importance, since they significantly affect the moral character of the act.

For example, let's take the case of buying groceries—a mundane and morally indifferent human act. Let's say, however, that a husband goes out to buy needed groceries because he sees that his wife is weary and he would like to spare her the added fatigue of buying the family foodstuffs. Here, the outing—now properly described as an act of charity, or even an act of mercy—becomes morally praiseworthy. But this isn't the only possibility. What if the husband offers to go buy groceries in order to get out of the house and away from the unpleasant task of preparing his income tax returns? In this case, the moral quality of his action grows cloudier, either as a merited break or an abdication of duty. Consider a third scenario. What if the husband offers to go buy groceries in order to seem helpful, while all the while intending to purchase a pornographic magazine at the same time? Here his shopping foray takes on a decidedly negative moral coloring. Yet in and of itself, the act of purchasing groceries is a morally neutral act, fully consistent with a morally excellent life but not contributing decisively to its excellence. It only draws a moral tone when considered together with the moral agent's intentions and the global circumstances of the act.

4. It would seem, however, that the traditional breakdown of acts into praiseworthy, blameworthy, and neutral does not exhaust the possibilities. There is a fourth category comprising those acts that should generally be avoided, and never pursued for their own sake, but which may be permitted or even enjoined for other reasons (as means to other ends). These could be termed "justifiable physical evils" (to distinguish them from moral evils), where "justifiable" means able to be justified under certain circumstances. For example, the principle of "lesser evil" refers to physical evils of this sort, since moral evils may never be permitted even to achieve a greater good.[15] Like acts that are indifferent in their moral species, justifiable physical evils draw heavily on circumstances and intentions for their moral meaning, but unlike indifferent acts, they already bear a negative moral value. Actions falling into this category are myriad and would include the decision to wage war, the mutilation of the human body, the confiscation of another's property, medical experimentation on humans, or—it would seem—physical violence. Such actions carry a presumption such that they cannot be pursued for their own sake and may only morally be chosen where circumstances and intentions are able to justify them and

order them to the good. They do not, in other words, carry an internal self-justification. Without an overriding reason to engage in these acts, they would be morally wrong.

Stated in another way, unlike morally indifferent actions, this sort of human act would always be reprehensible in the absence of justifying conditions. In and of itself (in the absence of these conditions), such an action would be immoral but could become moral when certain conditions are present. War, for example, does not contain a self-justification but can only be chosen when certain conditions are met. One should never confiscate another's property willy-nilly, but only with sufficient cause, such as in Aquinas' example of not returning a madman his sword.[16]

Aquinas does not speak of this category of acts, yet one can integrate this addition into his thought. In speaking about the sorts of acts a person can carry out, Aquinas says the following:

> Wherefore if the object of an action includes something in accord with the order of reason, it will be a good action according to its species; for instance, to give alms to a person in want. On the other hand, if it includes something repugnant to the order of reason, it will be an evil act according to its species; for instance, to steal, which is to appropriate what belongs to another. But it may happen that the object of an action does not include something pertaining to the order of reason; for instance, to pick up a straw from the ground, to walk in the fields, and the like: and such actions are indifferent according to their species.[17]

Aquinas refers to the species of the acts as being in accord with reason, repugnant to reason or outside the order of reason, and from this we derive three sorts of acts. Yet there are also actions that *in themselves* are repugnant to reason (such as mutilation of a human being), which, however, when taken in the fullness of the act and including its circumstances and intentions may become lawful and even praiseworthy.

When we speak of a "presumption against violence," one must be careful not to import a series of assumptions that may or may not hold true. The chief reason for distinguishing between exceptionless moral norms and justifiable physical evils is precisely to show that the latter can sometimes be virtuously engaged in whereas the former can not. Yet there is no doubt that such a presumption exists, and hence "just war theory" describes the conditions necessary to "justify" a choice that has no internal self-justification.

Several questions spring to mind here. First, what distinguishes an intrinsically evil act, a *malum intrinsece*, from a justifiable physical evil? Second, how can an act that could never be chosen as an end sometimes be chosen as a means? This seems to contradict the moral principle that the end doesn't justify the means. Third, what criteria does one employ to determine the sufficient reason to engage in such an act?

To sum up this short exposé, we could say that some acts are praiseworthy when chosen for themselves; other acts are fully compatible with human goodness and may be chosen as an end in themselves or as a means to some other good end; some actions may never morally be chosen as an end in themselves or as a means to something else; and some actions may not be chosen unless certain justifying conditions are present. Our question continues to be: does violence as earlier defined fall into the third category or the fourth?

How Can a Physical Evil Be Justified?

Traditional morality holds that *bonum ex integra causa, malum ex quocumque defectu.*[18] A good action must be completely good, in its object, intention and circumstances. Whereas any moral defect vitiates an action, only a totally good action is good. If this is the case, how can physical evils be morally justified? Can bad actions be made good? The answer clearly is no. A morally bad action may never be carried out, but other circumstances may come together to make the action not morally bad, but indifferent or good. If, as it is said, good intentions and good circumstances do not rectify a bad action, then in what sense is an action truly *bad* if it can be rectified by these causes? The confusion here stems from the analogy of evil. A physical evil is not a moral evil and could sometimes be chosen without engaging in moral evil. When we say that the end doesn't justify the means, we mean that an intrinsic evil cannot be made good by a good end. In reality, the end often does justify either indifferent actions or physical evils. The question is, how does this come about?

By a Change in the Object?

Sometimes apparently evil actions can be justified when it is seen that the action, though seeming to be of a moral species incompatible with human goodness, in reality belong to a different moral species. An act of lethal self-defense, though it involves the killing of a human being, is not an act of murder. Withholding information from a person who has no right to it is not lying, since it is not unjust to refuse to render to another that which is not his due. Sometimes the circumstances surrounding an action change the moral species of the act. "Sexual intercourse with a woman" includes everything from conjugal relations to adultery to fornication to rape to incest, and the circumstances here (the woman in question is another's wife, or girlfriend, or sister...) change the species of the moral act.[19] In fact, "sexual intercourse with a person of the opposite sex" is an insufficient description of a human act to define its moral species. We need further circumstances in order to know what sort of moral act we are dealing with, even though our description of the physical act seems clear enough.

At times, in other words, the circumstances surrounding an action are so important to the nature of the action that they define the moral species of the action. In these cases, the circumstances cease to be merely circumstances and become an essential part of the act itself. The identity of the person chosen as a tennis opponent does not affect the nature of the act, whereas the identity of the person chosen as a partner for sexual relations does define the nature of the act. Elements that may seem to be accidental to an act—such as place, identity, time, and other factors—can sometimes be essential to the nature of the act as a moral choice.

By a Change in the Intention?

Doing the right thing for the wrong reason vitiates human action. Sometimes intention colors an action sufficiently to make it either morally good or morally evil. For any action to be morally good, it must be done with a good intention. At the same time, a good intention can never make an intrinsically evil action good. For example, the intentional termination of the life of a sick patient with the intention of sparing him or her further suffering can never be a good act, despite the (misguided) compassion that motivates it.

On the other hand, slapping a child's hand simply out of anger or frustration, or doing so out of cruelty, or doing so with the loving intention of educating the child through proper discipline may radically alter a moral judgment of the act. Here it seems clear that a "physical evil" (slapping a child) should not be pursued for its own sake but may be pursued for the sake of a greater good (the child's formation of character). In this case, intention becomes paramount and actually justifies an action that in and of itself would be reprehensible. Yet here, too, the change in moral quality of the act may result from a change in its formal object. Slapping a child's hand out of malice and doing so as an act of discipline— out of love—actually constitute two different moral acts. The species of corporal punishment is a different sort of human act from a random act of cruelty. Here, a change in intention is sufficient to change the object of the act itself.

In other cases, however, a change in intention may change the moral quality of an act without altering its moral species. A declaration of war, for instance, may be just or unjust while still remaining specifically a declaration of war. The difference between a just war and an unjust war comes from a combination of intentions and circumstances (just cause, probability of success, etc.) that change the moral quality of the decision (to engage in war) without modifying its object.

By a Change in the Circumstances?

As we have seen, at times a change in circumstances means a change in the moral species of an act. Even when this does not happen, the circumstances of a moral act can significantly influence its moral quality, especially in the case of morally indifferent acts and physical evils. The Church forcefully rejects the premise of "situation ethics," by which the moral value of an action would depend primarily on the circumstances, because the theory downplays the value of the object of the act, which gives the action its moral specificity.[20] According to situation ethics, moral absolutes are impossible, since hypothetical situations can always be imagined whereby any action could at some point be morally good.

While avoiding such extremes, the importance of circumstance in determining the moral quality of actions that are not intrinsically evil cannot be gainsaid. For example, as we have seen in the choice to wage war (involving the *ius ad bellum*), a series of conditions are necessary to justify the decision. These conditions—such as prospects of success, the damage inflicted by the aggressor, etc.—are circumstances and do not change the species of the act, although they do alter the moral licitness of the choice and can actually determine its evil, lawfulness, or obligatory character.

Violence as the Will to Harm

We have described violence as the use of force with the intent to cause physical harm to another. Can such an action be integrated into a morally good life? At first blush it would seem that it cannot. One of the principal ethical precepts students learn in medical school is the Latin adage: *primum non nocere* (first, do no harm).[21] At least for medicine, before any obligation to assist another comes the negative mandate to avoid hurting another. The Hippocratic Oath states: "I will prescribe regimen for the good of my patients according to my ability and by judgment and never do harm to anyone." This principle of medical ethics would seem to apply to general ethics as well. An intent to harm would contradict the Golden Rule, as well as Jesus' command to love one's neighbor as one's self. No one wills harm to himself and thus cannot will it to another.

It is also clear that if willing harm to someone is synonymous with willing evil to someone, then such an act is simply evil in itself. We clearly cannot will harm for its own sake, since such a will is necessarily iniquitous. To will harm *tout court* is to will evil. Here, too, our definition of violence as willing physical harm is different from merely willing physical pain (for whatever reason), since it implies true damage rather than a sensitive or nervous experience. The two may overlap in a moral analysis, but they do not coincide.

There may be, however, limited exceptions to the general principle of not willing harm to another. To intend harm to another can never be chosen for its own sake, but may, in certain circumstances, be chosen as a means to a good end. As in the case of other justifiable physical evils, the choice to inflict harm may at times become morally licit in certain circumstances. The most obvious is the reason of self-defense, a topic we examine more closely in the next chapter. To deliberately harm an aggressor to protect oneself or another may be morally acceptable and sometimes praiseworthy. Here the harm to another is intended not as an end but as a means to defend oneself or another from harm. There must, of course, be some proportionality between the harm inflicted and the harm avoided, though an exact proportionality is not required. Self-defense is not incompatible with the moral exigency of always willing good to others, since even when inflicting harm in order to stop an aggressor, one wills good to them and intends only to impede them from doing harm.

Recent magisterial pronouncements regarding capital punishment have adopted a similar line of reasoning.[22] In *Evangelium Vitae*, Pope John Paul II chose to locate his discussion of the death penalty under the heading of legitimate defense. Here the ordinarily reprehensible act of deliberately killing another human being can occasionally be justified, but only where the offender is still in some way an aggressor. John Paul wrote:

> It is clear that, for these purposes to be achieved, the nature and extent of the punishment must be carefully evaluated and decided upon, and ought not go to the extreme of executing the offender except in cases of absolute necessity: in other words, when it would not be possible otherwise to defend society.[23]

A borderline case is that of corporal punishment. It would ordinarily be reprehensible to apprehend a human being and subject him to a drubbing. In and of itself such an act would be morally illicit. Yet this action—which has no internal self-justification and therefore can never be chosen for its own sake—may at times be licitly chosen as a means either of education or of retribution (proportionate both to the evil being punished and the good end envisioned). Here the distinction made above between intending pain and intending harm becomes especially necessary, since pain is momentary whereas physical damage is permanent. Corporal punishment (when licit) intends pain without intending harm.

Corporal punishment is in fact of a different moral species than wanton physical aggression. One should not infer from this difference that the right to punish provides moral justification for any sort of punishment. Punishment, corporal or otherwise, offers a moral case somewhat analogous to that of just war doctrine, in that it first requires sufficient reason to punish (analogous to *ius ad bellum*) and then requires other moral considerations in its application (analogous to *ius in bello*). Something similar must obtain in the case of violence, where the broad category of "physical harm" is not univocal but spans everything from piercing a person's earlobe to hewing off his head. Even where violence is morally permissible, it must respond to a principle of proportionality.

A thornier case, however, is that of torture. The United Nations claims in the clearest of terms that torture is never justifiable:

> Art. 2.2. No exceptional circumstances whatsoever, whether a state of war or a threat of war, internal political instability or any other public emergency, may be invoked as a justification of torture.

> Art. 2.3. An order from a superior officer or a public authority may not be invoked as a justification of torture.[24]

The Church's Magisterium has likewise reached a settled position that torture falls into the category of intrinsically evil actions.[25] Still, it is notoriously difficult to define torture with any exactitude. Everyone understands that the public authorities can apply pressure, for example, to criminals to induce them to reveal information necessary for the protection of citizens. Up to what point is this application of pressure a justifiable physical evil, which may be permitted when the gravest of circumstances require it? And then, when does it cross the line and become torture, ruled out by a moral absolute? Making a terrorist's life uncomfortable so that he will reveal the location of a bomb set to go off in a major city is surely justifiable (whereas simply making someone's life unpleasant is ordinarily morally reprehensible). But where does discomfort give way to torture? What sort of threats and actual pain can be administered in the name of self-defense or legitimate punishment and what actions fall under the category of intrinsically evil actions?

It would seem that the essential dividing line between the two must be more than just a question of degree, such as when one distinguishes between grave and light matter in the area of theft. Surely a light beating cannot be licit and a severe beating intrinsically evil. There must be another factor at work here to produce this bright line of difference.[26]

It would seem that torture as a definable moral act consists in the intentional infliction of extreme physical or psychological suffering on a non-consenting, defenseless person, entailing substantial curtailment of the exercise of the person's autonomy generally for the purpose of breaking the victim's will.[27] A distinguishing mark of torture begins to emerge as more than the infliction of pain, no matter how great, and rather as the curbing of personal autonomy and the breaking of a person's will so that he or she becomes willing to do what he or she would otherwise not choose to do. This is not simply the case of furnishing sufficient motivation to do so, but rather of making a person virtually incapable of not doing so.

A second justification for doing harm comes to us under the name of the "principle of totality," an expression coined by Pope Pius XII in an address to the First International Congress on the Histopathology of the Nervous System in 1952.[28] By this principle, the part only exists for the sake of the whole and thus can be sacrificed when absolutely necessary for the good of the whole. This principle was developed to explain how mutilation is morally permissible in certain cases. Mutilation of the human body, especially when causing irreparable damage to the organism, constitutes an evil to be avoided. Corporal mutilation refers to any procedure that temporarily or permanently impairs the natural and complete integrity of the body or its functions."[29] Yet the point of reference here is the person himself and his life, not the arm, the leg, or any other member.

Mutilation can at times be permitted, therefore, as a means to a greater good. Sometimes diseased limbs or organs, such as a gangrenous foot, must be removed for the sake of the entire organism. Moreover, this principle also allows for the removal of *healthy* body parts for the sake of preserving life, such as when a person cuts off a healthy foot stuck in a railway track in order to escape from an oncoming train.[30]

Formulations of this principle always specify that such mutilations are licit only when the good end sought is unattainable by other means. For example, Pius XII stated that one may destroy or mutilate parts of the body "when and in the measure which is necessary for the good of the being as a whole, to assure his existence, or to avoid or repair grave and lasting damage which cannot in any other way be avoided or repaired."[31] Partial harm is done to the person for his greater good.

This principle was also applied, however, to justify organ donation. During the 1940s organ transplants became medically possible. Moral theologians and ethicists debated the issue for decades and neither Pius XII nor John XXIII nor Paul VI issued any substantive or definitive statement on organ transplants from living donors. It was not until the promulgation of the 1992 *Catechism of the Catholic Church* that the Catholic papal Magisterium pronounced authoritatively on the subject. The Catechism sums up magisterial teaching with the simple expression: "Organ transplants are in conformity with the moral law if the physical and psychological dangers and risks incurred by the donor are proportionate to the good sought for the recipient."[32]

What could seem evident to us now proved a source of great vexation and discussion for moral theologians of the time. The problem was that unlike therapeutic mutilation, the principle of totality seemed ill-suited to justify what we could now call heterologous organ transplants (to distinguish from homologous organ transplant in the case of say, moving a piece of healthy flesh from the buttocks to the face in the case of burn victims). Strictly speaking, the procedure of heterologous transplanting of organs is not therapeutic, in the sense that the mutilation does not benefit the donor undergoing it. The principle of totality cannot be ethically applied because the relationship of one person to another or even to the community is not that of a part to the whole. One person does not exist for the sake of another, but each possesses an inviolable dignity as an end in himself.

Saint Thomas Aquinas famously described the relationship of the individual to the community as a part to a whole to justify capital punishment, but this analogy can only be taken so far.[33] In speaking of the limits of public authority over the physical being of citizens, Pope Pius XII distinguished between a physical organism, which "has a unity subsisting in itself" and whose members have no sense or finality outside the whole organism, and the moral community, which "is not a physical unity subsisting in itself and its individual members are not integral parts of it."[34]

An early defense of the morality of heterologous organ transplants came from Bert J. Cunningham in his doctoral dissertation at Catholic University in 1944.[35] In this work, Cunningham argues that what is permissible to do for the good of oneself one may also do for the good of another. He points out that the members of one's own body are directed not only to one's own good but in a certain way to the good of others. If the individual himself is ordered not only to his own good but to the good of others, then the parts of the individual are also ordered to the good of others. Since according to Catholic morality one may and indeed should sometimes risk one's life for another, for certain very serious needs of others one should be able to undergo the lesser evil of mutilation, Cunningham concludes.

A statement by Pope Pius XII in 1958 opened the door for applying the principle of totality to heterologous organ transplants. "To the subordination of particular organs to the organism and to its own finality," he wrote, "is added the spiritual finality of the individual himself."[36] Not only are members subordinated to the good of the body, but a person's corporal good does not exhaust his comprehensive good, which includes his spiritual good. Pius' words were later applied by ethicists to the case of organ transplants from live donors in that the spiritual good of self-giving toward one's neighbor justified what would otherwise have been illicit because such an act, though harming corporal integrity, contributes to the moral and spiritual good of the donor himself. In this way, and assuming the voluntary nature of the donor's gift, one person is not instrumentalized for the good of another but integrates his self-sacrificing act of charity into his overall end as a spiritual being.

It should be noted that other attempts to apply the principle of totality to justify otherwise illicit actions have been rejected by the Church's Magisterium, notably when applied to the use of contraception in marriage. Some argued that a single contraceptive act in the midst of a marital life devoted to childbearing and education could not constitute an intrinsic evil, since the act would be ordered to the ultimate good of marriage and family life. This position was rejected by Pope Paul VI.[37]

A similar rationale was typically invoked to justify corporal punishment for children, by which pain is intentionally administered though intended ultimately for the good of the one being punished. A parent's well-administered spanking does not intend permanent harm to the child but the child's overall good. In this case, something that ordinarily would be worthy of reproach (the intentional causing of physical pain to another) can become justifiable. Although here we are speaking about pain rather than physical harm (which differs from the definition of violence we proposed earlier on), the same principle seems to hold. If one or the other is chosen for the ultimate good of the person receiving it, it may be lawful.

A problem that immediately emerges in applying the principle of totality, however, is the question of how to overcome the rationale employed in ages past to justify torture and other actions now seen as morally abhorrent. If, as Christians, we understand eternal life to be infinitely more valuable than our earthly existence, how can we disallow actions that aim at the eternal good of persons even while restricting their temporal good? If it is morally permissible to amputate a gangrenous leg for the sake of saving a person's life, why should it be unlawful to do this or even more severe things for the sake of saving a person's soul? Why, for instance, would it be unlawful to kill a small child immediately after baptism, thus ensuring its final salvation rather than exposing it to the awful risk of losing this, its greatest good?

It would seem that the answer—necessarily brief and incomplete in this present study—lies in a twofold distinction. First, a consequentialistic calculus of goods is insufficient to determine the morality of a given act, and thus even if we were absolutely certain that our action would cause the intended finality, even this good end would not justify absolutely any means. The existence of moral absolutes means that certain sorts of action may never be morally chosen, no matter how great the perceived outcome. Second, in the case of torture, the outcome is never certain, and even where the outcome seems favorable (a person's conversion to the true faith, for instance, or a renunciation of past errors), such a result proceeds from psychological obligation rather than a true, human act of choosing. The person must always be treated as a person, which is another way of saying that the person's dignity must be respected at all times. This final condition is the least developed of all in classical moral theory, yet the one most often appealed to in contemporary moral discourse on these related topics.

A Prima Facie Judgment

The preceding considerations provide a contextualization for the problem of violence, as well as the necessary elements to arrive at a *prima facie* judgment regarding its morality. Understood as the use of physical force with the intent to cause physical harm to another person, such an action must be of the sort against which there is a true moral presumption but which does not constitute an intrinsic evil. Violence can never be undertaken for its own sake but requires a justification. Moreover, even when it is justified, it must be proportionate to the end sought and consistent with the dignity of the one suffering it.

One may morally use physical force with the intent to cause physical harm as a means of defending one's own or someone else's life. One may also do so when the good of the person suffering the violence requires it. This would seem to reflect Magisterial teaching that "[e]xcept when performed for strictly therapeutic medical reasons, directly intended amputations, mutilations, and sterilizations performed on innocent persons are against the moral law."[38] In this regard, it draws important moral principles from just war theory, just punishment theory, studies on torture and capital punishment, and the principle of totality.

The main problem with violence as a moral category continues to be its inherent ambiguity. Moral analysis demands precision, and "violence" suffers from an intrinsic lack of such precision. Still, by sufficiently narrowing down its definition, some sort of moral analysis may be fruitfully undertaken. The foregoing reflections are meant to initiate such an analysis and to provide one voice in a moral discussion to which other voices must be added. As the sort of action that requires moral justification, however, violence will continue to be held up by Catholic social doctrine as something to be avoided whenever possible, even to the point of its total practical exclusion. We will see that something similar occurs with the case of capital punishment, a particular case of lethal violence.

Chapter 5

Capital Punishment and the Just Society

The previous chapter sets the stage for a closer analysis of another key issue of Catholic social doctrine that has undergone substantial review in recent decades. Few issues today arouse such moral passion as capital punishment. Since capital punishment is an act of political authority, its moral analysis naturally falls squarely in social ethics rather than bioethics or other areas of moral study.

Unlike more abstruse theological disputes of ages past, capital punishment elicits opinions not only from professional academics but also from dentists, housewives, taxi drivers, accountants, and hairdressers. This nearly universal interest in the death penalty should not lead us to suppose, however, that any sort of unanimity has been reached—far from it. With equal vehemence and subjective certitude, one will argue in defense of capital punishment and another for its abolishment. And though the scales of public conscience seem to be tipping ever more in favor of the abolitionists, as of yet, neither side has secured an uncontested claim to the moral high ground.

Modern sensibilities clearly lean toward the prohibition of capital punishment. There was a time, not long ago, when people and nations considered the death penalty useful, moral, and necessary as a punishment for serious crimes. This is no longer the case. There has been a fundamental shift in attitudes regarding the death penalty in the last 50 years. Since World War II, nearly all democratic countries have outlawed capital punishment, except in the case of military law. On the global scene, 95 countries have abolished the death penalty, with the Netherlands and Gabon outlawing capital punishment as recently as 2010. In recent years, countries without capital punishment have outnumbered those that still permit the practice with an ever further tipping of the scales in favor of abolition.[1] The United States, where a majority of citizens favor the death penalty, stands out as an anomaly among democratic countries.

In the ubiquitous debate on the death penalty, theological propositions are often thrown together with philosophical, historical, political, juridical, emotional, and pragmatic arguments, resulting in an almost-anything-goes hodge-podge of answers. The incommensurability of these levels of reasoning (or feeling) snarls discussion and makes reaching any conclusion a formidable project.

Furthermore, among Catholic thinkers the death penalty presents particular difficulties not found in other contemporary areas of controversy. In the case of abortion, contraception, or women's ordination, for example, lines are clearly drawn between theologians loyal to the Magisterium and those who dissent from Church teaching. Regarding capital punishment, on the other hand, such black and white categories do not exist. By drawing on centuries of theological reasoning from monumental figures like St. Augustine and St. Thomas Aquinas, one can mount an impressive case for the legitimacy of the death penalty. Others, however, would compare capital punishment to issues like slavery, formally condemned by the Church only recently, and for centuries tacitly accepted, and even defended by many theologians. Such thinkers point to the pronouncements of Pope John Paul II—passages in the *Catechism of the Catholic Church* concerning capital punishment were modified to incorporate the Pope's words on the subject in his encyclical *Evangelium Vitae*—and forecast still further evolution in Catholic doctrine, to the point of proscribing the death penalty altogether. Pope John Paul II intervened publicly in several cases to appeal for a commutation of the death sentence, and as recently as September 9, 2010, Pope Benedict XVI joined several Catholic bishops to request clemency for Gregory Wilson, a prisoner scheduled for execution in Kentucky.

As in the case of many other moral quandaries, the road to a solution may lie in getting the question right. Maybe—as Walker Percy would say—the wrong questions are being asked. At the very least we must recognize that in the area of capital punishment a variety of questions could be asked, and answers will correspondingly vary.

In this chapter I propose to focus on the three questions I consider most important for a proper ethical analysis of capital punishment: (1) the questions of justice, (2) the question of legitimacy, and (3) the question of opportuneness. Although these three questions overlap, each involves particular nuances and merits a separate inquiry.

The Question of Justice

A 1998 issue of *Commentary* magazine featured an article by David Gelernter, bearing the provocative title, "What Do Murderers Deserve?"[2] Taken at face value, the question requires little deliberation: murderers deserve to die. They have intentionally taken the life of another and to restore the balance that justice demands, they must suffer a similar fate. Anything short of death cannot possibly satisfy the requirements of strict justice. Indeed, after several pages of rumination this is precisely the conclusion Gelernter reaches.

Such moral reasoning forms part of the patrimony of human civilization. The adage "let the punishment fit the crime" echoes the Old Testament injunction "an eye for an eye, a tooth for a tooth." The actual expression used by Scripture is still more explicit: "Anyone who maims another shall suffer the same injury in return: fracture for fracture, eye for eye, tooth for tooth; the injury inflicted is the injury to be suffered" (Lev 24:19-20).[3] As a principle of justice and taken by itself, this logic seems to make perfect sense. Yet such reasoning gives rise to several problems. First of all, do we really seek absolute justice? Would we like to see all crimes, sins, and offenses (including our own) punished as they truly deserve?

In a typical passage from Scripture, the Psalmist, reflecting on the universality of guilt and the consequent universal need for pardon, writes, "If you, O Lord, should mark our guilt, Lord, who would survive?" (Ps 130). Who, indeed, we may ask, is free from moral evil? Who among us deserves no punishment? Similar reflections have been incorporated into the First Eucharistic Prayer: "*Do not consider what we truly deserve*, but grant us your forgiveness." In these words of the Roman Canon, we entreat our Lord not only to refrain from *applying* the punishment we truly deserve but even from *considering* it. The fact is, as we acknowledge in the preceding line of the Canon, we are indeed sinners and therefore worthy of punishment. Clearly this argument in and of itself would not rule out the death penalty, but as Christians it should give us pause when we seek to exact full retribution for others' sins.

When St. Ambrose was asked in the 4th century about his opinion on capital punishment, the imperial prefect-turned-archbishop of Milan replied by making reference to Jesus' conduct with the adulterous women (Jn 8) as the example to follow.[4] Jesus doesn't address the question of the woman's guilt or the appropriateness of the Mosaic prescription of stoning, but instead invites her zealous accusers to examine their own innocence before meting out the prescribed penalty.

Secondly, must punishment necessarily correspond in species to the crime committed? If this were the case, the use of prisons would be limited to those who detain others against their will. As it stands, the practice of incarcerating thieves, rapists, and drunk drivers reflects our understanding that punishment, in order to be just, need not mimic the crime committed. As long as the penalty is proportionate to the gravity of the crime, it satisfies the demands of justice.

Many of our contemporaries deem it a genuine advance in human civilization that public authority no longer retaliates against criminals along the lines that strict justice would seem to mandate. For instance, the penalty of mutilation (e.g., amputating a thief's hand), still practiced in certain societies, is commonly considered to be a vestige of more barbarous times.

The opinion that murder, especially when premeditated and particularly cruel, necessarily requires the death penalty as the only commensurate chastisement cannot be sustained. Commensurability is relative, not absolute. Justice demands a proportionality between punishment and crime, but justice will always be approximate and imperfect in this life. There are crimes qualitatively or quantitatively worse than a single murder—such as certain forms of torture, mass murder or serial killing—which could not be redressed absolutely even by the death of the perpetrator.

Thirdly, can justice be taken as the sole criterion in dealing with malefactors? Is the restoration of equilibrium sufficient unto itself as a principle to guide human action in dealing with others' misdeeds?

On the one hand we recognize that "legitimate public authority has the right and duty to inflict penalties commensurate with the gravity of the crime."[5] The moral sense of mankind has always insisted that good actions merit praise and reward, while evil deserves reprobation and punishment. It likewise offends our sense of justice to think that all crimes should receive equal punishment, or that greater offenses should not receive correspondingly greater penalties. On the other hand we shun certain punishments as unworthy of truly human society. In so doing we implicitly invoke another standard to temper the principle of justice: the principle of respect for human dignity.[6] Thus Pope John Paul II insisted that public authority should limit itself to bloodless means whenever possible, since, as the Catechism puts it, they "are more in conformity to the dignity of the human person."[7]

The Second Vatican Council noted with approval the "growing awareness of the exalted dignity proper to the human person,"[8] together with his universal rights and duties. The question of the dignity of the person commands supreme importance because from this dignity spring man's natural rights, the most basic of which is the inalienable right to life.[9] Does this dignity, and hence this right, perdure in the criminal, or does he somehow forfeit his dignity? Does one's crime effectively alienate the inalienable right to life?

In this regard St. Thomas argued to the affirmative. According to Aquinas, by sinning man loses the dignity of his humanity and falls into the state of the beasts. "Hence," he concludes, "although it be evil in itself to kill a man so long as he preserve his dignity, yet it may be good to kill a man who has sinned, even as it is to kill a beast."[10] As Germain Grisez points out, Aquinas' reasoning here is flawed.[11] Carried to its logical conclusion, such a postulate would lead to moral chaos. Whereas according to Catholic doctrine man falls from grace by any mortal sin, and thus makes himself worthy of hell (which, fortunately, the State cannot impose), he does not thereby efface the image of God in his soul, which lies at the base of his personal dignity.[12] As St. Thomas rightly says, by sinning man "departs from the order of reason," but this departure does not destroy his inherent resemblance to his Creator nor his personhood, since it is not ontological but moral.

If things were otherwise we could rightly treat anyone in a state of sin (which, in any event, we can never ascertain with certainty) with the same impunity with which we treat animals. Not only would murderers be liable to the death penalty but under the right conditions, so would adulterers, heretics, fornicators, and those who willfully miss Mass on

Sunday. Moreover there could be no further talk of "humane" punishment for such perpetrators; they could be dispatched like a lame horse or a blind dog. Punishment itself, in fact, would lose all retributive meaning, since the very concept implies a free and willing wrongdoer, and consequently personal dignity.

Personal sinfulness, therefore, does not abrogate the sanctity of the life of the sinner nor his dignity as a person. In *Evangelium Vitae,* Pope John Paul spoke of the "great care [that] must be taken to respect every life, even that of criminals and unjust aggressors."[13] Likewise, when the same pope issued appeals for clemency in the cases of death-row inmates Karla Faye Tucker and Joseph O'Dell, he made no reference to the verdict of the court or of the possible innocence of the plaintiffs. Rather he appealed to the sanctity of all human life, which belongs to God and not to man.

In 1960, long before becoming Pope, Karol Wojtyla expressed what he called the personalist principle, which, as we saw earlier, states that "the person is a good towards which the only proper and adequate attitude is love."[14] That goes for good persons, bad persons, saints, and criminals. "To be just," wrote Wojtyla, "always means giving others what is rightly due to them. A person's rightful due is to be treated as an object of love." In this sense, he continued, "it can be said that love is a requirement of justice."[15] Obviously, this love takes different forms, not excluding punishment, but it is incompatible with willfully taking another's life. Love necessarily seeks the good of the other, and the first good is existence itself.

In summary, we conclude that capital punishment corresponds to a certain strain of justice, but a justice which is insufficient as a principle for ordering society because it fails to take into account the dignity of the person. For such a right ordering of society, justice must be tempered and perfected by love. In his 1980 encyclical letter *Dives in Misericordia*, Pope John Paul wrote that "[t]he experience of the past and of our own time demonstrates that justice alone is not enough, that it can even lead to the negation and destruction of itself, if that deeper power, which is love, is not allowed to shape human life in its various dimensions."[16] Pope Benedict further developed this line of thought in *Caritas in Veritate*, where he stated:

> *Charity goes beyond justice*, because to love is to give, to offer what is "mine" to the other; but it never lacks justice, which prompts us to

give the other what is "his", what is due to him by reason of his being or his acting… On the other hand, charity transcends justice and completes it in the logic of giving and forgiving.[17]

The Question of Legitimacy

As we see, the matter of strict justice does not exhaust the problem of capital punishment, and perhaps it is not even the most important question. A second area of inquiry could be expressed as follows: Is it *licit* for public authority to execute criminals? Here our interest centers on the juridical question: what is permissible and what is forbidden. Once again, besides responding to this particular question, we must also explore the appropriateness of the question itself.

To set the stage, a brief historical analysis is necessary. We must examine—albeit in a sketchy fashion—what Sacred Scripture, theology, and the Church's Magisterium have taught regarding the legitimacy of capital punishment.

With regard to Biblical teaching on the matter, we have already touched on the Old Testament understanding of retributive justice. For centuries many have defended the legitimacy of the death penalty based on its practice in the Old Testament, especially when tied to an important text from the New Testament, namely from Paul's letter to the Romans. In this letter Paul states,

> Let every person be subject to the governing authorities. For there is no authority except from God, and those that exist have been instituted by God. Therefore he who resists the authorities resists what God has appointed, and those who resist will incur judgment. For rulers are not a terror to good conduct, but to bad. Would you have no fear of him who is in authority? Then do what is good, and you will receive his approval, for he is God's servant for your good. But if you do wrong, be afraid, for he does not bear the sword in vain; he is the servant of God to execute his wrath on the wrongdoer. (Rom 13:1-4).

Nevertheless, though Jesus came "not to abolish the law… but to fulfill [it]" (Mt 5:17), in many cases provisions of the Old Law were in fact substantially modified by the New Law. In this regard we should bear in mind that the Old Testament prescribed the death penalty not only in the case of murder but also in the case of blasphemy (Lv 24:16), idolatry (Ex 22:19; Nm 25:5), working on the Sabbath (Ex 31:15; 35:2), kidnapping (Ex 21:16), homosexuality (Lv 20:13), bestiality (Ex 22:19; Lv 20:15-16), sorcery (Ex 22:18; Lv 20:27), striking or cursing one's parents (Ex 21:15, 17; Lv 20:9), and adultery (Lv 20:10). We have seen how Jesus himself declined to apply this prescription in the case of adultery (Jn 8:13). Moreover, the ethical finality of capital punishment in the Old Testament theocracy (safeguarding Israel's fidelity to the covenant with Yahweh) differs radically from its understood purpose in the modern state (protection of society and promotion of the common good).

Opponents of capital punishment frequently indicate God's dealing with Cain after his crime of fratricide as a counter-example to the mandate of the death penalty in the Pentateuch. Not only does God not punish Cain's crime with death, he also prohibits others from harming him. "Then the Lord said to him, 'Whoever kills Cain will suffer a sevenfold vengeance.' And the Lord put a mark on Cain, so that no one who came upon him would kill him" (Gn 4:15).

The above citation from Paul's letter to the Romans does not legitimate capital punishment but only upholds the authority of civil government and its power of coercion in general. In regard to this passage and specifically to the "sword borne by public authority," Pope Pius XII taught that Paul was referring to "the essential foundation itself of penal power and of its immanent finality" and not to the content of "individual juridical prescriptions or rules of action."[18]

For its part, theological reflection has generally affirmed the legitimacy of capital punishment, though this was not so from the beginning. In the first centuries of Christianity the Mosaic precept against killing was interpreted literally and without exceptions. Capital punishment was considered irreconcilable with the faith, and such occupations as judge and soldier were excluded from licit professions for Christians, in order to avoid having to pronounce or execute the death sentence. Among those who taught in this vein were Lactantius,[19] Tertullian,[20] St. Cyprian,[21] and St. Ambrose.[22] In tongue-in-cheek fashion, St. Cyprian writes: "A homicide committed for private interests is a crime; committed in the name of the State it is a virtue."[23]

From St. Augustine on, however, capital punishment was seen in a different light. In his *City of God*, for example, Augustine speaks of certain exceptions to the divine law forbidding killing of a human being, including "for the representatives of the State's authority to put criminals to death, according to law or the rule of rational justice."[24] As a rationale for these exceptions, Augustine referred to agents of authority as "a sword in the hand" of God and cites a series of examples from the Old Testament where men are justified in killing in obedience to God.

St. Thomas Aquinas' argument takes a slightly different tack. As we saw in the previous chapter, in the *Summa Theologiae* Aquinas affirms that the individual person is to the community as a part to the whole. Thus, just as a decayed member of the body may be excised for the good of the whole, so too "if a man be dangerous and infectious to the community… he may be killed in order to safeguard the common good."[25] Theologians after St. Thomas by and large followed his line on the death penalty, and alternative interpretations only began to surface in the late 18th century.[26] It should be noted that many of these theologians who argued in favor of capital punishment employed the same reasoning to justify public whipping and mutilation as well.[27] Such penalties were defended on the grounds that they are necessary for preserving the common good and safeguarding society.[28]

Finally, as regards the teaching of the Magisterium of the Church, until fairly recently the overall tenor of the scattered papal pronouncements or allusions to capital punishment tended toward acceptance of a practice firmly ensconced in society and in civil law and commonly defended by theologians.

The first Pope to take a stand in favor of the death penalty was Innocent I in the year 405, who in response to a query from the bishop of Toulouse bases his favorable position on Paul's letter to the Romans. Innocent wrote,

> In regard to this question we have nothing definitive from those who have gone before us. It must be remembered that power was granted by God, and to avenge crime the sword was permitted; he who carries out this vengeance is God's minister (Rm 13:1-4). What motive have we for condemning a practice that all hold to be

permitted by God? We uphold, therefore, what has been observed until now, in order not to alter the discipline and so that we may not appear to act contrary to God's authority.[29]

In the year 866, however, Pope Nicholas I adopted a different angle in his letter to the newly converted Bulgarian Christians. Nicholas urges the neophytes to promote life both of body and soul, and to "rescue from death not only the innocent, but also the guilty."[30] As grounds for his argument, Nicholas appeals to the example of Christ, who had saved the Bulgarians from their imprisonment to death and brought them to eternal life.[31]

After the turn of the millennium came another milestone in the Church's reflections on capital punishment. In dealing with Waldensian heretics who sought reentry into the Catholic Church, Pope Innocent III required the pronouncement of a profession of faith which included the statement: "The secular power can without mortal sin carry out a sentence of death, provided it proceeds in imposing the penalty not from hatred but with judgment, not carelessly but with due solicitude."[32]

The basic acceptance of the legitimacy of capital punishment continued through more recent pontificates, though usually in the form of indirect reference. In his brief 1891 encyclical letter to the bishops of the Austro-Hungarian Empire, *Pastoralis Officii*, Leo XIII wrote of the prohibition by divine and natural law of killing or wounding a human being, "except for a public cause [that is, by public authority] or in the necessity of defending one's own life."[33]

Pius XII presented a more explicit defense of the lawfulness of capital punishment. He states that "as long as a man is without guilt, his life is untouchable," and adds that "God is the sole lord of the life of a man not guilty of a crime punishable by the death penalty."[34] The Pontiff provides the moral reasoning behind his thought on capital punishment in an address to a congress of doctors: "Even in the case of the death penalty the State does not dispose of the individual's right to life. Rather public authority limits itself to depriving the offender of the good of life in expiation for his guilt, after he himself, through his crime, has deprived himself of the right to life."[35]

Despite these instances of support for the legitimacy of capital punishment on the part of the Magisterium, many theologians do not see in these pronouncements an unreformable teaching, at least prior to the publication of *Evangelium Vitae*. There has been considerable agreement that the received position on capital punishment was generally taken for granted but never formally declared by the Magisterium. As a representative example, Anselm Günthör wrote in 1979 that, regarding capital punishment, "the statements of the ecclesial Magisterium are occasional assertions and do not represent a fully definitive position; we must not undervalue them, but nor should we consider them to be unchangeable and perennially valid Magisterial statements."[36]

Here it is worth recalling the teaching of the Second Vatican Council regarding the interpretation of Magisterial statements. *Lumen Gentium* proposes three factors by which the "manifest mind and intention" of the Roman Pontiff can be known, namely "by the character of the document in question, or by the frequency with which a certain doctrine is proposed, or by the manner in which the doctrine is formulated."[37] In the case of capital punishment, the Magisterium has consistently upheld the legitimacy of the death penalty in principle, though with variance as to the underlying reasons and to the limits of its application. The pronouncements, however, were infrequent and of a less than solemn character and formulation, which has led to some theologians' speculation that the Magisterium has not intended to offer a definitive teaching on the question.

As we saw earlier, reflections on the legitimacy of capital punishment have stepped up particularly in the second half of this century. The publication of *Evangelium Vitae* in 1995 marked a watershed in the debate on this issue—both because of its authority (*EV* is the first papal *encyclical* to deal specifically with capital punishment, and thus the weightiest Magisterial statement on the subject to date) and because of the teaching it offers regarding the justification for the death penalty. This teaching warrants special attention.

The first element to be noted regards the *contextual placement* of the discussion on capital punishment. Pope John Paul expressly stated that the problem of the death penalty is to be placed in the context of legitimate defense. The Holy Father went on to say that recourse to the death penalty should be limited to "cases of absolute necessity: in other words, when it would not be possible otherwise to defend society."[38] The only legitimating factor for capital punishment, therefore, is the actual threat from an aggressor who cannot be rendered harmless by any other means.

When would these cases of "absolute necessity" come about? John Paul affirms that because of steady improvements in the organization of the penal system, today "such cases are very rare, if not practically non-existent."[39] That is to say, governments today nearly always have other means at their disposal to "defend the lives of human beings effectively against the aggressor."[40] One can call to mind extreme situations—for example small, underdeveloped countries with a weak, unstable government, corrupt officials, and powerful organized crime—where no other solution seems viable. There have been cases in recent years where drug lords have been captured but have continued to direct their operations and issue death sentences from their jail suites.

An important corollary to the placement of capital punishment in the context of legitimate defense is the commandment against taking human life and the preservation of the inherent dignity of the human person. In *Evangelium Vitae* the Pope speaks of a "genuine paradox" in which "the right to protect one's own life and the duty not to harm someone else's life are difficult to reconcile in practice."[41] In other words, the criminal (aggressor) forfeits neither his dignity as a human person nor his right to life. Rather, in a confrontation of two irreconcilable values the right to protect one's own life (or the "grave duty for someone responsible for another's life") outweighs the duty not to harm someone else's life.[42]

To wrap up, then, we can summarize the Church's teaching regarding the legitimacy of the death penalty as follows: in case of absolute necessity, when no other means is sufficient to render harmless an unjust aggressor who threatens the life of citizens, the death penalty may legitimately be applied. Where in theory these findings may furnish the data we need to form our Christian conscience on the death penalty, once again it would seem that this conclusion doesn't fully satisfy our desire to grasp the deeper meaning of what is at stake.

The Question of Opportuneness

The Second Vatican Council called for a renewal of moral theology, whose presentation should "throw light upon the exalted vocation of the faithful in Christ and their obligation to bring forth fruit in charity for the life of the world."[43] This renewal is exemplified in the focus of the third part of the *Catechism of the Catholic Church*, which deals with man's vocation to life in Christ. Instead of limiting moral theology to a juridical system of the permissible, the forbidden, and the obligatory—which, nonetheless, form a necessary part of morality—we are invited to fix our attention on our exalted Christian vocation, to move daily toward a greater conformity and union with Christ, our life. This forms the foundation of a just, loving civilization.

What is true for the individual is, *servatis servandis*, true for society at large. In *Evangelium Vitae* Pope John Paul encourages the faithful to view the death penalty "in the context of a system of penal justice ever more in line with human dignity and thus, in the end, with God's plan for man and society."[44] This sentence, I think, contains a profound truth which must not be overlooked.

In an interview with the Italian daily *Avvenire* in September 1998, then-theologian of the papal household, Fr. Georges Cottier, affirmed that the development of the Church's teaching on capital punishment (as reflected in the modifications to the Catechism) "illustrates how throughout history the Christian conscience becomes more aware of the demands of the Gospel and their consequences." He further explained that "Christianity arose in a society which included slavery, the death penalty, and many other practices that today we consider aberrant. Christianity didn't invent them. Little by little, an awareness of the demands of the Gospel and their application in the field of morality have profoundly matured, through theological reflection."[45]

A larger and more complete question on capital punishment, which embraces but transcends the issues of justice and legitimacy, is the question of opportuneness. Rather than stop at what is permissible, we should look to our ideal and take effective steps to move toward it. What sort of society are we striving to create? Would the "civilization of justice and love" envisioned by the recent papal Magisterium include the death penalty? We must not ingenuously disregard the cold facts of crime and the sad state of fallen human nature. We must not succumb to utopian musings that perhaps one day mankind will outgrow his need for a system of laws and public chastisement.[46] At the same time this sober realism must not lower our gaze or deter our pursuit of what is most noble and blessed. Catholic social doctrine calls us to find ways for "charity in truth" to become practical realities of the social order.

As Christians, we are called to point out the greatness to which man is called, and to challenge our contemporaries to bring human society into conformity with our true dignity. Pope John Paul went so far as to place the promotion of the dignity of the person at the heart of the Church's mission. "To rediscover and make others rediscover the inviolable dignity of every human person makes up an essential task, in a certain sense, the central and unifying task of the service which the Church and the lay faithful in her are called to render to the human family."[47]

In 1980 the National Conference of Catholic Bishops in the United States published a statement on capital punishment in which they urged Christians and all Americans to support the abolition of the death penalty. Their convincing line of reasoning follows the "opportuneness" argument. Rather than attempt to prove that capital punishment is unjust or illicit, the bishops indicate values to be pursued. "We maintain," the bishops wrote, "that abolition of the death penalty would promote values that are important to us as citizens and as Christians." The document proceeds to enumerate four key values that would be advanced by the prohibition of the death penalty.

"First, abolition sends a message that we can break the cycle of violence, that we need not take life for life, that we can envisage more humane and more hopeful and effective responses to the growth of violent crime....

"Second, abolition of capital punishment is also a manifestation of our belief in the unique worth and dignity of each person from the moment of conception, a creature made in the image and likeness of God....

"Third, abolition of the death penalty is further testimony to our conviction, a conviction which we share with the Judaic and Islamic traditions, that God is indeed the Lord of life. It is a testimony which removes a certain ambiguity which might otherwise affect the witness that we wish to give to the sanctity of human life in all its stages....

"Fourth, we believe that abolition of the death penalty is most consonant with the example of Jesus, who both taught and practiced the forgiveness of injustice and who came 'to give his life as a ransom for many' (Mk 10:45)."[48]

The abolition of capital punishment would clearly not remedy our social ills. Its effects on the crime rate would likely be negligible. But this isn't the point. To bring about the culture of life, a culture "ever more in line with human dignity and... with God's plan for man and society," Christians must proclaim the truth of the human person. Such a proclamation demands a concerted effort at the level of families, educational systems, the media, and the Church to attack the root of crime and moral decay. But it also includes an unswerving affirmation of the value and sanctity of all human life.

Some would argue that with the serious social and moral problems we face, most especially the scourge of abortion, and with all the truly innocent victims of violent crime and the modern tendency to turn criminals into victims and vice-versa, efforts to abolish capital punishment are wrongheaded, or at least misdirected. While accepting the premises of such an argument, I would refute the conclusion. We must indeed fight against the heinous crime of abortion with all the moral means at our disposal. We must indeed extend our pity and support first and foremost to innocent victims of crime, and guilt must be recognized and punished. Yet these causes do not preclude attention to capital punishment as well. In all sectors of society and in all our decisions, public and private, we must proceed with consistency, without lowering our standards or betraying the cause of Christ.

Though the life issues we have been considering clearly stand at the forefront of contemporary concerns of Catholic social thought, a more classical area of this doctrine continues to demand attention and development. The economic question, with its perennial areas of debate as well as its more recent permutations, continues to shape our moral culture. To properly envision *the world as it could be*, we must necessarily come to a deeper understanding of the implications of Gospel principles for the economic life and structures of society. To this fascinating topic we now turn.

Chapter 6

The Church and Economic Development

Though I have already argued that the economic question has perhaps assumed an overly monopolizing role in Catholic social thought—sometimes overshadowing other important social justice issues—it remains a significant area of the Church's social doctrine.[1] Regarding the issue of human progress and development, the Church has insisted that such development must be integral and not merely economic. Nonetheless, she has also consistently included the issue of *economic* development as an essential component of true progress. Here we will examine *development* and its twin sister *progress* especially in the light of Paul VI's 1967 encyclical *Populorum Progressio*,[2] held up by Benedict XVI as the "*Rerum Novarum* of the present age."[3]

We commonly associate the idea of progress, and especially the *ideology* of progress, with the Enlightenment. This is understandable since Enlightenment and post-Enlightenment writers cherished the idea of progress and did their best to arrogate it to themselves as an idea that could only have become possible after Western thought had thrown off the fetters of Christian dogma and classical cosmology.[4] The idea of progress, however, has a far more distinguished pedigree than its Enlightenment proponents were prepared to admit.[5]

The ancients, beginning at least with Hesiod and proceeding through Xenophanes, Protagoras, Aeschylus, Sophocles, Thucydides, and Plato, had traced an idea of humanity's progress from primitive origins to an ever more developed civilization.[6] It was a Christian, however, rather than a pagan philosopher, who formulated the most complete account of human progress. St. Augustine's *The City of God* has been rightly called the first comprehensive philosophy of world history. In it Augustine insists upon the unity of mankind and introduces the conception of human history that, although predetermined by God in the beginning, has unfolded through the activity of forces immanent in humanity itself, striving for perfection. As Robert Nisbet has written, "Augustine fused the Greek idea of growth or development with the Jewish idea of a sacred history."[7]

As a result, Nisbet further notes, "Augustine sets forth the history of mankind in terms of both the stages of growth understood by the Greeks and the historical epochs into which the Jews divided their own Old Testament history."[8] Thus, in a celebrated and influential passage, Augustine writes: "The education of the human race, represented by the people of God, has advanced, like that of an individual, through certain epochs, or, as it were, ages, so that it might gradually rise from earthly to heavenly things, and from the visible to the invisible."[9]

In much of the later history of the idea of progress the basic structure of Augustine's thought remains intact, with the noteworthy exception of the displacement of God. The Enlightenment's specific contribution to earlier notions of human progress consisted in a removal of God as the *grounding* for human progress, followed by outright hostility to religion as the *enemy* of progress. Whereas Augustine's idea of progress depended upon God's providential care for mankind, the French *Philosophes* and later theorists, notably Auguste Comte, posited a progress that stamped out religion altogether. Comte's famous law of the three stages—the theological (or fictitious), the metaphysical (or abstract) and the scientific or positive—supplanted one another successively in an inexorable forward march.[10]

The nineteenth century was, by and large, a time of naïve belief in the necessity of progress. With the passing of time, it was supposed, things necessarily got better. This optimism burgeoned as the fruit of scientific advances, political stability, and the end of the wars of religion seemed to usher in an age of reason and human dominion over nature.

The Ambiguity of Progress

I begin with these general reflections on progress, since much of twentieth-century Magisterial social teaching regarding progress reflects a reaction to Enlightenment Progress as an ideology. This brief background allows us to better appreciate the legacy of *Populorum Progressio* at a distance of forty years, especially as regards the importance of economic progress. The Magisterium never speaks in a vacuum, and especially where ideologically charged concepts come into play, some familiarity with the cultural context is essential. This is decidedly the case with the Church's relationship to "progress."

In each of his three first encyclicals Benedict has carried on a theme of his earlier writings, namely a critique of unsatisfactory theories of progress, grounded in the Enlightenment.[11] In *Deus Caritas Est*, Benedict noted that the modern world, beginning in the 19th century, "has been dominated by various versions of a philosophy of progress whose most radical form is Marxism."[12] As an offspring of Hegelianism, Marxism sees progress as a dialectical process moving from thesis to antithesis to synthesis. Any acceptance of the status quo "slows down a potential revolution and thus blocks the struggle for a better world."[13] In this model, Christian charity itself is unacceptable, since it makes the present situation more tolerable. Benedict reacts strongly to this theory. "One does not make the world more human by refusing to act humanely here and now," he writes. "We contribute to a better world only by personally doing good now, with full commitment and wherever we have the opportunity, independently of partisan strategies and programmes."[14]

In *Spe Salvi* Benedict returned to the theme of progress, noting its ambiguity and need for purification. "First we must ask ourselves," he writes, "what does 'progress' really mean; what does it promise and what does it not promise?"[15] Benedict notes that in writers such as Francis Bacon "progress" not only proves incompatible with a vigorous Christianity—it threatens to assume the place of God. A hitherto unknown "faith in progress" is convinced that "through the interplay of science and praxis, totally new discoveries will follow, a totally new world will emerge, the kingdom of man."[16] With Marx, the ideology of progress adds a political dimension to that of science and reason. As an ideology, progress fails since it places blind hope in the liberating potential of technological or scientific advancement, identifying these with human development. If progress is true, it signifies improvement, and not merely change. It is not guaranteed with the passage of time. Things do not necessarily get better—they can also get worse.

Progress therefore also requires truth, an understanding of what is good and what is better. Without these objective reference points in man's nature, one cannot ascertain progress at all or distinguish it from mere alteration. Above all, progress must include a moral dimension. Benedict insists that "progress, in order to be progress, needs moral growth on the part of humanity."[17] And he concludes: "If technical progress is not matched by corresponding progress in man's ethical formation, in man's inner growth, then it is not progress at all, but a threat for man and for the world."[18] This moral growth cannot be assumed; forward progress in time does not guarantee progress in morals, and there is no reason to think that the present generation is more morally enlightened than our parents' or grandparents' generation or that of the Middle Ages, for that matter. To do so would be to fall into historical arrogance.

This Magisterial skepticism isn't exclusive to Benedict, of course. Pope John Paul II, despite his well-known openness to all the goodness modernity has to offer, was especially guarded in his evaluation of progress.[19] He observed that "the constant progress of medicine and its ever more advanced techniques" encourages people to think they are their "own rule and measure," with the right to demand that society should guarantee them "the ways and means of deciding what to do with [their lives] in full and complete autonomy."[20] So, too, the media often portray pro-life advocates "as enemies of freedom and progress" while contraception, sterilization, abortion, and even euthanasia are interpreted "as a mark of progress."[21] According to John Paul, this distortion occurs because "[p]rogress usually tends to be measured according to the criteria of science and technology"[22] by those who "advocate a false civilization of progress."[23] And he warned that although technical advances "can supply the material for human progress," of themselves alone "they can never actually bring it about," since along with material advancement it requires a "more humane ordering of social relationships."[24]

It is not surprising, then, that in his encyclical letter dedicated expressly to the question of progress, Pope Paul VI exhibited more than a little diffidence toward the ideology of material progress. It is, in fact, expressly to Enlightenment notions of progress that Paul VI responded in *Populorum Progressio*.[25] Paul reacted strongly to a material progress devoid of God and spiritual values, posited simply on man's scientific and technological dominion of the world. He wrote: "Every kind of progress is a two-edged sword. It is necessary if man is to grow as a human being; yet it can also enslave him, if he comes to regard it as the supreme good and cannot look beyond it."[26] Here, though Paul speaks of "every kind of progress," he refers specifically to a one-dimensional progress, understood as "pursuit of material possessions."[27]

In the section of that encyclical called "Christian Vision of Development," Paul began with the sober statement: "Development cannot be limited to mere economic growth,"[28] and throughout the encyclical one notes Paul's efforts to distance himself from materialistic notions of progress. In this, he was completely in line with the approach taken by the Second Vatican Council, especially in the Pastoral Constitution on the Church in the Modern World, *Gaudium et Spes*.[29]

To embrace the good of human progress while distancing himself from defective ideologies, Paul proposed a full-blown, Christian idea of progress. He insisted especially on the idea of *integral* development, understood as improvement of the whole person, in every facet of his being. "To be authentic," Paul wrote, development "must be well rounded; it must foster the development of each man and of the whole man."[30] Throughout *Populorum Progressio* Paul insisted that economic and technical development alone is insufficient to meet the deepest needs of humanity and must walk hand in hand with development in other areas, notably the cultural and spiritual.

The "Vexed Questions" of *Populorum Progressio*

Paul's insistence on integral development, with special emphasis on the importance of human and spiritual values, successfully distinguished the Christian sense of progress from that of Enlightenment ideology. On the downside, however, it may also have fostered doubt regarding the Church's position toward economic development in itself. To garner a better understanding of the legacy of *Populorum Progressio* for Catholic social thought it is necessary to examine in greater depth three vexed questions treated in the encyclical.

First, what is the Church's real appraisal of economic progress? Is economic growth a good in itself, to be sought and aspired to, or is it rather an unworthy desideratum, whose pursuit necessarily vitiates man? Second, how central is the issue of economic *equality* to the Catholic idea of progress? Is the overriding economic evil to be avoided that of an unbalanced distribution of the world's goods? Third, how is international assistance to be reconciled with personal accountability in assuring sustainable development? Who is ultimately responsible for economic progress and what are the respective roles to be played by domestic and foreign players in this process?

Material Progress: A Good for Mankind?

So much has been made of the need to broaden our vision of progress to include all the aspects of the human person, that in an ecclesiastical context it has become increasingly difficult to simply speak of material or economic progress without immediately introducing a series of qualifications. Advocating economic progress *tout court* would seem to carry with it the materialistic worldview that the Magisterium has struggled mightily to resist. This has understandably led some to wonder whether the Catholic Church considers economic development to be a boon to be sought or a temptation to be avoided.

Moreover, it is easy to see how some, with all our proper emphasis on a preferential love for the poor, infer that the Church somehow favors poverty. As Ernest Fortin waggishly wrote some years ago, in an essay provocatively titled "The Trouble with Catholic Social Thought," "if the poor are really closer to God, I suppose one should think twice before robbing them of their poverty."[31]

This is not the Church's position. Perhaps in her emphasis on love for the poor, the Church has not stated in plain enough terms that she considers economic prosperity to be a true human good worthy of pursuit. A certain conflation of the virtue of spiritual poverty with the state of material destitution has further obscured Christians' approach to economic development.[32] Let's be clear. The Church loves the poor, but does not love their poverty, just as the Church has a special love for sick persons, while hating their sickness all the while.[33] Material poverty is an evil, just as physical illness is. So the Church's love for the indigent and needy moves her to help them out of their situation rather than keeping them there. This is implicit in Church teaching regarding aid to the poor but perhaps merits a more explicit exposition.

The Church believes in material progress as a good to be pursued and achieved.[34] While the Catholic Church has never preached a Calvinistic "prosperity Gospel" ("adhere to Jesus Christ and his teaching and you will receive abundant material benefits"), she has nonetheless taught that material prosperity is a true human good worthy of pursuit. Thus in *Populorum Progressio*, Paul wrote that material progress "is necessary if man is to grow as a human being." In other words, man cannot fully develop without it. He furthermore adds that material prosperity does not preclude the activity of the human spirit but may even have the contrary effect. "Indeed," Paul wrote, "with it, 'the human spirit, being less subjected to material things, can be more easily drawn to the worship and contemplation of the Creator.'"[35] In other words, material progress is a good, yes, but it is not the supreme nor ultimate good of man.[36] And so Paul also stated that "neither individuals nor nations should regard the possession of more and more goods as the ultimate objective."[37]

The encyclical warns over and over against the ideology of materialism, which makes an idol of wealth. Greed (or avarice), one of the "seven deadly sins," is a constant temptation against which human beings must do battle. Yet Paul also recognized that the wealthy have no monopoly on greed. "Rich and poor alike—be they individuals, families or nations—can fall prey to avarice and soul-stifling materialism," he wrote.[38]

According to the Second Vatican Council, economic development is interwoven with man's overall advancement. The Pastoral Constitution on the Church in the Modern World stated that "progress in the methods of production and in the exchange of goods and services has made the economy an instrument capable of better meeting the intensified needs of the human family."[39] The text goes on to note that "technical progress must be fostered, along with a spirit of initiative, an eagerness to create and to expand enterprises, the adaptation of methods of production—in a word, all the elements making for such development."[40] Moreover, though material progress cannot be identified with the advent of Christ's Kingdom, the two are not wholly unrelated: "While earthly progress must be carefully distinguished from the growth of Christ's kingdom, to the extent that the former can contribute to the better ordering of human society, it is of vital concern to the Kingdom of God."[41]

Further along, the Constitution draws the necessary conclusion that Christians engaged in economic development are doing something morally good and providing a worthy service to humanity as a whole. "Christians who take an active part in present day socio-economic development and fight for justice and charity should be convinced that they can make a great contribution to the prosperity of mankind and to the peace of the world."[42]

Integral human progress, as understood by the Church, is determined by an ever greater achievement of the common good, understood explicitly as the sum total of social conditions that allows persons—both as individuals and in societies—to achieve their own perfection.[43] These conditions explicitly include the material elements necessary for the person's all-around welfare. The *Catechism of the Catholic Church* sums up the components of the common good in three categories, the second of which reads:

> The common good requires the social well-being and development of the group itself. Development is the epitome of all social duties. Certainly, it is the proper function of authority to arbitrate, in the name of the common good, between various particular interests; but it should make accessible to each what is needed to lead a truly human life: food, clothing, health, work, education and culture, suitable information, the right to establish a family, and so on.[44]

The common good is not exhausted by material advancement, but it does include such advancement as a fundamental component. Material progress itself, however, must benefit *persons*—all persons—and not just the state or a select economic elite. Quoting L.-J. Lebret, Paul wrote: "We cannot allow economics to be separated from human realities, nor development from the civilization in which it takes place. What counts for us is man—each individual man, each human group, and humanity as a whole."[45] To truly contribute to the common good, then, economic development cannot consist only in the growth of a nation's GDP, or increased production at the macro level. The fruits of this growth must redound to the benefit of all. In this regard, *Populorum Progressio* echoes the words of Pope Pius XII, who stated in 1941:

> The economic wealth of a nation does not consist properly in the abundance of goods, measured by a simple calculation of their

material worth, but rather that such abundance truly and effectively serves as the material base for the personal development of its members. If such a just distribution of goods didn't happen, the true purpose of the national economy wouldn't be achieved, since despite an abundance of material goods, the people, unable to participate of them, would not be economically rich, but poor.[46]

Economic Disparity

A second "vexed question" raised by *Populorum Progressio* concerns the importance of economic equality as a parameter for development. Like other twentieth-century popes, Paul VI spoke of economic development not only in absolute terms, but also in *relative* terms, of one nation or people in comparison with others. In *Populorum Progressio*, Paul VI insists repeatedly on the significance of a growing economic disparity among peoples and nations. He speaks of the "scandal of glaring inequalities"[47] and issues the following dire warning:

> Unless the existing machinery is modified, the disparity between rich and poor nations will increase rather than diminish; the rich nations are progressing with rapid strides while the poor nations move forward at a slow pace. The imbalance grows with each passing day: while some nations produce a food surplus, other nations are in desperate need of food or are unsure of their export market.[48]

Paul is not alone in this moral analysis. His words echoed those of his immediate predecessor, Blessed John XXIII, who wrote in his 1961 encyclical *Mater et Magistra*, that in certain lands "the enormous wealth, the unbridled luxury, of the privileged few stands in violent, offensive contrast to the utter poverty of the vast majority."[49] The Second Vatican Council itself had noted with evident disapproval that while "an immense number of people still lack the absolute necessities of life, some, even in less advanced areas, live in luxury or squander wealth. Extravagance and wretchedness exist side by side."[50] It also urged that "strenuous efforts" be made "to remove as quickly as possible the immense economic inequalities."[51] Pope John Paul II likewise decried a widening gap between "the so-called developed North and the developing South."[52] As in Jesus' parable of the rich man and Lazarus (Lk 16:19-31), the papal Magisterium has consistently held up the juxtaposition of opulence and indigence as a moral scandal demanding rectification.[53]

Nonetheless, Paul's texts on economic inequalities must be read in the context of the entirety of Catholic social doctrine. The social Magisterium has consistently recognized the natural differences among persons and nations and insisted that economic homogeneity is an unworkable utopia. In *Rerum Novarum*, Leo XIII called for a healthy realism, bearing with "the condition of things inherent in human affairs," as opposed to the Socialists' utopian efforts, since "all striving against nature is in vain."[54] Leo calls to mind that manifold differences naturally exist among persons: "people differ in capacity, skill, health, strength; and unequal fortune is a necessary result of unequal condition." At the same time, Leo insists that these natural inequalities are not necessarily evil, either for individuals or for the larger community. In fact, he writes, social and public life "can only be maintained by means of various kinds of capacity for business and the playing of many parts; and each man, as a rule, chooses the part which suits his own peculiar domestic condition."[55]

The 1992 *Catechism of the Catholic Church* picked up on this same theme, reiterating Leo's arguments. The "incompleteness" of each human brings to light our mutual dependence, which corresponds to God's will for humanity. "On coming into the world," we read, "man is not equipped with everything he needs for developing his bodily and spiritual life. He needs others."[56] This mutual dependence, in turn, relates to the very real differences and "inequalities" that exist among persons. Yet these inequalities do not indicate sin. "Differences appear tied to age, physical abilities, intellectual or moral aptitudes, the benefits derived from social commerce, and the distribution of wealth. The 'talents' are not distributed equally."[57]

The Catechism, moreover, declares that these natural differences are willed by God and notes that they encourage the practice of "generosity, kindness, and sharing of goods" and "foster the mutual enrichment of cultures."[58] Still, the Catechism observes that there also exist "sinful inequalities that affect millions of men and women" and that these inequalities stand "in open contradiction of the Gospel."[59]

How are Catholics to understand this teaching? Where the rich advance *at the expense of* the poor, a negative ethical judgment seems unquestionable. If a given economic system produces a situation where the rich get richer and the poor get poorer, the system is clearly unjust.

Other situations, however, demand a more nuanced judgment. Several questions may well be asked in this regard: What happens when the rich get richer and the poor also get richer, but at a slower pace? Some would argue that the increased wealth of the rich is a prerequisite for the slower but inexorable growth of the poor, along the lines of the adage that "a rising tide lifts all boats."[60] If this is so, is it evil? Paul Collier, for example, argues persuasively that for Africa's landlocked countries to develop, its coastal neighbors must develop first, among other things in order to provide a market for the former's goods.[61] Must global development proceed at a uniform pace in order to be morally just? Second, what is the role of superfluous wealth—invested or used for growing one's own firm—in a healthy economy? There is a consensus among economists that superfluous wealth is a requirement for economic growth, such that the presence of the wealthy, rather than making the poor poorer, actually contributes to their prosperity as well. Finally, is the problem principally one of economic equality or the guarantee of at least a sufficiency for all? Without taking away from the need for the Church to denounce scandalous economic imbalances, it would seem that the moral priority of Christians must be the latter.

Aid and Personal Responsibility

A third "vexed question" brought out by *Populorum Progressio* is the matter of assistance to the developing nations, combined with the personal responsibility of developing nations to take their destiny into their own hands. Paul insisted in no uncertain terms: "Advanced nations have a very heavy obligation to help the developing peoples."[62] He stated that "the superfluous wealth of rich countries should be placed at the service of poor nations."[63] In practice, however, how is this to be accomplished? In part, Paul offers this practical advice: "an advanced country [should] devote a part of its production to meet their needs," and "train teachers, engineers, technicians, and scholars prepared to put their knowledge and their skill at the disposal of less fortunate peoples."[64]

Despite these repeated calls for solidarity and aid, Paul also recognized a key element of what would later be called "sustainable development." For sustainable development to occur, development must not be momentary or tied to a single contingent cause, but rather stable and enduring. It must not depend on ongoing external intervention, but attain a certain self-sufficiency and interdependence.

On repeated occasions in *Populorum Progressio* Paul insisted on the need for the developing nations to take personal responsibility for their own advancement. He declared that "[t]he peoples themselves have the prime responsibility for their own development."[65] He stated, moreover, that man, endowed with intellect and free will, "is responsible for his fulfillment even as he is for his salvation. He is helped, and sometimes hindered, by his teachers and those around him; yet whatever be the outside influences exerted on him, he is the chief architect of his own success or failure."[66] And Paul concludes that: "[m]an is truly human... only if he is the architect of his own progress,"[67] and that world unity "should allow all peoples to become the artisans of their destiny."[68]

These principles suggest that for outside intervention to truly contribute to a poorer nation's sustainable development, it must not create dependencies or encourage an abdication of personal responsibility but rather provide the tools necessary for a nation to become "the architect of its own progress."[69] As a perpetual, institutional reality rather than a sporadic, targeted endeavor, international economic aid easily creates such dependencies and stifles development.[70] On the other hand, perhaps insufficient attention has been given to the factors necessary to bring about this development in a sustainable way. In *Populorum Progressio*, Paul underscored a critical element in this equation that merits special consideration.

The factor in question is *education*. An uneducated populace lacks the most fundamental tool for social and economic improvement. Without hyperbole Paul stated that "basic education is the first objective for any nation seeking to develop itself."[71] He goes on to say: "Lack of education is as serious as lack of food; the illiterate is a starved spirit. When someone learns how to read and write, he is equipped to do a job and to shoulder a profession, to develop self-confidence and realize that he can progress along with others... Literacy is the 'first and most basic tool for personal enrichment and social integration; and it is society's most valuable tool for furthering development and economic progress.'"[72]

The need for education has not become less acute in the intervening years since *Populorum Progressio*. If anything, the process of economic globalization has heightened this need as the relationship between knowledge and wealth creation has grown tighter. In this regard, Pope John Paul II wrote in his 1991 encyclical *Centesimus Annus*: "In our time, in particular, there exists another form of ownership which is becoming no less important than land: *the possession of know-how, technology and skill*. The wealth of the industrialized nations is based much more on this kind of ownership than on natural resources."[73] And a little further along he adds:

> Whereas at one time the decisive factor of production was *the land*, and later capital—understood as a total complex of the instruments of production—today the decisive factor is increasingly *man himself*, that is, his knowledge, especially his scientific knowledge, his capacity for interrelated and compact organization, as well as his ability to perceive the needs of others and to satisfy them.[74]

Education and technology are not only a form of wealth in themselves. More importantly, they guarantee the possibility of continued wealth creation for the people that possess them. Immaterial wealth has value especially because it is a source of renewable wealth. Nations experience "sustainable economic development," when wealth generation devolves on the nation itself and no longer depends on external subsidies. Modern wealth consists less and less in the possession of natural resources and more and more in the possession of human resources and infrastructure. These human resources are not a finite, physical entity that belongs to one and not another, but the intangible good of know-how, education, and method, which are communicable goods.

Along with academic and technical education, Paul further includes *education in virtue* as a necessary component in the process of industrialization. In this way, too, he underscores practical ways in which a nation can effectively take charge of its own development:

> The introduction of industrialization, which is necessary for economic growth and human progress, is both a sign of development and a spur to it. By dint of intelligent thought and hard work, man gradually uncovers the hidden laws of nature and learns to make better use of natural resources. As he takes control over his way of life, he is stimulated to undertake new investigations and fresh discoveries, to take prudent risks and launch new ventures, to act responsibly and give of himself unselfishly.[75]

In *Centesimus Annus,* Pope John Paul echoed and expanded upon Paul's list of virtues, offering a clear path toward internally driven development:

> Important virtues are involved in this process, such as diligence, industriousness, prudence in undertaking reasonable risks, reliability and fidelity in interpersonal relationships, as well as courage in carrying out decisions which are difficult and painful but necessary, both for the overall working of a business and in meeting possible set-backs.[76]

Education is clearly a central factor in economic development, although it represents the first item on a longer list of requirements. Since *Populorum Progressio* it has become increasingly clear that, along with illiteracy, other factors such as political corruption, undiversified economies, insecure property rights, unstable currency, and isolation from world markets constitute serious impediments to a nation's economic development.[77] This last obstacle merited special attention both from Pope John Paul II and Pope Benedict XVI. In 1991, John Paul noted that even in recent years "it was thought that the poorest countries would develop by isolating themselves from the world market and by depending only on their own resources," whereas the contrary has proved true. And thus he concludes: "It seems therefore that the chief problem is that of gaining fair access to the international market."[78] In a similar vein, Benedict noted that in the economic sphere, "the principal form of assistance needed by developing countries is that of allowing and encouraging the gradual penetration of their products into international markets, thus making it possible for these countries to participate fully in international economic life."[79]

In his commemorative encyclical, *Caritas in Veritate,* Pope Benedict picks up where Paul left off, bringing out important points regarding the traps that retard countries' economic development and the effective use of economic aid to achieve truly sustainable development. To this end, Benedict insists on the need for "investing in rural infrastructures, irrigation systems, transport, organization of markets, and in the development and dissemination of agricultural technology,"[80] all of which can contribute effectively to sustainable development. Yet among the different factors that make such development possible, Benedict singles out the issue of legal structures and the rule of law as a guarantor of political and social stability. The focus of international aid, Benedict asserts, should be on "consolidating constitutional, juridical and administrative systems in countries that do not yet fully enjoy these goods."[81] Alongside economic aid in the traditional sense, he adds, there needs to be "aid directed towards reinforcing the guarantees proper to the State of law: a system of public order and effective imprisonment that respects human rights, truly democratic institutions."[82] Moreover, Benedict notes importantly that strengthening state structures should be accompanied "by the development of other political players, of a cultural, social, territorial or religious nature, alongside the State."[83] In this way, shoring up civil society will complement the strengthening of the rule of law to ensure effective, long-term development.

Yet Paul's initial analysis still holds true: effective means must be sought and obstacles overcome to allow peoples to achieve an internally driven economic development. The better we can identify these means and obstacles, the more effective our efforts will be.

Paul VI's Contribution

Progress—both economic and social—deals with both ends and means. Catholic social teaching offers clear guidelines regarding the ends of progress—namely the common good and its requirements—while embracing a plurality of possible means to arrive at these ends. Catholic social doctrine, while ruling out certain *immoral* means as incompatible with true human goodness, never intends to canonize any means in itself, but only approves of them insofar as they contribute to the ends toward which they are ordered. Thus while Paul, relying on the best sociological and economic counsel of his time, advocated financial aid to poorer nations, this advocacy was clearly contingent on the efficacy of this means to achieve true development. If economic aid were shown to be adverse to economic development (as some economists have recently suggested), the Church would no longer support such means but would seek more efficacious measures to achieve the same end.[84] Here, merely sentimental arguments are insufficient; the goal is not to *feel* as if one is helping others, but effectively to do so. To be real, charity must be tied to truth—*caritas in veritate*.

The task of Catholic social thought does not lie so much in engineering the most apt tactical remedies to the problem as it does in providing a moral analysis of social realities and indicating possible paths to a solution. The Church sees it as her duty to exhort the faithful and all "men and women of good will" to the practice of virtue, and in this case, to the social virtues that form the necessary groundwork for the reform of social and economic structures.

Some of Paul's contingent analyses and solutions may now seem out of date, or have shown, with time, to be impracticable. His prognosis that the price of manufactured goods would steadily increase while the price of raw materials would decrease, for example, proved to be backward.[85] His judgments on the relation between agriculture and industry, his suggestions regarding the imposition of trade tariffs, his proposal for a great *World Fund*—were prudential judgments offered as examples to stimulate practical initiative in this area.

Other proposals showed themselves to be prescient and would have been beneficial had they been carried out. If effected, his proposition that international loans be accompanied by guarantees that the capital would be put to use "according to an agreed plan and a reasonable measure of efficiency"[86] surely would have prevented many of the default loans and credit swaps witnessed in the past decades.

Where some of Paul's more concrete proposals may be conscientiously left aside, the crux of his message and the principles he articulates hold true.[87] His call for world solidarity and a greater attention to the plight of the poor and underdeveloped is as timely today as in 1967. As we come to an ever clearer knowledge of what works and what doesn't work to stimulate development, our responsibility grows greater for acting in accord with this knowledge.

One wonders, however, whether and up to what point traditional categories for understanding economic justice require revision. Along with the "vexed questions" of *Populorum Progressio*, we could ask whether more fundamental concepts still provide the best coordinates for understanding and evaluating the economic life of society. One such concept is that of *distribution*, a theme that merits a chapter all its own.

Chapter 7

Beyond Distributive Justice

Of the many areas of Catholic social thought requiring serious study and development, one of the most urgent could very well be the age-old concept of distributive justice.[1] As we have seen in the last chapter, the hundred years of social Magisterium spanning from Leo XIII's *Rerum Novarum* to John Paul II's *Centesimus Annus* were marked by a concern for the growing divide between rich and poor. Although the Church steadily steered Catholics away from the socialist reading of the class phenomenon and the solutions offered by the Marxist school, she nonetheless called attention to the gulf between wealth and poverty as a scandal to be remedied. Not only does such disparity exist within nations, however, but it is even more acute on a global scale.

Though a little international travel suffices to bring home the truth of these observations, proposals for solutions vary considerably. Here the Church's social Magisterium restricts itself to offering a moral analysis of the situation, while depending on the creativity and initiative of well-formed laity engaged in the economic and political realms to come up with effective, concrete solutions. The Church sees it as her duty to exhort the faithful and all men and women of good will to the practice of virtue, and in this case to the social virtues that form the necessary groundwork for the reform of social and economic structures. This is where the concept of distributive justice comes in.

Following Aristotle, Thomas Aquinas divided justice first into general (or legal) justice and particular justice, and then further divided particular justice into two types, commutative justice and distributive justice. Whereas commutative justice regulates exchange and aims at maintaining a just balance between individuals, distributive justice would be the virtue by which "a ruler or a steward gives to each what his rank deserves"[2] and represents the proper order displayed in ruling a family or any kind of social grouping. The one who has responsibility for the common good ought to practice justice in the distribution of the divisible goods of the community.

Two major socio-economic changes of the modern age have made necessary a serious reconsideration of this virtue, both in its formulation and in its application. In the first place, the agents directly responsible for the common good have multiplied exponentially. In the past, this responsibility was seen as the nearly exclusive domain of public authority or those who held political office—in Aquinas' time, this was nearly always a monarch. Thus, relatively few concerned themselves with practicing distributive justice, which was the task of state authorities. While politicians clearly continue to exercise this responsibility, they share it more and more with businesses and private individuals who act as stewards of common stock. According to Catholic social teaching, property bears a double dimension, private and social. The use of possessions exceeding one's personal and family needs should be ordered to the common good. In the past when most people lived at subsistence levels, few needed to concern themselves with the responsible stewardship of common goods, since their duty was limited to the sphere of their own families. Now, with steadily increasing numbers of people and groups who possess goods in excess of their actual needs, the virtue of distributive justice has become ever more relevant on a broad scale. The virtuous administration of wealth has come to the fore as an important issue for Christian conscience.

The second socio-economic change affecting distributive justice has been the evolution of principal forms of wealth and the accelerating process of wealth creation in determined sectors of society. Up until just prior to the Industrial Revolution, wealth was properly measured in durable goods, such as land, livestock and gold. While still important, these indices of wealth have ceded more and more ground to less tangible riches, such as technology, know-how, and education. In past centuries, basic productive know-how (like an agricultural technique) was handed on from generation to generation, and incremental advances were relatively small and infrequent. Since the time of the Industrial Revolution, however, rapidly changing technology has played an increasingly central role in the productivity of nations and peoples. One key factor behind the dramatic material development that certain countries have experienced in the past century has been technological progress, which has made possible the production of a superfluity of goods and the consequent possibility of a diversification of trades and professions.

These two phenomena—the multiplication of subjects of distributive justice and the evolution of wealth—underscore certain shortcomings of appealing to distributive justice as the proper category for understanding and solving modern problems of poverty and development. In the first place, problems plague the very concept of distribution itself. The first definition of the word "distribute" offered by the Random House-Webster's Dictionary reads: "to divide and give out in shares; allot." According to this definition, wealth distribution would refer to the allotment of resources according to a given proportion. In fact, Aristotle specified that those in charge of common stock should dole out divisible goods by a "geometric proportion" according to each one's rank.[3] The whole idea of distribution, and consequently of just or unjust distribution, may bring to mind an enormous warehouse of resources controlled by a central power structure. Distribution would involve the apportionment of finite goods, and therefore would demand choices which necessarily benefit some while slighting others. According to this paradigm, the just nation would be the nation that first allocates its material wealth equitably among its own citizens and then to the rest of the world. The unjust nation would be the one that hoards its riches internally or squanders them on luxurious living while the rest of the world agonizes in its indigence. Of course, distribution can also mean the spread of a determined entity throughout an area, but generally distribution calls to mind the deliberate apportioning of finite, divisible goods among a group. When we add to the language of distribution an accent on reducing the "gap between rich and poor" rather than on alleviating the suffering of the poor, the problem of sustainable development is further muddled. When framed in this way, the central problem would seem to be more one of inequality than of development, and if this were the case, redistribution would indeed be the solution. This does not, however, exhaust the Catholic understanding of economic justice.

Secondly, the responsible management of common stock involves much more than how much will be distributed to the poor and how much will be retained for personal use. Ordering property to the common good goes well beyond a restrictive concept of distribution and involves ethical investment, job creation, increased productivity, and responsible savings for the future. While the ancient custom of almsgiving has lost none of its moral weight, it does not exhaust the ethical responsibilities of the wealthy. Responsible investment and job creation can be explained in terms of distribution in a broader sense, but this is not what springs to most modern minds on hearing the word "distribution."

In the third place, distribution as allotment likewise snags on the question of immaterial wealth. In his *Nichomachean Ethics*, Aristotle already recognized that the object of distributive justice went beyond material riches and included other divisible goods, such as honors. Yet intangible goods are not distributed in the way that material wealth is, since giving to one does not imply taking from another. A typical zero-sum mentality that still reigns in the minds of many assumes that one man's riches somehow cause another's poverty, and the solution to this inequity would lie in the redistribution of this wealth. Such a redistribution need not occur, however, in the case of intangible goods, since the communication of knowledge or technology does not impoverish the giver—except in terms of short-term competitive advantage. In a world where the wealth of nations depends less and less on material resources and more on intangible resources, notions of distribution must also be updated.

Moreover, the zero-sum mindset that sees the world's wealth in terms of a fixed, divisible quantity falls short in other important ways as well. Education and technology are not only forms of wealth in themselves, but, more importantly, they guarantee the possibility of continued wealth creation for the people that possess them. Immaterial wealth has value precisely because it is a source of renewable wealth. Nations experience "sustainable development," at least in the material sphere, when wealth generation devolves on the nation itself and no longer depends on external subsidies. Modern wealth consists less and less in the possession of golden eggs, so to speak, and more and more on the possession of the goose that lays them. This goose is not a finite, tangible entity that belongs to one and not to another; it is rather the intangible good of know-how, education, technology and method.

Finally, in its strict sense, distributive justice obliges those with responsibility for the common stock to divide this stock among those under their charge, but this vertical obligation would not extend to the transversal interdependence of a globalized world. The idea of distributive justice could be stretched to meet these new situations, but restrictive notions of distribution are certain to persist.

The Development of Catholic Social Thought

Since the time of Leo XIII, most of Catholic magisterial teaching regarding international distributive justice has focused on underscoring the problem and appealing to the conscience of wealthier nations to find ways of assuring a more equitable distribution of goods. Efforts have certainly been made to pinpoint the causes of poverty, and Leo himself emphasized the function of a just wage in building up a middle class capable of economic independence and freedom. With great realism, Leo also recognized that certain inequalities are inherent to the human condition and that attempts to eradicate them would be both ineffectual and counterproductive. Nonetheless, little was proposed on an international scale besides the need for wealthier nations to share with their less fortunate brethren. Typical is the summons from Pope John XXIII that now is the time "to insist on a more widespread distribution of property, in view of the rapid economic development of an increasing number of States."[4] Pope Paul VI took a significant step forward in Catholic social thought by shifting emphasis to the international scene in an increasingly globalized world and by stressing the importance of education and co-responsibility in working out solutions to economic and social problems.

Pope John Paul II carried the question of equitable economic development still further, beyond the notion of distribution to a more proactive approach to international economic relations. Especially in his encyclical letter *Centesimus Annus,* John Paul offered a helpful appraisal of the causes of wealth in developed nations, rather than focusing on the causes of poverty. For instance, along with the external conditions needed for economic growth such as a stable political environment and favorable tax structures, John Paul indicated the virtues of businesspeople that make such growth possible, "such as diligence, industriousness, prudence in undertaking reasonable risks, reliability and fidelity in interpersonal relationships, as well as courage in carrying out decisions which are difficult and painful but necessary, both for the overall working of a business and in meeting possible setbacks."[5] In this way, he holds up an ideal for those engaged in business and signals a virtuous path to those who seek to work toward sustainable economic development.

Instead of framing the question of underdevelopment in terms of the causes of poverty, John Paul asks what positive factors have been lacking such that certain societies have not experienced growth similar to their more developed neighbors. In other words, why have certain countries not shared in the same economic growth enjoyed by others? What has been missing? The principal reason he discerns does not rest on an analysis of equitable distribution but rather on participation and integration into circles of productivity and exchange. With all due respect to the no-global movement, isolationism does not benefit the poor.[6]

Often exclusion and marginalization are self-imposed, sometimes out of fear of economic exploitation and sometimes as a means to keep absolute control over the people. Other times, marginalization is exacerbated by protective fiscal policy of the wealthier nations, such as high trade tariffs that discourage importation of more economical foreign products. Regardless of its causes, such exclusion from international commerce hampers economic development and needs to be addressed.[7] As Thomas Friedman observed in his analysis of globalization, *The Lexus and the Olive Tree*, our goal should not be to stop globalization (because in the end it cannot be stopped), but rather to assist those countries presently on the margins to develop the cultural, economic, and legal "software" necessary to benefit from it.[8]

Pope Benedict XVI has renewed the call for the "redistribution" of wealth but in a nuanced fashion that requires careful examination. Though respectful of economic processes, Benedict has insisted that political authority—ever vigilant for the common good—must also intervene. Commutative justice alone is insufficient. Thus in *Caritas in Veritate*, Benedict suggests that in the global era, economic life "also needs just laws and forms of redistribution governed by politics."[9] One assumes here that Benedict is referring especially to redistribution through taxes and subsidies, both national and international, since taxation is the ordinary medium for redistribution. Yet this is not all. At the same time, Benedict makes it clear that government alone can never be the answer to equitable redistribution and calls for the exercise of subsidiarity and coordination between private, civil and public entities. While advocating that more economically developed nations allocate larger portions of their gross domestic product to development aid, he suggests that this take place in tandem with a review of internal welfare policies, "applying the principle of subsidiarity and creating better integrated welfare systems, with the active participation of private individuals and civil society." He suggests that by doing so much bureaucratic waste can be eliminated and resources saved, "which could then be allocated to international solidarity." He furthermore proposes the application of "fiscal subsidiarity," which would allow citizens "to decide how to allocate a portion of the taxes they pay to the State" that could result in "obvious benefits in the area of solidarity for development as well."[10]

Benedict's employment of the concept of redistribution merits special attention, however, not only as regards the *means* of carrying it out but even more as regards its *significance*. In several instances in *Caritas in Veritate* it becomes clear that "redistribution" means something other than the literal reapportioning of existing wealth. In fact, it would seem to refer to a spreading of prosperity, involving wealth creation and participation, rather than a straightforward taking from one so as to give to another. Benedict states, for instance: "In the search for solutions to the current economic crisis, development aid for poor countries must be considered a valid means of creating wealth for all."[11] In other words, Benedict envisions development aid as a sort of investment, whereby wealth is created and not merely moved around, and where, moreover, this creation benefits all—both givers and receivers ("all"). He similarly calls for a renewal of the field of finance, so that it will "go back to being an *instrument directed towards improved wealth creation and development.*"[12]

Another expression of Benedict's backs up this interpretation of "redistribution." He notes that the processes of globalization, suitably understood and directed, "open up the unprecedented possibility of large-scale redistribution of wealth" globally while warning that malfunctions must be corrected "to ensure that the redistribution of wealth does not come about through the redistribution or increase of poverty."[13] Now if by "redistribution" Benedict meant simply the reallocation of existing wealth, then he would not warn against a *redistribution* of poverty. Literally speaking, a redistribution of wealth and a redistribution of poverty are the same thing. In order to understand this, let's take a simple case, assuming for a moment that the global geo-political reality consists of only two countries, one wealthy (Reichland) and one poor (Armensland). Let's further suppose that Reichland's assets total $1000 and Armensland's total

$100. Now in a generous effort at redistribution, Reichland bestows a gift of $450 to Armensland, leaving each country with an identical net worth of $550. This transaction could be accurately described as a redistribution of *wealth,* but it could also be accurately described as a redistribution of *poverty,* since the two terms are perfectly correlative. Armensland has grown wealthier by $450 while Reichland has grown poorer by the same amount. Yet Benedict insists that we must bring about a redistribution of wealth *without* a redistribution of poverty. The only way that this can come about is through wealth creation, where one's gain does not proceed from another's loss. A few sentences later Benedict rephrases this phenomenon as a "world-wide diffusion of forms of prosperity."[14] So by wealth *redistribution* Benedict means a *diffusion* of prosperity, which has a very different ring to it.

Benedict states that economic activity needs to be directed toward the pursuit of the common good, for which the political community in particular must take responsibility. He notes that "grave imbalances are produced when economic action, conceived merely as an engine for wealth creation, is detached from political action, conceived as a means for pursuing justice through redistribution."[15] In other words, wealth creation alone is also insufficient when it ends up excluding persons, communities and nations. Political action is necessary to ensure redistribution, understood as equitable and universal wealth creation that truly serves the common good.

Beyond Distribution: Solidarity, Participation and the Universal Destination of Goods

For all the reasons enumerated, it would seem that the time has come to rework our moral lexicon. If modern notions of distribution are fraught with misconceptions that no longer reflect today's socio-economic situation, our vocabulary should undoubtedly move toward more appropriate language. The Church has already shown itself capable of this in others aspects of her social doctrine. A good example of this creative development can be found in John Paul's proposal of the virtue of solidarity. In his 1987 encyclical *Sollicitudo Rei Socialis,* the Pope defines the virtue of solidarity as "a firm and persevering determination to commit oneself to the common good."[16] Despite the novelty of the term, John

Paul's definition sounds remarkably similar to a much older virtue that Thomas Aquinas called "legal justice." Aquinas, again following Aristotle, writes that legal (or general) justice is that virtue "which directs human actions to the common good."[17] Instead of speaking about solidarity, therefore, we could simply speak about the more classical concept of legal justice without introducing new terminology. Yet who would deny that for the modern mind, "solidarity" captures the idea that the Pope is endeavoring to express far better than the phrase "legal justice," and skirts some of the misconceptions that the latter could provoke?

Distributive justice must hold fast to its well-earned place in ethical theory. For millennia it has helped humans parse the ethical demands of administering common stock and furnishes an important counterpoint to commutative justice. Nonetheless, Catholic social thought is now in need of new ethical categories to better comprehend and explain the moral requirements of individuals, associations and countries with regard to the sustainable development of peoples and nations.

One possible candidate for such a category is the Catholic understanding of "participation" as developed so beautifully by Karol Wojtyła in *The Acting Person* and subsequently laid out in the 1992 *Catechism of the Catholic Church*. If the major obstacle restraining the development of underdeveloped nations is marginalization, then participation in networks of knowledge, education, communications and exchange can provide a viable access ramp to fuller integration in development. This demands, of course, a will to do good and a generosity that exceed purely economic interest, since investment in participation and inclusion in markets may not offer financial advantage, at least in the short run. This is why Benedict insists so vigorously that economic decisions and activity demand *gratuitousness*, "which fosters and disseminates solidarity and responsibility for justice and the common good among the different economic players."[18] The virtue of solidarity itself plays a fundamental role in reframing global moral questions, especially since it extends our gaze beyond national borders to embrace the entire human family, as well as transcending the strict demands of justice to include the concept of "social charity."

Another helpful concept at the core of Catholic social teaching is that of the *universal destination of goods*. This theologically rich principle recognizes that in creating the universe, "God intended the earth with everything contained in it for the use of all human beings and peoples."[19] As a result, in using the goods that he possesses, man should regard them "not only as his own but also as common in the sense that they should be able to benefit not only him but also others."[20] The connection of this principle with that of solidarity emerges immediately. Analogically, a Christian must consider that even the *intangible* goods and talents he has received are meant not just for himself but for the good of all.

The universal destination of goods in no way negates the right to private property but rather complements and grounds it. Thus Leo XIII could write that the "fact that God has given the earth for the use and enjoyment of the whole human race can in no way be a bar to the owning of private property."[21] Leo observed that God had granted the earth to mankind in general, not in the sense that everything was to be held in common, but "rather that no part of it was assigned to any one in particular, and that the limits of private possession have been left to be fixed by man's own industry, and by the laws of individual races."[22] He also clarified that even though material goods were apportioned among private owners, they did not therefore cease to minister to the needs of all, since all derive some benefit from the property of others. At the same time, the right to private property is by no means absolute. Rather, as Pope John Paul noted, "the right to private property is subordinated to the right to common use, to the fact that goods are meant for everyone."[23]

In commenting on the universal destination of goods, the Council Fathers wisely advised that customs and traditions proper to the community ought not be regarded as altogether unchangeable, "if they no longer answer the new needs of this age."[24] Creativity and innovation should continually be applied to discover effective ways for the earth and all that is in it to truly provide for the needs of all, amidst constantly changing temporal realities.

In analyzing economic problems and possible solutions, oversimplification must be avoided at all costs. The manifold and complex processes at work elude simple diagnoses and quick fixes. At the same time a veritable paradigm shift must occur if we are to escape from sterile models of distribution that threaten to hamstring a Catholic theory of sustainable development. Direct subsidies can remedy urgent economic crises, but they can never substitute for shared methods and technology or for insertion into networks of exchange and trade. The best assistance does not create dependencies but enables peoples and nations to fend for themselves and to participate fully in the international community.

If it is true that the problem of poverty and underdevelopment requires much generosity on the part of those who possess greater resources, it is equally true that this generosity should be directed in such a way as to genuinely benefit others in the long run. Thinking in terms of participation, solidarity and the universal destination of goods can generate creative responses that go beyond mere distribution in their efficacy, reach and duration.

These considerations must be evaluated in terms of their real, effective contribution to human development, an important touchstone of Catholic social thought. Moreover, they must be considered in a global manner, as they affect the whole of mankind and not merely given social or geographical sectors. How can the economy be effectively guided to promote the wellbeing of all, and not just a few? The question of global governance has come up again and again, in particular as a remedy for economic abuses and as a way of promoting the global common good. Yet the idea of global governance raises problems as well, some of which do not admit of easy answers. Let us explore this idea in greater depth.

Chapter 8

Global Governance and the Universal Common Good

Benedict XVI's reproposal of the need for a world political authority in his social encyclical *Caritas in Veritate* drew a predictable outcry from many quarters.[1] Resistance to such an idea has numerous causes, not least of which is the experience of the United Nations Organization in the past half century. The fact that Benedict speaks of a renewal of the United Nations in the same section of the encyclical where he treats of global authority, and that in so doing he expresses hope that the concept of the family of nations can acquire "real teeth," only served to exacerbate the consternation of those who consider the idea of international political authority utopian at best and perilous at worst.[2] As the closest thing we have to an international authority, the United Nations has not exactly shone as a beacon either of efficiency or of disinterested defense of international justice;[3] Often the UN has found itself a pawn to manipulation from lobbyists and special interest groups that have pushed its positions far left of the mainstream on questions such as "reproductive rights," marriage and radical feminism.[4]

Skepticism concerning the United Nations is not the only cause of opposition to the idea of global governance, however. As political authority moves further from the people who are governed, it risks disconnecting itself from their real concerns and wishes, as we have seen in recent years in the case of the European Parliament. One of the mainstays of representative government is its accountability to the people it serves. This accountability, in turn, relies on the people's ability both to follow the activity of their representatives and to replace those who do not responsibly and effectively carry out this service. Such accountability has been next to non-existent in the case of the United Nations and is hard to envision at the international level. The inner workings of faraway governments (when one need go no farther than Brussels) tend to become less transparent and murkier than most people are accustomed to in their own countries.[5]

The problems don't stop here. In order to handle even minimal tasks on a world scale, a global government would necessitate yet another immense bureaucracy, which would almost certainly be less efficient than existing national governments. Citizens who did not agree with the policies of such an entity would end up paying for them anyway. In addition, they would have no ultimate recourse except submission to such policies, since the possibility of migration—which has always been an extreme escape hatch for the disgruntled—would cease to exist in a one-government world.

Americans have exhibited particular hostility to global governance for the above reasons and others as well. For one thing, Americans tend to trust their own elected officials more than a hypothetical body of international bureaucrats with power to meddle in U.S. affairs. For all the criticism of U.S. politicians, American citizens still tend to consider them more reliable than other figures that do not share their national values, education and principles. Many Americans believe that the United States has served as a force for good in the world, such as effectively putting an end to the Second World War and uniquely in history helping defeated enemies to rebuild, as well as defending other nations from the threat of Soviet Communism during the long Cold War. In addition, Americans perhaps rightly suppose that they have more to lose than any other country if they were to submit to international governance, while having virtually nothing to gain. It is hardly a secret that some other nations harbor envy toward the United States and would love to start issuing directives regarding how it should manage its political, military and economic affairs. There is also the economic factor. Many reason that taxes are already high enough; support of a bureaucratic international body would further drain limited resources and allocate them in a way some would consider unfair.

So how are we supposed to view Benedict's call for an international political authority? Should we simply ascribe his views to a benighted European, quasi-socialist mindset that refuses to die, despite its evident failures where it has been applied? Furthermore, how do our changing socio-political landscape and the inexorable advance of economic and cultural globalization affect our traditional understanding of law, national sovereignty, war, and the common good, especially as they relate to development and the growing threat and reality of terrorism? Benedict's encyclical *Caritas in Veritate* provides a helpful stimulus to revisit these questions, as well as furnishing some surprising insights that can help better orient our attitudes toward and understanding of these issues.

Political Authority and the Universal Common Good

Some of the criticism leveled against Benedict has grown out of mistaken suppositions, which must be cleared away before we can serenely evaluate his proposal. The first necessary clarification concerns the consistent nature of the Church's teaching on the need for political authority, even on an international level. From the tone of some commentaries on *Caritas in Veritate,* one could get the impression that Pope Benedict was proposing something quite innovative in calling for a world political authority. He wasn't. This is a basic tenet of Catholic social doctrine and represents an application of perennial Christian teachings regarding the common good. Its present articulation goes back to Pope Leo XIII (1878–1903), a devoted Thomist, and received a decisive push during the pontificate of Blessed John XXIII (1958–1963).

Following the doctrine of St. Thomas Aquinas and the classical tradition he draws from, Catholic political philosophy teaches that the purpose of all law, and of the public authority that promulgates and enforces it, is promotion of the common good.[6] Political authority exists for the sake of the common good, and the common good, in turn, calls out for an authority to safeguard it.[7] Above and beyond the particular good and particular interests of individuals exists the common good of society.[8] This common good is not the good of the abstract collectivity or the state, nor is it merely the amalgamation of the particular goods of the individual members but rather the good of every person both as an individual and as a social being in relation to others.

Catholic social teaching defines the common good as "the sum total of social conditions which allow people, either as groups or as individuals, to reach their fulfillment more fully and more easily."[9] It is the specific mission of the law and public authority to guarantee these social conditions and opportunities for the good of all. This ensemble of conditions comprised by the common good can be broken down into three component categories: (1) respect for the dignity of the person as such and the protection and satisfaction of his rights, (2) social well-being and development of the group itself (material prosperity, health, education, culture, etc.), and (3) peace—the stability and security of a just order.[10]

The common good does not exist only on the level of the state or nation, however, but at the level of every human group or community.[11] Thus we can speak of the common good of families, associations, local communities, the Church, states and nations, and of any other human groups that fall somewhere in between. Moreover, along with the *particular* common good of these different human groups, we can also recognize the *universal* common good of the entire human family. A constant teaching of Catholic social doctrine has been that wherever a human society exists, some sort of authority must also exist to safeguard and promote the common good of that society. This goes for the world society as well.

As long as the universal "family of mankind" remained something of a theological and sociological abstraction, the need for an authority to effectively secure the universal common good remained similarly nebulous and theoretical. The inexorable process of globalization has altered that, effectively creating a true global community and heightening the need for care of the universal common good.[12] Christians have always believed in the idea of a common human family, united under the common fatherhood of God. Yet until quite recently nation-states were relatively autonomous and independent. With the exponential growth of communications and transportation, however, the world's nations have become more and more interdependent and interrelated, and the decisions of each nation affect the others much more powerfully than in centuries past.[13]

Benedict characterizes the "explosion of worldwide interdependence, commonly known as globalization" as the "principal new feature" of the world situation in recent decades.[14] And where he readily acknowledges that globalization has been "the principal driving force behind the emergence from underdevelopment of whole regions" and in itself "represents a great opportunity," he also recognizes that without proper guidance, "this global force could cause unprecedented damage."[15]

Solidarity and Global Governance

How, then, can the universal common good be provided for and furthered? How can globalization be "guided" to its proper end? What is to keep the particular interests of the stronger members of human society—whether they be individuals, robber bands, states, or other social or economic institutions—from unjustly trampling the interests of weaker members? The Catholic Church proposes two solutions to this problem, one at the level of *virtue* and the other at the level of *structures*.

The first, "virtuous" solution goes by the name of *solidarity*. In his 1987 encyclical *Sollicitudo Rei Socialis*, Pope John Paul II wrote that the growing economic, cultural, political and religious interdependence characteristic of the contemporary world constituted a moral category to which corresponds the moral *virtue* of solidarity. Solidarity, he wrote, "is not a feeling of vague compassion or shallow distress at the misfortunes of so many people." It is, rather, "a firm and persevering determination to commit oneself to the common good; that is to say to the good of all and of each individual, because we are all really responsible for all."[16] In *Caritas in Veritate*, Pope Benedict added his reflection regarding "the implications of our being one family," which includes the need to embark upon a new trajectory, "so that integration can signify solidarity rather than marginalization."[17]

Solidarity, therefore, as a virtue, impels persons and communities to expand their horizons of moral concern, looking beyond individual interests to include the needs of other individuals and groups and to act with their interests in mind. Each decision we make has a moral dimension, which derives not only from the object of the act, but also from the consequences of that action on others. As these consequences become more significant, they assume a greater weight in evaluating our choices. And so as human beings and societies become more interconnected, our decisions affect others more broadly and deeply, and the virtue of solidarity becomes more and more necessary.

Though the virtue of solidarity must be cultivated by all persons, it is especially important for those in public authority and for those whose actions most directly affect the situation of others.[18] Public authority is responsible first to its own citizenry, that is, the portion of humanity under its tutelage, according to the Augustinian principle of *ordo amoris*.[19] There is nothing wrong with public authority looking first and foremost for the good of its own people, in the same way that parents are called to focus first and foremost on the good of their own children. At the same time, this priority is not exclusive, and public authority must widen the scope of its interest and concern to the whole of humanity. The Catechism does not mince words when it declares: "International solidarity is a requirement of the moral order."[20] Where the virtue of solidarity is assimilated and practiced, tensions between nations and peoples are reduced and the universal common good is promoted.[21]

In addition to this "virtuous" reaction to the phenomenon of globalization the Church proposes a second "structural" solution to ensure the universal common good: an international political authority. Every human community needs an authority and a rule of law "*supra partes*" to govern it and disinterestedly provide for the common good.[22] Leo XIII observed that no society can hold together "unless someone be over all, directing all to strive earnestly for the common good," and so every body politic "must have a ruling authority."[23] Whereas there is a political authority that watches over the particular common good of individual nations,[24] there is no such authority to provide for the universal common good of the world community.[25] Moreover, no one nation can arrogate to itself this responsibility.

In his 1963 encyclical *Pacem in Terris*, Pope John XXIII commented on the growing interconnectedness of nations and the need to watch over the good of the world community. "Today the universal common good poses problems of worldwide dimensions," he wrote, "which cannot be adequately tackled or solved except by the efforts of public authority endowed with a wideness of powers, structure and means of the same proportions: that is, of public authority which is in a position to operate in an effective manner on a world-wide basis. The moral order itself, therefore, demands that such a form of public authority be established."[26]

So whereas Benedict XVI unmistakably shares this same vision regarding the need for a global political authority, he did not invent it—it is part of a legacy that precedes him. While this surely will not alleviate all real doubts regarding the advisability of such an authority, it should at least place Benedict's statements in the broader context of Catholic social thought, which highlights the real continuity of the Church's teaching in this area. As we will see, however, though Benedict speaks from within the tradition on this point, he does not merely repeat the ideas of his predecessors but adds some significant modifications that show an awareness of and response to some of the problems associated with such a global authority.

Government or Governance?

A second cause of the understandably severe reactions to Benedict's reproposal of an international political authority seems to come from an important misunderstanding: the conflation of the terms "global governance" and "world government." The two are radically distinct proposals. Unlike world government, global governance does not imply a single, centralized authority to decide on world affairs; in fact, many theorists of global governance are staunchly opposed to the idea of world government.

Global governance has been defined as "the nexus of systems of rule-making, political coordination and problem-solving which transcends states and societies."[27] Because of this variegated matrix, global governance has moreover been described as "multilayered" in that it has no single locus of authority but operates at various levels at the same time: the supranational level (such as the United Nations and its various offshoots); the regional level (EU, MERCOSUR, ASEAN, etc.); the transnational level (civil society, business networks, etc.); and the sub-state level (community associations, city governments, etc.).[28] In the midst of these different levels we find that of national government. We also note that the age-old and venerable idea of international law, or *ius gentium*, is also included in this broader notion of global governance.

As we will see, this multilayered description of global governance seems very close to the sense in which Benedict employs the term. In fact, in his remarkably nuanced discussion of the topic, he moves beyond the less developed understanding of global governance as expounded by his predecessors John XXIII and Paul VI.

Global governance involving international cooperation, public authority and rule of law can take a variety of practical forms, and the Church's Magisterium has refrained from specifying what sort of structures need to be instituted. The path to greater legal cooperation among nations will necessarily involve overcoming substantial hurdles, such as the perception mentioned earlier that international bodies are as susceptible to lobbying and particular interests as their national counterparts, if not more so.

Furthermore, on the international level as well as the national level, the Church consistently reaffirms the vital principle of subsidiarity, which determines that "a community of a higher order should not interfere in the internal life of a community of a lower order, depriving the latter of its functions, but rather should support it in case of need and help to co-ordinate its activity with the activities of the rest of society, always with a view to the common good."[29] Therefore, any international law or authority should not be all-encompassing or invasive regarding the internal life of nations, but should be strictly limited to areas of life that cannot practically and effectively be governed by the nations themselves. The sovereignty of nations should not be compromised by overly aggressive international legal structures. A more concrete proposal of how this subsidiarity is to be applied in practice constitutes one of the original contributions of *Caritas in Veritate*.

The Originality of *Caritas in Veritate*

John XXIII had observed that the universal common good could only be assured "by a public authority with power, organization and means co-extensive with these [global] problems, and with a world-wide sphere of activity."[30] He also noted that the very same principle of subsidiarity that governs relations between public authorities and individuals, families and intermediate societies in a single state "must also apply to the relations between the public authority of the world community and the public authorities of each political community."[31] His analysis went no further, however, and one struggles to see how he meant for this public authority to be constituted.

Paul VI, too, had spoken pointedly—in an address to the United Nations that he cites in *Populorum Progressio*—of the need and importance of "gradually coming to the establishment of a world authority capable of taking effective action on the juridical and political planes."[32] Yet once again, Paul makes no attempt to explain what this authority would look like in practice or how subsidiarity was to be concretely applied.

Benedict XVI picks up the same theme in *Caritas in Veritate*, and seems in large part to be echoing the thought of his predecessors. He notes, for instance, that "there is urgent need of a true world political authority," that such an authority would "need to be regulated by law, to observe consistently the principles of subsidiarity and solidarity, to seek to establish the common good," and that it would "need to be universally recognized and to be vested with the effective power to ensure security for all, regard for justice, and respect for rights."[33] Up to this point, his analysis seems rather standard.

But Benedict's proposal presses further. He not only expressly invokes the importance of subsidiarity but also lays out practical means by which it can be applied. In a key paragraph of the encyclical, Benedict appraises the principle of subsidiarity and its application to international society, noting that this principle "is particularly well-suited to managing globalization and directing it towards authentic human development." The reason for its special suitability, Benedict contends, is that it is able "to take account both of the manifold articulation of plans—and therefore of the plurality of subjects—as well as the coordination of those plans."[34] Benedict asserts that subsidiarity is "the most effective antidote against any form of all-encompassing welfare state," an affirmation that has immediate practical applications at the international level as well.

Benedict explicitly calls for a "dispersed political authority, effective on different levels,"[35] a far cry from a Big-Brotheresque, one-world government. So, while he reaffirms the need for an international authority to promote "a global common good," he immediately adds that such an authority "must be organized in a subsidiary and stratified way, if it is not to infringe upon freedom and if it is to yield effective results in practice."[36] Benedict rejects outright the proposal of a single, overweening international government, in favor of a coordinated, stratified authority. "In order not to produce a dangerous universal power of a tyrannical nature," he writes, "the governance of globalization must be marked by subsidiarity, articulated into several layers and involving different levels that can work together."[37] For instance, he cites the "articulation of political authority at the local, national and international levels" as an important means to ensure that globalization does not "undermine the foundations of democracy."[38] In other words, he envisions a political authority truly accountable to the citizenry it was set up to serve. Benedict's call for a "stratified" and "dispersed" authority marks an authentic advance in the vision of global governance put forward by the social magisterium.

Moreover, Benedict calls for a reevaluation of the *role* and *powers* of public authorities, suggesting that they be "reviewed and remodeled" so as to better suit the characteristics of contemporary society. This new model, Benedict suggests, could involve "an increase in the new forms of political participation, nationally and internationally, that have come about through the activity of organizations operating in civil society" in order to promote greater citizen participation in the *res publica*.[39] In applying this idea to international governance, Benedict offers a further development of the thought of his predecessors.

In fact, Benedict's insistence on subsidiarity, his rejection of a single world power, and his advocacy of a multi-tiered approach to global governance combine to offer a more refined, realistic and developed notion of how an international public authority could be structured than previously seen from the papal magisterium. So while Benedict's suggestions still remain somewhat preliminary and heuristic, they begin to offer a sense of specific direction that was absent in the Magisterium of his predecessors.

Specific Areas of Global Governance

In the past century the need for international law or a supra-national public authority was invoked by the Church's Magisterium principally (though not exclusively) in the context of two practical aims: (1) the arbitration and peaceful solution of international conflicts, and (2) a coordinated effort to assure economic development throughout the world. Both of these aims are component parts of the universal common good, and both are still seen by the Church as requiring the coordination of political authority at the global level.

Arbitration of International Conflicts

The first area of concern arises from humanity's long history of armed conflict and the especially bitter experience of the past century's bloodshed. The Church exhorts the peoples of the world to seek long-term solutions to conflict resolution that will obviate the need for war. One such solution is global governance. Since the universal common good includes the security and stability of a just international social order, creative steps must be taken to facilitate cooperation among nations and the creation of structures to ensure long-term peace.

This specific reflection finds its roots in the Second Vatican Council's Pastoral Constitution on the Church in the Modern World, *Gaudium et Spes*. This text treats the role of the Church in the world, referring principally to the role of the Catholic laity in the evangelization of the temporal order, so that the diverse components of society will conform more and more to the requirements of the common good. The document was promulgated on December 7, 1965 by Pope Paul VI at the height of the Cold War, twenty years after the end of the Second World War, fifteen years after the outbreak of the Korean War, nine years after Soviet Premier Nikita Khrushchev's UN outbreak in which he wagged his finger and shouted to U.S. Representatives "We will bury you!", and just four years after the Cuban Missile Crisis.

At this time fears revolved around an all-out nuclear conflagration between the major superpowers, and it seemed to many that the only thing preventing war was the assurance of mutual destruction in which no single side could win. If we read this document carefully, we see that many of the Church's statements then and afterward rested on these fears. In *Gaudium et Spes*, the Council Fathers noted that the "horror and perversity of war is immensely magnified by the addition of scientific weapons."[40] The reason for this magnification is that acts of war involving these weapons "can inflict massive and indiscriminate destruction," thus going far beyond the bounds of legitimate defense.[41] From this text we can glean a first factor in the magnification of the horror of war: the near impossibility of safeguarding the *ius in bello* criterion of discrimination, which requires the limiting of bellicose aggression to military targets, while avoiding the civilian population. By their very nature, it would seem, weapons of *mass destruction*, such as atomic warheads, eliminate the possibility of such discernment.[42]

A second cause of the magnification of the horror of war brought about by the development of nuclear weapons was the sheer magnitude of destruction that was envisioned. Again, *Gaudium et Spes* noted that if the weapons then found in the armories of the great nations were to be employed to their fullest, "an almost total and altogether reciprocal slaughter of each side by the other would follow, not to mention the widespread devastation that would take place in the world and the deadly after-effects that would be spawned by the use of weapons of this kind."[43] Such vast destruction would be virtually impossible to justify by the traditional criteria of just war theory. For one, "probability of success" (another condition for a just war) seemed extremely doubtful (with the very idea of "success" put in jeopardy), and any sort of "proportionality" between the evil cost of the war and the wrongs it sought to rectify seemed unthinkable.

These considerations led the Council Fathers to suggest "an evaluation of war with an entirely new attitude."[44] In other words, it was specifically the new possibilities of mass destruction occasioned by the advent of nuclear weapons, and effectively demonstrated by the bombings of Hiroshima and Nagasaki, that spurred the Council to embark on a stricter analysis and application of the conditions for a "just war" than hitherto considered. This document followed closely on the heels of John XXIII's 1963 encyclical, *Pacem in Terris*, where he had written that "in this age of ours which prides itself on its atomic power, it is irrational to believe that war is still an apt means of vindicating violated rights."[45]

It is in this context that we find the Council's call for the creation of a global political authority, specifically for the purpose of resolving armed conflicts. In *Gaudium et Spes* the Council Fathers noted that the goal of eliminating war "requires the establishment of some universal public authority acknowledged as such by all and endowed with the power to safeguard on the behalf of all, security, regard for justice, and respect for rights."[46]

Though these Magisterial statements undoubtedly reflected the feeling and fears of the times, the far-reaching effects of modern weaponry continue to provoke serious concern. As recently as 1991, just two years after the fall of the Berlin Wall, Pope John Paul II wrote:

> It is not hard to see that the terrifying power of the means of destruction—to which even medium and small sized countries have access—and the ever closer links between the peoples of the whole world make it very difficult or practically impossible to limit the consequences of a conflict.[47]

Where recourse to war as a means of resolving international disagreements or repairing injustices is never ruled out as a matter of principle, the Church considers such recourse to be a last resort, one which should be arrived upon in a coordinated manner. Again, Pope John Paul II wrote: "Just as the time has finally come when in individual States a system of private vendetta and reprisal has given way to the rule of law, so too a similar step forward is now urgently needed in the international community."[48] John Paul insisted on the importance of global governance in this endeavor and noted: "What is needed are concrete steps to create or consolidate international structures capable of intervening through appropriate arbitration in the conflicts which arise between nations."[49] Again, what seems needed is coordination and arbitration rather than an all-powerful, international overlord.

Benedict took up the same theme in *Caritas in Veritate*, though he limited himself to listing the practical reasons that global governance is especially necessary in our times, among which is found conflict resolution. His reflection that "in the face of the unrelenting growth of global interdependence... there is urgent need of a true world political authority" specifically references the aim to "bring about integral and timely disarmament, food security [sic] and peace."[50]

Interestingly, Benedict's reflections on the matter seem to flow not so much from the fears of global conflagration as from awareness of a more recent phenomenon: the increasing danger and scope of terrorist attacks. The World Trade Center and Pentagon attacks of September 11, 2001 and the Madrid train bombings of March 11, 2004 provide just three examples of the real threat that international terrorism imposes on modern civilization. The fears and insecurity that have arisen in the civilian population as a result of these atrocities—without mentioning the consequences on travelers and heightened racial strife—are simply beyond calculation.

Shortly before his election to the papacy, then-Cardinal Joseph Ratzinger wrote that today, "it is not so much the fear of a large-scale war that causes us sleepless nights but rather fear of the omnipresent terrorism that can become operative and strike anywhere."[51] This led him to conclude that because of this change, the questions about law and ethics have "shifted focus."[52] It is critical to note that in the face of this heightened threat of terrorism, international cooperation becomes *more*, rather than less, important, while a nation's right to legitimate self-defense must be consistently upheld. Especially since terrorist groups are frequently international themselves and not identifiable with any national political authority, the individual nations must in some way combine forces, share intelligence and coordinate efforts if terrorism is to be effectively combated and overcome.

Development and Economic Solidarity

A second practical area where the Church has repeatedly advocated global governance is the sphere of economic development. In contrast to the developed world, where legal structures exist to protect the rights of workers and demand accountability from economic enterprises, such structures are often lacking in less developed nations, making the latter enticing targets for exploitation by unscrupulous business interests. International trade itself also requires legal structures and authorities capable of redressing injustices. Furthermore, some nations are effectively excluded from development because they do not offer interesting market opportunities and are thus passed over for investment and trade. In order for the market to effectively serve the common good on a global level, it requires some sort of regulation and direction from political structures.

Once again it was *Gaudium et Spes* that brought this question to the fore, noting that "the apt pursuit and efficacious attainment of the universal common good now require of the community of nations that it organize itself in a manner suited to its present responsibilities, especially toward the many parts of the world which are still suffering from unbearable want."[53] The Council urged that economic development not be left to the judgment of "certain more powerful nations," but that it engage the largest possible number of people, and that "all nations have an active share in directing that development."[54]

In *Centesimus Annus*, Pope John Paul brought the two most critical reasons for global governance together, likening the "collective responsibility for avoiding war" to a "collective responsibility for promoting development."[55] He also compared the regulatory role of *national* business law to that of laws needed to orient *international* markets. Just as within individual societies it is possible and right to organize a solid economy that will direct the functioning of the market to the common good, he reasoned, "so too there is a similar need for adequate interventions on the international level."[56]

John Paul II noted that the globalization of the economy "can create unusual opportunities for greater prosperity" but that the "increasing internationalization of the economy ought to be accompanied by effective international agencies which will oversee and direct the economy to the common good."[57] He further observed that this task cannot be left to an individual state, since even if it were the most powerful on earth, it would not be in a position to undertake it. In order to achieve this result, he concludes, "it is necessary that there be increased coordination among the more powerful countries, and that in international agencies the interests of the whole human family be equally represented."[58] One notes how John Paul speaks of "coordination" and "international agencies," rather than global government, much as his successor Benedict would do.

In *Caritas in Veritate* Pope Benedict picked up the same call, insisting on the need for international coordination to meet the real problem of economic underdevelopment still experienced by so many peoples. He begins his reflection on international cooperation with the premise that the development of peoples depends, above all, *on a recognition that the human race is a single family* working together in true communion, not simply a group of subjects who happen to live side by side."[59] This is, admittedly, a theological principle, since as Benedict notes, the unity of the human race "is called into being by the word of God-who-is-Love."[60] At the same time, it is a vital sociological reality, manifested by the interconnectedness we have come to call globalization. It is essential for understanding the very nature of the universal common good.

As Pope John Paul did before him, Benedict asserts that greater interconnectedness calls for greater solidarity. In the course of *Caritas in Veritate*, Benedict invokes the principle of solidarity no fewer than 28 times, most often in the context of international development. Nowhere does he speak of the need for anything akin to a top-down, global economic plan but continues to apply his multi-tiered approach to global governance, often proclaiming the need for greater cooperation among the various sectors of society. He invokes, for example, the "need for a system with three subjects: the *market*, the *State* and *civil society*."[61] He further reasons that since solidarity is a sense of responsibility on the part of everyone with regard to everyone, "it cannot therefore be merely delegated to the State."[62] Benedict never embraces the simplistic narrative that one encounters elsewhere, namely that economic powers, driven by greed, are the cause of the world's problems, whereas politics, driven by a disinterested concern for the common good, is the solution. Rather, he expressly notes that the "actors and causes of both underdevelopment and development are manifold" and that "the faults and merits are differentiated," which means that we must "liberate ourselves from ideologies, which often oversimplify reality in artificial ways."[63]

So while Benedict readily points out that large multinational companies and local producers "sometimes fail to respect the human rights of workers,"[64] he notes that wrongheaded and overly aggressive politics has also often been part of the economic underdevelopment, such as in the case of Eastern Europe where "politics withdrew resources from the economy and from the culture, and ideology inhibited freedom."[65] Checks and balances are needed everywhere. And just as mismanaged political action and mismanaged economic activity both contributed to today's problems, both must contribute to the solution. He recognizes that whereas *Populorum Progressio* assigned a central role to "public authorities" in this task, today's world requires a reevaluation of the role of these authorities, especially through the increased engagement of civil society.[66] He asserts that three different "logics"—contractual logic, political logic and the logic of the gift—must all work together to achieve true development and an international economy that truly serves the common good.[67] Each has an irreplaceable role to play. Rather than a uniform, mono-dimensional reality, "economic life," Benedict insists, "must be understood as a multi-layered phenomenon."[68]

Despite Benedict's clear belief in the importance of global governance to promote economic development, he envisions this governance in a refreshingly variegated way, insisting, for instance, that development programs "be accomplished with the involvement of local communities in choices and decisions that affect the use of agricultural land."[69] It is specifically in the context of "constructing a new order of economic productivity," in fact, that Benedict proposes "a dispersed political authority, effective on different levels."[70] He likewise espouses the articulation of political authority at the local, national and international levels as "one of the best ways of giving direction to the process of economic globalization."[71]

As we will see in greater detail in Chapter 12, time after time in *Caritas in Veritate* Benedict manifests an openness to innovative solutions for remedying problems both old and new. Part of this intellectual openness means the rediscovery of perennial principles that can be reapplied to good effect in contemporary circumstances. Part of it means a willingness to engage new partners in dialogue and new modes of cooperation that can produce effective results. Part of it also means looking at completely new proposals to confront the unprecedented social, political and economic realities of the present day.

Benedict's understanding of global governance and its necessity for guiding the process of globalization provides an apt example of this openness. Resisting an attitude of laissez-faire resignation to be swept along by forces beyond our control, Benedict expresses confidence in the ability of the human spirit to properly orient these processes. Globalization, he reminds us, is neither good nor bad. It will be what people make of it. "We should not be its victims," Benedict proclaims, "but rather its protagonists, acting in the light of reason, guided by charity and truth."[72] While this orientation requires the effective and responsible engagement of political authority at both the national and international levels, it is ultimately the responsibility of all of us, acting in concert for the common good.

This increasing concern for the global common good, brought on in part by a heightened consciousness of our interconnectivity, has given rise to other social concerns as well. One particularly critical area is that of religious liberty and freedom of conscience. For many nations, religious pluralism is a new reality, after decades or even centuries of a more uniform religious landscape. For almost everyone, a greater awareness of existing differences not only of religious creeds, but also of their particular understandings of the human person, society and moral principles, has led to concern for the future of society. While we instinctively recoil from the idea that religious tolerance must obliterate the real differences among religions, we also wonder where proper lines are to be drawn if the common good is to be promoted. A first question that must be asked is whether religious tolerance as a concept is up to the task.

Chapter 9

"Tolerance" and Religious Liberty

Whereas Catholic social thought regarding economic theory and practice has evolved slowly, and, at times, only by fits and starts, it leapt forward dramatically in the area of religious liberty in the mid-twentieth century, though not without resistance.[1] The very resistance, in fact, turned out to be part of its success. The vehement, sometimes acrimonious debates that accompanied the drafting of the Vatican II declaration on religious freedom, *Dignitatis Humanae*, yielded an exceptionally precise and carefully worded document. Noteworthy in the 5,700-word declaration is the absence of even a single reference to religious "tolerance" or "toleration."

The choice of religious "freedom" or "liberty" as the proper category for discussion and the exclusion of "tolerance" flies in the face of the societal trend to deal with Church-State issues in terms of religious tolerance. One notable example is the United Nations "Year for Tolerance" (1995). That year, Federico Mayor, director-general of UNESCO, made the following remarks in New York:

> Fighting intolerance takes both state action and individual responsibility. Governments must adhere to the international standards for human rights, must ban and punish hate crimes and discrimination against all vulnerable groups, must ensure equal access to justice and equal opportunity for all. Individuals must

become tolerance teachers within their own families and communities. We must get to know our neighbors and the cultures and the religions that surround us in order to achieve an appreciation for diversity. Education for tolerance is the best investment we can make in our own future security.

If the umbrella of tolerance necessarily covers hate crime legislation and "appreciation for diversity" with all that has come to signify, these remarks may well give pause. In modern discourse tolerance is never just tolerance, and even if it were, it would hardly present the best category for describing attitudes to religion. In the following paragraphs I will highlight five arguments that illuminate the inadequacy of the notion of tolerance to convey the attitude that states should adopt in their relationship with religion, and the wisdom of the Council Fathers in avoiding this problematic language.

1. Tolerence in Itself as an Inadequate, and Indeed Inappropriate, Category for Approaching Religion

Religion is a good to be embraced and defended, not an evil to be put up with. No one speaks of tolerating chocolate pudding or a spring walk in the park.[3] By speaking of religious tolerance, we make religion an unfortunate fact to be borne with—like noisy neighbors and crowded buses—not a blessing to be celebrated.

Here it is instructive to recall that modern ideas of religious tolerance sprang from the European Enlightenment project. A central tenet of this project was the notion of *progress*, understood as the overcoming of the ignorance of superstition and religion to usher in the age of reason and science.[4] In the words of Voltaire, "Philosophy, the sister of religion, has disarmed the hands that superstition had so long stained with blood; and the human mind, awakening from its intoxication, is amazed at the excesses into which fanaticism had led it."[5]

Since religion was the primary cause of conflict and war, only through a lessening of people's passion for religion and commitment to specific doctrines could peace be achieved. As Voltaire wrote in his *Treatise on Toleration*, "The less we have of dogma, the less dispute; the less we have of dispute, the less misery."[6] Toward this stated end many mechanisms were put into play, among them the selection of proper words to modify people's views toward religion.

The language of tolerance was first proposed to describe the attitude that confessional states, such as Anglican England and Catholic France, should adopt toward Christians of other persuasions.[7] The assumption was that the state had recognized a certain confession as "true" and put up with other practices and beliefs as a concession to those in error. This led, however, to the employment of tolerance language toward religion as such. The *Philosophes* would downplay or even ridicule religion in the firm belief that it would soon disappear altogether. Thus, separation of Church and state becomes separation of public life and religious belief. Religion should be excluded from public conversation and relegated to the intimacy of home and chapel. Religious tolerance is a myth, but a myth imposed by an anti-religious intellectual elite.

This "tolerant" mentality is especially problematic when applied in non-confessional states, such as the United States, where an attitude of tolerance is not that of the state religion toward un-sanctioned creeds but of a non-confessional secular state toward religion itself. Language of religious toleration of Christianity in Saudi Arabia would be a marked improvement over present conditions and consistent with a confessional Muslim state's belief that Christianity is a false religion. In a non-confessional state, such language is more pernicious.

Dignitatis Humanae, on the contrary, taught that religion is a human good to be promoted, not an evil to be tolerated. While government should not presume to command religious acts, it should "take account of the religious life of the citizenry and show it favor."[8] Religious practice forms part of the common good of society and should be encouraged rather than marginalized.

2. The Insurmountable Dichotomy between "Tolerance" and "Toleration"

Along with the conceptual error of tolerating the good of religion, the meaning of tolerance has evolved still further, and has now come to be taken as a virtue. The United Nations "Declaration of Principles on Tolerance" states outright that tolerance is a *virtue* and defines it as "respect, acceptance and appreciation of the rich diversity of our world's cultures, our forms of expression and ways of being human."[9]

This definition mirrors that of the *American Heritage College Dictionary*, which states that tolerance is "(1) a fair and permissive attitude toward those whose race, religion, nationality, etc., differ from one's own; freedom from bigotry. A fair and permissive attitude toward opinions and practices that differ from one's own."

If tolerance is a virtue, it is a decidedly modern virtue. It appears in none of the classical treatments of the virtues: not in Plato, not in Seneca, not even in Aristotle's extensive list of the virtues of the good citizen in his *Nichomachean Ethics*. Indulgence of evil or error, in the absence of an overriding reason for doing so, has never been considered virtuous. Even today, indiscriminate tolerance would not be countenanced. A public official tolerant of child abuse or tax evasion would not be a virtuous official.

The closer one examines tolerance and strives to apply it across the board, the more its insufficiency as a principle to govern society becomes apparent. Even if it were possible to achieve total tolerance (which it is not), it would be exceedingly undesirable and counterproductive to do so.[10]

Moreover, as a virtue, tolerance seems to have distanced itself so far from its etymological roots as to have become another word altogether. Thus the *virtue* of "tolerance" no longer implies the *act* of "toleration" but rather a general attitude of permissiveness and openness to diversity. Implicitly, this diversity is treated as something positive to be embraced rather than an evil to be suffered in regard for a greater good. Tolerance, therefore, now has two radically incompatible meanings that create space for serious misunderstandings and abuse, both deliberate and unintentional.

In isolation from an objective referent, tolerance and intolerance can and indeed must be applied arbitrarily. In point of fact, a tolerant person will not tolerate all things but only those things considered tolerable by the reigning cultural milieu. Thus the accusation of intolerance has become a weapon against those whose standards for tolerance differ from one's own, and our criteria for tolerance depend on our subjective convictions or prejudices. Voltaire was able to defend the actions of the Roman Empire in persecuting Christians and blamed the Christians themselves for their martyrdom because they failed to keep their religion to themselves. He avers that the Christians' death was a consequence of *their own intolerance* towards Rome and not the other way around.[11] Such sophistry is part and parcel of many of today's debates on tolerance as well and flows from the ambivalence of the term.

The affair grows even muddier when the "acceptance of diversity," present in modern definitions of tolerance, is thrown into the mix. The UN *Declaration of Principles on Tolerance* incorporates a prior statement from the UN *Declaration on Race and Racial Prejudice*, which states: "All individuals and groups have the right to be different" (Article 1.2).[12] Taken at face value, that is a ridiculous claim. Suicide bombing is different, as are genocide and sadomasochism. To say that one person has a right to be bad, simply because another happens to be good, is the ludicrous logic of diversity entitlement.

The sloppiness of these definitions is unworthy of the lawyers who drafted them and cannot but lead to the suspicion that such ambiguity is intentional. This vagueness allows tolerance to be applied selectively—to race, sexual orientation, or religious conviction—while other areas—such as smoking, recycling or animal experimentation—stand safely outside the purview of mandatory diversity.

This arbitrariness is not new. John Locke (1632-1704) himself, in the midst of his impassioned appeal for religious toleration, notes that of course toleration does not extend to Catholics, Muslims or atheists. "To worship one's God in a Catholic rite in a Protestant country," he writes, "amounts to constructive subversion."[13]

In the end, the question for everyone necessarily becomes not "Shall I be tolerant or intolerant?" but rather "What shall I tolerate and what shall I not tolerate?"

3. The Relativistic Underpinnings in Modern Notions of Tolerance

Voltaire, Locke, Gotthold Lessing, and other Enlightenment figures downplayed the importance of *doctrinal belief* in favor of *morals*. Unlike today, in eighteenth-century Europe a general agreement regarding fundamental moral principles could be counted on in contrast to the fierce debates surrounding questions of dogma. So moral orthodoxy was deemed necessary while doctrinally, a broad heterodoxy was countenanced. In doing so, Enlightenment thinkers couldn't avoid a creeping relativism and epistemological uncertainty regarding religious doctrine. Voltaire, for example, contends that in order for true tolerance to be established, theological controversy (which he describes as a "plague" and "epidemic illness"[14]) must disappear.

Locke, on the other hand, dismissively notes that "everyone is orthodox to himself."[15] His own ecclesiology that lacked belief in the existence of any one true church led Locke to the conviction that all Christian churches (except the Catholic Church) should be tolerated. "Nor is there any difference," he confidently wrote, "between the national Church and other separated congregations."[16]

Locke further appeals to the "Business of True Religion." A true Christian, Locke asserts, will dedicate himself principally to a life of virtue and piety, which are the chief concerns of religion. He relegates to a lower tier "outward pomp of worship, reformed discipline, orthodox faith."[17] His own theological prejudices and political concerns led him to arbitrarily place morals above doctrine, since morals at the time garnered greater unanimity and generated fewer disputes. Their roles have been somewhat reversed today.

Locke's disdain for "orthodoxy" and Voltaire's diatribes against religious "fanaticism" find an echo in contemporary descriptions of tolerance. The UN *Declaration on Principles of Tolerance* states that tolerance "involves the rejection of dogmatism and absolutism."[18] Popular wisdom holds that true tolerance entails not only *respect* for others, but the acknowledgement that *we don't know* for certain who is right. Such skepticism flows as a necessary consequence of "the rejection of dogmatism and absolutism."

In his 1995 encyclical *Evangelium Vitae*, Pope John Paul II wrote that some today "consider such relativism an essential condition of democracy, inasmuch as it alone is held to guarantee tolerance, mutual respect between people and acceptance of the decisions of the majority, whereas moral norms considered to be objective and binding are held to lead to authoritarianism and intolerance."[19] Although the U.N. Declaration does not employ the language of "relativism," it is a necessary corollary to its assertions.

4. The Ambiguity Surrounding the Proper Object of Toleration

A fourth argument against the language of tolerance is the widespread confusion regarding the proper *object* of tolerance. These days, tolerance for persons, ideas and behavior are generally lumped together under the general heading of "tolerance," but they are hardly the same thing.

Much as tolerance fails as a category for dealing with *good things*, which are embraced rather than tolerated, so, too, tolerance is an inappropriate category in regard to *persons*. From a Christian perspective, all persons deserve unconditional respect and love for the simple fact that they are persons. We may tolerate their irritating *behavior*—such as knuckle-cracking or gum-snapping—but it is insulting to suggest that we tolerate the persons themselves.

Nor are *ideas* the proper object of toleration. Ideas come in all shapes and sizes: true and false, ridiculous and compelling, brilliant and commonplace, diabolical and divine. Each must be evaluated in relation to the truth and accepted or rejected accordingly. Those ideas that convince by the strength of their inner consistency are embraced; those found to be untenable are rejected.

If goods, persons, and ideas fail as the proper object of tolerance, the only possibility remaining is annoying human behavior, error or evil situations. Here, too, the criterion for discerning what is to be tolerated must be determined by the superior good that justifies it. In the case of *Dignitatis Humanae*, the Council Fathers avoid the claim that error has rights by appealing to the truth that people "cannot discharge these obligations [the pursuit of truth] in a manner in keeping with their own nature unless they enjoy immunity from external coercion as well as psychological freedom."[20] Thus even when they fail to live up to their duty to seek the truth or fail in their attempts to discover it, the right to religious liberty persists.[21]

Just as the term "tolerance" does not appear in *Dignitatis Humanae*, it is likewise absent in the *Catechism of the Catholic Church*. In fact, of the scant five times that the verb "tolerate" appears in the *Catechism*, two refer to the moral legitimacy of accepting foreseen but undesirable evil consequences of human actions, if the evil is not intended either as an end or a means.[22] The other three concern the moral tolerableness of civil divorce in certain limited cases, and the intolerableness of trial marriages and a life of duplicity.[23] The precision of this language provides a refreshing contrast to much of the vague tolerance language of our day.

5. Slouching Toward Indifference

Although tolerance doesn't necessarily entail indifference, modern formulations of tolerance as acceptance or celebration of diversity would seem to imply at least a placid resignation and sometimes even an enthusiastic celebration of religious diversity. This has led to theologies of pluralism incompatible with the divine mandate to "go out to the whole world and make disciples of all the nations" (Mt. 28:19-20), as well as Peter's declaration that "There is no other name under heaven given among men by which we must be saved" (Acts 4:12).[24]

Voltaire took Thomas Aquinas to task as being intolerant for having dared to say that he wished all the world were Christian. But for Thomas that was the same as saying he wished all men to be happy. Few would consider it intolerant to wish all people to be healthy or well educated (though this implies "intolerance" toward ignorance and illness), and for Thomas the Christian faith was a greater good than health and education.

Blessed Mother Teresa of Calcutta, who devoted her entire life to spreading the love of Christ, expressed her motivation with the utmost simplicity: "I want very much for people to come to know God, to love Him, to serve Him, for that is true happiness. And what I have I want everyone in the world to have. But it is their choice. If they have seen the light they can follow it. I cannot give them the light: I can only give them the means."[25]

The *fact* of a plurality of religions doesn't imply the *ideology* of religious pluralism. Saint Paul undauntedly preached the Gospel of Jesus Christ to King Agrippa, who declared: "A little more and you would make a Christian of me," to which Paul replied, "I wish that not only you, but all those that hear me might become as I am" (Acts 26: 28-29). Though other religions may contain elements of truth, it is to be hoped that all come to the fullness of truth. As Cardinal Ratzinger wrote, the duty to evangelize stems from the Christian's conviction of the truth of Christianity, which is fundamentally different from other religions.[26]

Voltaire, building on Locke's arguments, arrived at relativism's logical end: indifference. Live and let live. Not only should we tolerate others' behavior and beliefs, it is wrong to try to change them. In this regard St. Pius X wrote: "Catholic doctrine teaches us that charity's first duty is not in the tolerance of erroneous opinions, sincere as they may be, nor in a theoretical or practical indifference toward the error or vice into which our brothers or sisters have fallen, but in zeal for their intellectual and moral improvement, no less than in zeal for their material well-being."[27]

This zeal, however, must express itself in ways consonant with the dignity of persons. In practice, this means absolute respect for the freedom and inviolability of conscience, especially in matters of religious belief. In his letter on the missions, Pope John Paul II penned these memorable words: "On her part the Church addresses people with full respect for their freedom. Her mission does not restrict freedom but rather promotes it. *The Church proposes; she imposes nothing.* She respects individuals and cultures, and she honors the sanctuary of conscience. To those who for various reasons oppose missionary activity, the Church repeats: *Open the doors to Christ!*"[28] In other words, to be true to her mission the Church cannot refrain from proclaiming the truth of the gospel of Jesus Christ, and those who hear are free to embrace this truth or reject it.

Similarly, in his 1994 book *Crossing the Threshold of Hope*, the Pope wrote, "The new evangelization has nothing in common with what various publications have insinuated when speaking of *restoration*, or when advancing the accusation of *proselytism*, or when unilaterally or tendentiously calling for *pluralism* and *tolerance*... *The mission of evangelization is an essential part of the Church.*"[29]

Dignitatis Humanae re-emphasized perennial convictions of Christianity, including the obligation to seek the truth and to bear witness to the truth we have received. In doing so, however, it underscored the deep respect that must be borne in every instance for the dignity and freedom of the person. "Truth," we read, "is to be sought after in a manner proper to the dignity of the human person and his social nature. The inquiry is to be free, carried on with the aid of teaching or instruction, communication and dialogue, in the course of which men explain to one another the truth they have discovered, or think they have discovered, in order thus to assist one another in the quest for truth."[30]

This respect for religious freedom stands head and shoulders above a supposed tolerance for religious belief, with the relativism, indifference and subtle disdain for religion it so often comprises. Yet despite its superiority as a category, religious freedom itself requires prudence and discernment in its application. Though it is indeed a fundamental human right, it is not a trump that can be played to justify any and all actions. Pope Benedict XVI has had the remarkable courage and insight to foresee the problems attending an incorrect reading of religious freedom, with its consequences for *the world as it could be*. His thoughts on this issue merit closer study.

Chapter 10

A Case for
Religious "Discrimination"?

W hen we speak of the relationship between "church and state," or "religion and politics," or, more broadly, "faith and reason," we naturally explore their legitimate autonomy and proper competencies. But we also inevitably find ourselves asking about their relationship, complementarity and mutual utility.

This topic has been at the forefront of many of Pope Benedict's addresses and writings, notably his Regensburg address of Sept. 12, 2006 and his first encyclical *Deus Caritas Est* (2005).[1] Even prior to his election to the See of Peter, however, Joseph Ratzinger returned often to this topic when considering questions regarding Catholic social doctrine.

In this chapter I wish to focus on a particular aspect of church-state relations, namely, the proper attitude that political authority should have toward religion in general and the state's differentiated evaluation, tolerance or promotion of specific religious bodies. This discussion will take as its point of departure a provocative statement from Pope Benedict's social encyclical, *Caritas in Veritate*. In it, while discussing religious liberty as a fundamental component of integral human development, Benedict also offered a remarkable qualification of this fundamental freedom and invokes the State's right and duty of discernment vis-à-vis concrete religious realities.

Benedict makes the case that although "religion" and the acknowledgement and worship of God is a good for humanity that ought to be promoted, not all religions are the same, and not all religions contribute equally to the development of individuals and societies. Some, in fact, may obstruct it. "Religious freedom does not mean religious indifferentism," he wrote, "nor does it imply that all religions are equal."[2]

Benedict's analysis does not end here, however. He makes the bold proposal that in order to safeguard and promote the common good, political authority must in some way engage in the task of *discernment among religions*. "Discernment is needed regarding the contribution of cultures and religions," Benedict states, "especially on the part of those who wield political power."[3]

The Pope places "cultures" and "religions" side by side, in part to show that his analysis is not so much theological as humanistic. He notes that certain cultures and religions "teach brotherhood and peace and are therefore of enormous importance to integral human development," yet other traditions "do not fully embrace the principle of love and truth and therefore end up retarding or even obstructing authentic human development."[4]

The Pope was no doubt aware of the hornet's nest he stirs up when suggesting that government is competent to judge ("*iudicium*") between one religion and another. His juxtaposition of religion and culture helps to obviate the criticism that the Pope was somehow inviting politicians to make theological judgments. In fact, Benedict went on to say that the discernment needed has to be "based on the criterion of charity and truth" and that this criterion for evaluating cultures and religions is the "whole man and all men."[5] It is, in other words, an anthropological judgment, based on universal principles of the common good—which rightly falls in the province of political authority.

Despite these important attenuations, Benedict's statement still raises serious questions. In the first place, it is at very least politically incorrect to distinguish among religions. We shy away from speaking of the errors of a particular religion and prefer to speak of the errors and excesses of some religious people or of religious fanaticism and fundamentalism. Moreover, this cultural sensibility is not based on whimsy but also experience. The tendency in contemporary society to treat religions equally is motivated in part by the awareness that any criticisms leveled against a particular religious group or institution could just as easily be used against one's own religion. If an exemption is denied today to the

Jehovah's Witnesses, Mormons or Shiite Muslims, who is to say whether the same might happen to Catholics tomorrow? In fact, because of the Catholic Church's extensive social engagement, it may be the most common target of religious discrimination.

Second, it would seem to be the nature of religious liberty that the possibility of some error is included in the search for God. Doctrinal errors could be more or less grave, but the liberty itself cannot be contingent on the absence or minimization of error; otherwise, it makes no sense. If the right to religious freedom were only the right to *true* religion, it would seem to be no right at all. Hence the Second Vatican Council taught that the right to immunity from coercion in matters religious "continues to exist even in those who do not live up to their obligation of seeking the truth and adhering to it."[6] If the right exists for those who do not seek the truth, how much more for those who sincerely seek it, even if their findings wind up missing the mark? Therefore, it would seem, proponents of any religious tradition merit identical respect and defense. After all, what many Catholics may consider to be silly doctrines, deserving only derision, may seem to others as reasonable as the Virgin birth, the Immaculate Conception, or the multiplication of loaves and fishes.

A third problem concerns the proper competence of civil government. We rightly fear depositing too much authority in the state regarding religions. Public authority is incompetent to judge the truth of religions, and even if it could, this discernment seems to fall outside its proper jurisdiction. How, after all, can political authority judge the authenticity of particular religious institutions or traditions? In this regard John Locke rightly noted in his *Letter Concerning Toleration*: "Neither the right nor the art of ruling does necessarily carry along with it the certain knowledge of other things, and least of all of true religion."[7]

When government exceeds its competence concerning religion, abuse is sure to follow. Though examples are hardly needed here, one could simply think of the biblical case narrated in the Book of Esther describing the precarious state of the Jews during the Babylonian exile. Under the reign of King Ahasuerus, the evil minister Haman says: "There is a certain people scattered and separated among the peoples in all the provinces of your kingdom; their laws are different from those of every other people, and they do not keep the king's laws, so that it is not appropriate for the king to tolerate them."[8] Eventually Haman gets his way, and only through divine intervention does Esther manage to save her people. In substance, these same arguments continue today, for example in debates concerning conscientious objection for Catholic healthcare workers or government attempts to oblige Catholic adoption services to place children in same-sex households.

The problems don't end here, however. Doesn't the Pope's suggestion contradict the teaching of the Council, which explicitly says that "government is to see to it that equality of citizens before the law, which is itself an element of the common good, is never violated, whether openly or covertly, for religious reasons. Nor is there to be discrimination among citizens"?[9] Isn't "discernment" just another name for discrimination? How can the Pope propose that public authorities challenge the equality of citizens or engage in religious discrimination?

Cases today abound where church-state relations are put to the test. Everything from Tony Blair's suggestion that Sharia Law could coexist with Britain's civil law and Germany's banning of Scientology, to debates regarding the use of headscarves by Muslim women in France and the referendum concerning the building of minarets in Switzerland—these examples underscore the importance of this question for contemporary society. In the majority of cases, Catholics find themselves siding with religious traditions against an overly invasive secular establishment, even when Catholics do not share the ideals or doctrines being argued about. This makes Benedict's invitation for "those who wield political power" to engage in "discernment" regarding the contribution of various religious traditions sound particularly jarring. What could he possibly mean by this? How would it be safely enacted without trampling on hard-won religious liberty for all? How can government authentically evaluate the "contribution" of religions?

To accurately assess Benedict's intentions here, it may prove helpful to sift through some of his prior writings in order to see what else he has said on the topic in different venues. We will therefore try to synthesize his thought on the correct relations between the state and religion in order to come to a clearer understanding of his meaning in *Caritas in Veritate* no. 55.

The Role of Political Authority vis-à-vis Religion

The Healthy Separation of Church and State

Christianity has always asserted that the religious and temporal orders are distinct, and that the legitimate authorities that govern each enjoy a proper jurisdiction in what pertains to their particular sphere.[10] Rooted in Jesus' words that man must give to Caesar what is Caesar's, but to God what is God's, Christians have always distinguished between these two orders.[11] Saint Augustine famously described them as the City of God and the City of Man.

For his part, Joseph Ratzinger has stated his conviction that the idea of "the separation of Church and state came into the world first through Christianity."[12] He even recognized the contribution of the Enlightenment to this healthy separation, gently noting that "the development of the Enlightenment, with which the model of the separation of Church and state appears, definitely has a positive side."[13] This positive evaluation of a certain separation between church and state extends to more recent times, even when such separation wasn't fully appreciated at the moment. For example, Ratzinger likewise wrote that on the whole, "the Church benefitted by being forced to detach herself from the state Church systems after the First World War."[14]

Important as it is, however, this separation is far from total. "The two spheres are distinct, yet always interrelated," Benedict has written.[15] Church and State contribute differently to the good of the human person, and complement one another's proper functions.[16] The Church benefits from its exchange with society, and the state benefits from the contributions of the Church. Reason purifies faith, just as faith purifies reason. The Church teaches the world but also learns from it, even when the lessons are tough to accept.[17]

The Role of the Church

What are these respective roles, and where do they overlap or intersect? The Council taught that the Church is "a sign and a safeguard of the transcendent character of the human person."[18] The Church is not just a humanitarian project, an NGO or a program of social reform. In this regard, Ratzinger has criticized as one-sided "the idea that all religions are basically just instruments for advocating freedom, peace, and the conservation of creation, so that they would have to justify their existence through political success and political goals."[19] The mission of religion must transcend worldly structures. The Church seeks above all the salvation of the human person in Jesus Christ, and all other objectives are subordinate to this one.[20]

Yet in her solicitude for the whole man and every man, the Church's mission is not solely otherworldly either. In the words of Benedict, "*the whole Church, in all her being and acting—when she proclaims, when she celebrates, when she performs works of charity—is engaged in promoting integral human development.*"[21] The Christian moral code is summed up in charity, which seeks the comprehensive good of every person, and of society itself. While the good of the person culminates in his or her eternal communion with the Holy Trinity and the community of the blessed in heaven, it is not limited to this.

The Church's mission of human promotion involves preaching the truth about man, and about what constitutes his true and integral good. The anthropological vision she has received from her Savior helps society itself to better understand the ethical requirements that issue from the dignity of the human person. In this way, the Church also provides a *public* service, and assists the State itself in coming to grips with the requirements of justice. In Ratzinger's words, "Christianity... has always *publicly* claimed to be... a truth that is spoken *publicly*, establishes *public* criteria, and that in a certain measure also binds the state and the powerful of this world."[22]

In *Deus Caritas Est*, Benedict declares that the state needs help in discerning the nature of this good and its concrete requirements.[23] The Church "is called to contribute to the purification of reason" especially as regards the nature of justice, since practical reason "can never be completely free of the danger of a certain ethical blindness."[24] Justice has to do with giving each person what he is due, but the practical content of this "due" is far from evident, and depends on one's understanding of the nature of the person. Here the Church's understanding of man proves invaluable to society. Other religions, too, even when not proposing a comprehensive theory of morality or social ethics, often provide their adherents with a worldview that conditions their understanding of these issues.

The Role of Government

What, then, is the proper role and competency of government, especially as regards its interaction with religion? According to Catholic teaching, which garners a broad consensus even outside our own tradition, political authority exists for one reason only: to promote and safeguard the common good.[25] What distinguishes a legitimate state from a mere power structure is this commitment to the common good and to justice itself. Thus, though we are not used to speaking in these terms, the role of the state is fundamentally moral in nature.[26]

Ratzinger has noted that Christian revelation holds "a very sober view of the state" and observed that the state "has its own sphere, within which it must remain."[27] Later he added that in Sacred Scripture, "the task of the state is formulated in an exceptionally sober, indeed almost banal, manner: it must ensure peace at home and abroad."[28] Yet this peace also demands that "the fundamental legal rights of the individual and of society are guaranteed."[29] The state will always have the temptation of overextending its proper jurisdiction, but this tendency must be resisted. As Ratzinger has written: "It is not the task of the state to create man's happiness, nor is it the task of the state to create new men. It is not the task of the state to change the world into a paradise—nor can it do so."[30] Moreover, he warns: "Wherever politics tries to be redemptive, it is promising too much. Where it wishes to do the work of God, it becomes, not divine, but demonic."[31]

On the other hand, the common good does not mean merely defense of "public order." It entails a more substantive notion of the human good at the level of both individuals and societies. There is a tendency to substitute the strong and content-filled notion of "the common good" with the much lighter idea of "public order," and thus political authority, rather than defending and promoting the common good, would assume the much simpler task of mere arbitrage among particular interests.[32]

According to Catholic social doctrine, the common good comprises three essential elements. The first component of the common good is respect for the liberties of citizens, especially freedom of conscience and religion.[33] Government should not arbitrarily curtail the free action of citizens and should only do so when demanded by a higher good. Yet this respect for liberties is not the sum total of the common good either. It also entails "the social well-being and development of the group itself" as well as "the stability and security of a just order."[34] In short, the common good comprises all those conditions of social life that permit human persons as individuals or in association to reach their plenitude.[35]

The Common Good and Religious Freedom

The first essential element of the common good, then, is respect for human liberty in its different manifestations. Basic freedoms, understood as human rights, should be defended by public authorities. Yet among the many possible human freedoms, the right to religious liberty enjoys an exalted status because of the importance of religion itself, both for individuals and society. In Ratzinger's words, religion's role is central to the overarching good of the person, since it serves "to integrate man in his entirety, to unite feeling, understanding, and will and to mediate between them, and to offer some answer to the demand made by everything as a whole, the demands of living and dying, of society and myself, of present and future."[36] Therefore Catholic teaching has never reduced the practice of religion to a neutral activity, like bungee jumping or skeet shooting, and has never seen the Church as a simple voluntary association like a chess club or PTA.[37] Therefore, the state's attitude toward religion in general should never be one of mere tolerance or permission but appreciation and support. Religion deserves from the state formal recognition, respect and encouragement. While not canonizing a particular creed, the state should promote religious practice as an essential aspect of the common good. As the Council stated, government "ought indeed to take account of the religious life of the citizenry and *show it favor*, since the function of government is to make provision for the common welfare."[38] Government has no reason to *favor* neutral activities but only such activities as contribute positively to the common good.

At the same time, while religious freedom is a fundamental human right, it is not absolute. While the Second Vatican Council forcefully declared that the human person has a right to religious freedom, and that all people should be immune from coercion to act against their beliefs, it added the important phrase "within due limits."[39] Likewise, when asserting that religious communities rightfully claim freedom of self-governance, it again added the clause "provided the just demands of public order are observed."[40] In other words, religious freedom must be balanced against other goods. In Ratzinger's words, human freedom "is a shared freedom, freedom in a coexistence of other freedoms, which are mutually limiting and thus mutually supportive."[41]

It is here that we get a glimpse of the underlying sense of Benedict's claim that political power must engage in discernment regarding particular religions. While government ought to show favor to the religious life of the citizenry, it does so *in virtue of religion's contribution to the common welfare.* The common welfare is already served by the protection of religious liberty, but religions themselves can also contribute positively to the common weal as well. If different religions contribute differently to this welfare, it could be argued that they merit differentiated recognition or support. At the same time, as we have seen, the contribution cannot refer simply to the supernatural good of different religious traditions, since the state is incompetent to determine this. It must, rather, refer to the *cultural contribution* made by religions. This discernment supposes that real differences exist among religions, even on the level of temporal society.

Religion and Religions

It has become commonplace to speak of "religion" as if it were a monolithic, undifferentiated reality. Take, for instance, the work of neo-atheistic writers who condemn "religion" as fundamentally harmful for individuals and negative for society. Christopher Hitchens subtitles his book *God Is Not Great* with the expression "How Religion Poisons Everything," and the second chapter bears the unqualified title: "Religion Kills."[42] Organized religion, Hitchens writes, is "[v]iolent, irrational, intolerant, allied to racism and tribalism and bigotry, invested in ignorance and hostile to free inquiry, contemptuous of women and coercive toward children."[43] Richard Dawkins, evolutionary biologist and celebrated atheist, takes a similar approach and writes quite explicitly: "I am not attacking any particular version of God or gods. I am attacking God, all gods, anything and everything supernatural, wherever and whenever they may have been or will be invented."[44]

The tendency to lump all religious traditions together under the broad banner of "religion" is not limited to atheists. It seems almost to be a mark of respect for others' traditions and a requirement of social etiquette. Or, in Ratzinger's words, the "notion that all religions are ultimately equivalent appears as a commandment of tolerance and respect for others."[45] Clearly the phenomenon of religion is a legitimate category, including the search for the divine and for transcendence, as well as an attempt to respond "justly" to God as he is recognized.[46] Yet for good and for ill, religion does not refer to one homogeneous, undifferentiated reality. Thus Ratzinger writes that the proposal that all religions are fundamentally the same, "which has been made since the early days of the science of comparative religions in the Enlightenment (though it had come up even before that), is already self-contradictory with respect to the religions themselves, for these are plainly not the same."[47]

Not all religions deserve equal approval, nor do they deserve equal condemnation. In this regard, Ratzinger could write that "anyone who sees in the religions of the world only reprehensible superstition is wrong" but also "anyone who wants only to give a positive evaluation of all religions... is equally wrong."[48] He goes on to say that not only is discernment possible but it is also necessary. He writes that religion itself "demands the making of distinctions, distinctions between different forms of religion and distinctions within a religion itself, so as to find the way to its higher points. By treating all content as comparably valid and with the idea that all religions are different and yet actually the same, you get nowhere."[49] In a sense, to say that religion requires the making of distinctions means that religion requires the application of the intellect. True religion should never descend into absolute fideism but should engage reason.

The differences among religions regard not only their theological truth value (their understanding of God) but also their underlying anthropology and outlook on human society. This means that their contribution to human culture will vary. Not all religions contribute equally to the common good or integral human development, and, as Benedict has noted, some may even obstruct it in important ways.

Possibility of Problems in Religion

In his own critical considerations of religions, Ratzinger writes with brutal honesty. He observes that there are "deviant, esoteric forms of religion on offer."[50] He speaks of "pathological" forms of religion.[51] He mentions religions that are "obviously sick" and of religions that are "destructive for man."[52] He asserts, moreover, that with the detachment of religion from reason, "pathological forms of religion are constantly increasing."[53] In this sense, he even expresses agreement with the Marxist critique of religion, which "is correct insofar as there are religions and religious practices that alienate man from himself."[54]

The problem goes still deeper than religious practice. Ratzinger notes that beyond differences among religions, "even the gods are not all alike," and that there are, in fact, some "decidedly negative divine figures."[55] A brief glimpse at the history of religions, Ratzinger suggests, is sufficient to disprove the idea that all religions are the same or merit equal approval. These differences affect the way that a person relates to the world and to other people, since they color his perception of reality as a whole and his understanding of the purpose of human existence. Some religious traditions will encourage a person in his pursuit of virtue and moral goodness, whereas others can retard these efforts. Ratzinger admits that it is definitely possible "for someone to receive from his religion directives that help him become a pure person, which also, if we want to use the word, help him to please God and reach salvation." On the other hand, it is equally possible that religion can "make it harder for man to be good." And Ratzinger once again draws the conclusion that there is always a need to purify religion "so that it does not become an obstacle to the right relation to God but in fact puts man on the right path."[56]

Which Religions Are We Talking About?

Perhaps the clearest idea concerning which elements of religions require discernment and purification comes from Ratzinger's reflections over the years regarding specific cases and particular religious traditions. The following paragraphs will elucidate several of these cases.

Islam

Pope Benedict's Regensburg address of September 12, 2006, just a year and a half into his papacy, garnered more public attention than any other activity of his papacy had since his election. In it, he cited the 14th-century Byzantine emperor Manuel II Paleologus, whom he refers to as "an educated Persian on the subject of Christianity and Islam, and the truth of both," regarding the relationship between religion and violence. "Show me just what Mohammed brought that was new, and there you will find things only evil and inhuman, such as his command to spread by the sword the faith he preached."[57] Despite his warning remarks that the emperor addresses his interlocutor with "a brusqueness that we find unacceptable," the Pope found himself in the middle of a media maelstrom with political and social repercussions, including several acts of violence against Catholics. In point of fact, in the very same paper, Benedict observes that many experts hold that surah 2, 256, which reads "There is no compulsion in religion" probably comes from the early period, when Mohammed was still powerless and under threat. Benedict has made no secret of his conviction that violence can never be justified in the name of religion, but he seems to harbor reservations regarding Muslims' commitment to the same principle.[58]

Benedict's various critiques of Islam recognize the difficulty of separating authentic religious fervor from nationalism and other human passions. Ratzinger has written, for example, that it is not clear to what extent "the new surge forward of the Islamic world is fuelled by truly religious forces." In many places, he continues, "there is the danger of a pathological development of the autonomy of feeling, which only reinforces that threat of horrifying things."[59]

Yet Ratzinger's reflections on Islam go deeper than the interplay of religion and violence and its attendant expressions in international terrorism. He invites readers to look deeper at the nature of Islam itself and its understanding of the human person and society. One question that comes immediately to the fore is the very issue of the separation of church and state. If this concept is foreign to or even incompatible with Islam, to what degree is Islam compatible with Western democracy? For instance, Ratzinger has noted that "the interplay of society, politics, and religion has a completely different structure in Islam" than it does in the West. He goes on to say that much of today's discussion in the West regarding Islam "presupposes that all religions have basically the same structure, that they all fit into a democratic system with its regulations and the possibilities provided by these regulations."[60]

Yet this is not consistent with the facts. Rather, it "contradicts the essence of Islam, which simply does not have the separation of the political and the religious sphere that Christianity has had from the beginning."[61] Ratzinger fears that discussions regarding Islam and its integration into

Western society necessarily adopt Western, and even Christian, suppositions about Islam that do not correspond to the way Islam views itself.

This underlying difference in understanding goes well beyond political or social theory regarding the nature of the state. It touches virtually every aspect of human existence. Ratzinger continues: "Islam has a total organization of life that is completely different from ours; it embraces simply everything. There is a very marked subordination of woman to man; there is a very tightly knit criminal law, indeed, a law regulating all areas of life, that is opposed to our modern ideas about society."[62] The conclusion he reaches, while an obvious outcome of this linear logic, still could strike us as remarkably severe. He states that we must have a clear understanding "that it is not simply a denomination that can be included in the free realm of a pluralistic society."[63] While he goes no further regarding the practical ramifications of this inference, he leaves the door open for serious questions regarding correct Western political policy concerning Islam.

Primitive Religions

The year 1992, with its commemoration of the 1492 "discovery" of America, brought with it a wave of anti-European sentiment and a revived nostalgia for the pre-Columban religions that flourished in America prior to its colonization and Christianization. In his book *Truth and Tolerance*, Ratzinger cites Brazilian liberation theologian Leonardo Boff as an example of this nostalgia. Boff wrote that the European Christians "conquered bodies with the sword and dominated souls with the cross," so that for many natives "Christianity appeared as the religion of the enemy." He goes on to express the hope that "1992 could be the year that represents the resumption of their religions, which were just and worthy."[64]

In his response, Ratzinger makes the altogether apt suggestion that at the very least, "in the face of such demands, one ought to look carefully at each religion to see whether its restoration would really be desirable."[65] He reminds readers of some important considerations that often go unnoticed amid ideological fervor. He recalls, for instance, that on the occasion of the most recent rebuilding of the main Aztec temple in 1487, a minimum of 20,000 people bled to death over four days as human sacrifices to the sun god. This sacrifice took place because the sun lived on the blood of human hearts, and the end of the world could only be prevented through human sacrifice.

All of this derived, Ratzinger reflects, not from some inborn inclination to bloodthirstiness but from a fanatical belief in the duty of men to provide for the continuation of the world in this manner. In other words, it was a requirement of their religious convictions and not merely an expression of senseless cruelty. In the face of this, he wryly surmises, "it will be difficult for us to encourage the restoration of this religion." And he concludes that although this represents an extreme instance, it still "shows that one cannot simply see in any and every religion the way for God to come to man and man to God."[66] If we can think of examples where discernment among religions is patently necessary, we can infer that it is always necessary in some degree.

New Age

In *Caritas in Veritate* Benedict declares that some religious cultures, rather than advancing communion among people, focus on "individual well-being, limited to the gratification of psychological desires."[67] Although he does not mention them by name, the Pope seems to refer in this passage to New Age or self-help spiritualities as especially dangerous for development, since they fail to foment the interpersonal communion that is integral to true development. At other times, Benedict continues, religious cultures manifest their deficiencies as a kind of syncretism, which not only alienates persons from each other but may also "distance them from reality."[68]

This is not the first time that Ratzinger has taken on the phenomenon of New Age in his writings. In his 1997 work *Salt of the Earth*, he had said that New Age "aims at a fusion of all religions," thus highlighting the syncretistic character of this movement.[69] He also noted New Age ties to an anti-Christian spirit that divinizes the cosmos.[70] In *Truth and Tolerance*, he confronts the New Age movement as one of the "new questions that arose in the nineties" and devotes an entire section to the topic.[71] Here he discerns problems with this movement that undermine the foundations of a truly just society. New Age, in Ratzinger's estimation, is an anti-rationalist response to the dilemma of relativism—so rather than search for a common truth, people find meaning "in a re-entry into the dance of the cosmos."[72] In the end, however, this trend signals not a liberation of the human person, but an abdication of responsibility for the world by seeking refuge in "the pleasure of infinity."[73] Ratzinger suggests that the more the pointlessness of political absolutisms becomes obvious, "the more powerful will be the attraction of irrationalism, the renunciation of everyday reality."[74] Here, too, is a religious phenomenon that requires discernment and evaluation, since its contribution to authentic human progress is questionable at best, promoting as it does isolationism and flight from the world.

Hinduism

Early religions of the east, such as Hinduism, demand a more nuanced analysis. Ratzinger has observed that Hinduism "is actually a collective name for a whole multitude of religions" in which there are some marvelous elements but also some negative aspects that bode poorly for the future of society. Among these, Ratzinger mentions the caste system, self-immolation (suttee; sati) for widows, and offshoots of the cult of the goddess Sakti.[75] Similarly, in *Caritas in Veritate*, Pope Benedict noted that religious traditions that "ossify society in rigid social groupings" impede authentic development.[76] Both the caste system itself and the practice of self-immolation underscore a completely different understanding of human dignity and basic human equality from that which undergirds Western civilization. How these assumptions about the human person can coexist with a society built on radically different premises is not self-evident.

Because of its heterogeneous nature, Hinduism doesn't lend itself to a simple appraisal. As Ratzinger observes, within Hinduism exists a multiplicity of forms, "very high and pure ones that are marked by the idea of love, but also wholly gruesome ones that include ritual murder."[77] At best, Hinduism requires purification; at worst, one could question its suitability for building a truly just society.

Animist Religions

In the case of animist religions (typically of African provenance), Ratzinger warns of the temptation of romanticism, an uncritical approach to a complex reality. To look at such primitive religions through rose-colored glasses, Ratzinger suggests, is to distort their historical reality. Naturally, he says, "they contain 'grains of truth', but in their concrete form they have created a world of fear, from which God is far removed and in which the earth is at the mercy of arbitrary spirits."[78] This has certainly not been a contributing factor to Africa's development and may indeed have been an impediment.

In fact, in a later work Ratzinger expressed his conviction that in Africa, "belief in spirits continues to be a great obstacle to the development of the land and to the construction of a modern economic organization."[79] Rather than empower the human person and society for responsible development, such beliefs drain human energies. "If I constantly have to protect myself against spirits," Ratzinger writes, "and an irrational fear governs my whole sense of life, then I am not rightly living what religion at its depth should be."[80] In *Caritas in Veritate* as well, Benedict observed that religious traditions espousing "magical beliefs that fail to respect the dignity of the person" and "attitudes of subjugation to occult powers" make it difficult for love and truth to flourish and tend to obstruct development.[81] Again, it should be noted that his judgment here does not merely concern the salvific or theological value of these religious traditions but rather their contribution to human development, which is the concern of public authorities.

Christianity

Among the many religious traditions, Ratzinger does not simply place Christianity as an equal. He asserts its real superiority. Again, this is based not solely on its truth claims regarding salvation and the nature of God but especially on its superiority for organizing human society. "Christian faith has proved," he states, "to be the most universal and rational religious culture."[82] Moreover, it "furnishes the basis of a rational moral faith without which no society can endure."[83] This leads him to cite with evident agreement that "the source of truth for politics is not Christianity as revealed religion but Christianity as leaven and a form of life which has proved its worth in the course of history."[84]

Yet in the self-critical spirit that characterizes him, Benedict has also noted that Christianity itself is in no way exempt from the need for purification. Here it is not just a case of "throwing stones" but rather of working together for the betterment of all. Just as there are pathological forms of other religions, so, too, there are diseased forms of Christianity. Because of "false ways of living the Christian reality, sectarian deformations, and so forth," Christianity, too, can "make it harder for man to be good."[85] Ratzinger notes, for instance, that witch burning was a "recrudescence of Germanic customs" which had, with difficulty, been overcome by the early medieval missionaries, but then "reemerged in the late Middle Ages as faith began to grow weak."[86] Another example Ratzinger cites of distortions of the true Christian spirit is "when the crusaders, on capturing the holy city of Jerusalem, where Christ died for all men, for their part indulged in a bloodbath of Moslems and Jews."[87] Religion, even authentic religion, doesn't guarantee freedom from sickness and fanaticism, and the give-and-take between reason and faith benefits both sides of the dialogue.

Atheism as Religion

In a particularly incisive passage Ratzinger notes that the pathology of religion (which he calls "the most dangerous sickness of the human spirit") also exists "precisely where religion as such is rejected and relative goods are assigned an absolute value."[88] Though atheists ostensibly reject the existence of God, they are not exempt from fanaticism of a religious nature. Ratzinger thus writes that "the atheistic systems of modern times are the most frightful examples of passionate religious enthusiasm alienated from its proper identity."[89] The disastrous fruits of the institutional atheism of both Marxism in the Soviet Union and national socialism in Germany bear witness to the extremes to which this anti-theistic ardor may arrive.

Whereas Locke had asserted that atheism ought not be tolerated by the magistrate since atheists could not be trusted to keep their oaths,[90] Ratzinger's analysis goes much deeper. "When the existence of God is denied," he writes "freedom is, not enhanced, but deprived of its basis and thus distorted."[91] Although atheism may present itself as the greatest of liberations—that of the creature from its Creator—it undermines the very foundations of freedom itself. It also undermines the nature of human equality and the essence of morality.

Ratzinger cites the case of evolutionary biology. While accepting the idea of some evolutionary processes, especially at the micro level, he criticizes the materialistic "development of evolutionary theory into a generalized *philosophia universalis*, which claims to constitute a universal explanation of reality."[92] Where the theory of evolution has been expanded to a *philosophia universalis*, Ratzinger contends, it has been used for an attempt at a new ethos based on evolution. Yet since this evolutionary ethic inevitably takes as its central concept the model of selectivity—that is, the struggle for survival—it offers little comfort. "Even when people try to make it more attractive in various ways," Ratzinger continues, "it ultimately remains a bloodthirsty ethic. Here, the attempt to distill rationality out of what is in itself irrational quite visibly fails."[93]

The most obvious example of this is the denial of free will proper to scientific materialism. In a 2006 essay, Richard Dawkins wrote that scientists believe that human brains are governed by the laws of physics just like man-made computers are. He noted that when a computer malfunctions, we do not punish it, we track down the problem and fix it. "Isn't the murderer or the rapist," Dawkins asks, "just a machine with a defective component? Or a defective upbringing? Defective education? Defective genes?" He goes on to write:

> But doesn't a truly scientific, mechanistic view of the nervous system make nonsense of the very idea of responsibility? Any crime, however heinous, is in principle to be blamed on antecedent conditions acting through the accused's physiology, heredity and environment.[94]

This wholly mechanistic view, which ultimately leaves no room for free will, destroys the possibility of morality, since morality hinges on personal freedom and responsibility. The very notions of praise and blame, reward and punishment—which are inherent to morality—have no place in a materialistic world bereft of spirit where everything has a material cause. If one were to take Dawkins's statements to their logical conclusion, people would be treated as things, as "machines" (in his terminology), and right and wrong would simply disappear as nonsensical constructs. Such scientific "progress" is hostile to human society and diametrically opposed to true development.

Conclusion

In light of the foregoing considerations it would seem that there are two fundamental ways that religious traditions require the discernment of public authorities. First, there is the fairly evident case of overt damage to society or disdain for lawfulness. Whereas religion is a good for humanity, it is not an unmitigated or unqualified good. In certain instances it can also become a justification for evil, such as terrorism.[95] In this same vein, the Council Fathers wrote that "society has the right to defend itself against possible abuses committed on the pretext of freedom of religion" and that it is "the special duty of government to provide this protection."[96] Here, the state's action against unlawful activities carried out in the name of religion simply applies to the activities the same norm that would govern any citizen.[97] The obvious exception here regards conscientious objection, by which no one should be obliged to act immorally, though to do so may require an exemption from the law.

The second case is far more subtle, difficult to articulate and even more difficult to apply in practice. Ratzinger has written that in all known historical cultures, "religion is an essential element of culture, is indeed its determinative center." Indeed, he argues, "it is religion that determines the scale of values and, thereby, the inner cohesion and hierarchy of all these cultures."[98] Yet cultures are not static; they evolve.[99] This evolution can be a positive or negative thing, but it is rarely indifferent. Since culture and its evolution are closely related to the common good of society, public authority cannot be indifferent to the progress or corruption of culture. Thus public authorities must be attentive to the influence of religions not only on the immediate social order but also on the future of society.

Democratic societies are grounded in certain nonnegotiable principles, which are not themselves products of the democratic process, but its conditions and guarantors. There is a determined cultural "soil" that makes democracy possible. The fundamental equality of persons, the dignity of the human person, healthy separation of church and state, and principles of justice and fairness are some of these conditions. Since these cultural foundation stones are themselves fruit of a particular worldview, a Christian worldview in point of fact, what happens when other religious traditions with competing visions of man and society enter the stage? In what ways would opposing scales of values threaten the survival of a given society? Perhaps more importantly, what would happen if populations were to shift in such a way that non-Christian religions became predominant in countries of Christian inspiration? If everything were left up to consensus and majority opinion, democratic society itself could very well be jeopardized.

It seems essential that the pillars of Western society that guarantee its survival be subtracted from the political process and enshrined as non-negotiable absolutes. In Ratzinger's words: "Ultimately the democratic system can only function if certain fundamental values—let us call them human rights—are recognized as valid by everyone and are withdrawn from the competence of the majority."[100] A distinction is needed between what is subject to the will of the majority and what forms the untouchable underpinning of Western society.

Though Benedict has said a fair amount regarding the correct rapport between church and state—enough to glean a fairly precise understanding of his call for "discernment" at the theoretical level—he has said very little about the practical consequences that such discernment should generate. He does not speak about public authorities banning religions, curtailing their activities, or anything else of the sort. He doesn't even comment on the recognition and concession of special status to purportedly "religious" bodies and institutions, which could involve everything from fiscal exemptions to favored standing.

What he does contend quite clearly is the need for people and governments to actively pursue truth, including moral truth, according to their competencies. In the case of civil governments, this means seeking a more substantive notion of justice and the common good that goes beyond consensus and the mere avoidance of disruption of the public order, since "a justice that is more than the regulation of group interests must be subordinate to a universal criterion."[101] The aim of public debate is not only to persuade others of our opinions, but the pursuit of truth, both theoretical and moral. This is society's common endeavor and we must believe that it is possible. Civil society is called to apply reason once again to religion, to make religion responsible to reason. In the name of the common good, public authority should participate actively in this discernment.

Perhaps one of Benedict's goals in proposing the need for discernment among religions is simply to stimulate this public debate. When people start discussing deeper questions, questions of moral truth rather than mere expediency, we are already making progress. There is also a practical side to this. For where Ratzinger forcefully argues that majority opinion can never be a standard for truth, education of the public is significant, since "law cannot be permanently effective unless it has some kind of public credibility."[102] Public credibility is achieved in large measure through public argument.

This discernment further implies that freedom, including religious freedom, must be linked more and more closely to truth, and to responsibility. Ratzinger has argued that the growth of freedom can no longer consist simply in the demolishing of barriers to individual rights, since such a practice will eventually yield the destruction of those very individual rights. Growth of freedom, rather, must consist in the growth of responsibility, which "includes the acceptance of ever greater ties, as demanded by the claims of human coexistence, by what is appropriate for the essence of being human."[103] Acknowledging what is appropriate for humanity, in turn, demands a renewed discussion of natural law principles, without which only positive law exists.

Throughout his pontificate, Benedict has shown himself to be unafraid of controversy. In the ongoing debates concerning the correct relationship between religion and public authority, his call for "discernment" will provide ample fodder for healthy debate about one of the most pressing issues of our times. One thing is clear, religions are not all the same, and not everything done in the name of religion merits the same respect and protection. As Christians continue to call for worldwide regard for the fundamental right to religious liberty, they will do well to welcome helpful dialogue between faith and reason as a sure benefit to both.

In this chapter we have had the opportunity to examine Pope Benedict's critical contribution to one of the most critical social issues of our day, religious liberty, much of which has roots in his writings prior to his election to the See of Peter. We now turn specifically to Benedict's pontificate, to his specific contribution as Pope to the ongoing corpus of Catholic social teaching. We begin with his first encyclical, *Deus Caritas Est*.

Chapter 11

Deus Caritas Est and Catholic Social Thought

As we saw in chapter three, the category of "social encyclicals" is now well ensconced in magisterial nomenclature. It distinguishes Papal teaching letters that deal expressly with social questions from other encyclicals that touch on social issues only tangentially or treat other subjects entirely. The established corpus of social encyclicals begins with Leo XIII's groundbreaking *Rerum Novarum*, passes through Pius XI's *Quadragesimo Anno*, John XXIII's *Mater et Magistra*, Paul VI's *Populorum Progressio*, and ends, as of this writing, with Benedict XVI's 2009 encyclical *Caritas in Veritate*.[1]

While perfectly understandable, this custom of drawing a bright line between "social encyclicals" and other Magisterial texts leads to the regrettable consequence of downplaying the important social teachings contained in other papal texts or ignoring these documents altogether when examining Church doctrine on particular social questions. Pope John Paul II's apostolic exhortation *Familiaris Consortio*, for example—a masterful treatise on marriage, the family and society—is habitually excluded from the catalogue of social magisterial texts, as is his encyclical letter *Evangelium Vitae* and the post-synodal apostolic exhortation *Christifideles Laici*, despite their invaluable teaching regarding pressing social justice issues.

Similarly, Pope Benedict XVI's encyclical *Deus Caritas Est* will never be considered a "social encyclical." As his first encyclical, *Deus Caritas Est* is considered "programmatic," in that it lays out fundamental themes that Benedict considers of prime importance for the Church of today, themes he is expected to refer back to in the future.[2] In the first of two parts of the encyclical Benedict examined the fundamental theological truth of God as love, along with the relationship between divine love and human love and the possibility of truly loving God and neighbor. Those familiar with the theological works of Joseph Ratzinger found a text in line with his previous writings, both in style and content. The true surprise of the encyclical came with the second part, which focuses on the charitable work of the Church as a community of believers.

In this second part of the encyclical, Benedict expressly referenced the Church's social doctrine and elaborated on it in new and innovative ways. He listed some of the key social encyclicals, as his predecessors had often done, and recalled the origins of modern social teaching in the pressing need for a new approach to a just structuring of society in the aftermath of the industrial revolution. His careful consideration of the social question, in light of the theological virtue of charity, offered an original contribution to Catholic social doctrine and merits serious study.

Church and State

The central insight of Benedict's social teaching in *Deus Caritas Est* concerns the complementary relationship between Church and State, between faith and reason, and between charity and justice—topics he would develop further in *Caritas in Veritate*. In his extended reflections on the topic, which comprise nearly the entire second half of the encyclical, Benedict offers an innovative contribution to Catholic social thought, while remaining firmly rooted in the tradition. The Church lives by faith and dedicates herself to charity, while the state is called to live by practical reason and dedicate itself to justice. As the Church cannot guarantee justice, neither can the state guarantee charity. Despite this clear distinction, however, Benedict insists that the two realities are closely interrelated and mutually enriching. Although we must distinguish between Church and state and their respective roles, we must not seek to separate them. "The two spheres are distinct, yet always interrelated."[3]

Benedict begins his discussion on justice and charity as a response to theories like Marxism that posit a necessary antagonism and incompatibility between justice and charity. According to this ideology, justice can only be achieved when charity is abolished, since insistence on charity only serves to preserve and propagate the *status quo* with its injustices.[4] To this criticism, Benedict responds that charity and justice complement one another and must advance hand in hand, as allies rather than adversaries. One cannot supplant the other since both are truly necessary. Even in a perfectly just political environment, charity would not be superfluous.

Benedict takes up the perennial message of Catholic social teaching, that the state exists for the sake of the common good to ensure a just ordering of human society. He notes that "the pursuit of justice must be a fundamental norm of the State and that the aim of a just social order is to guarantee to each person, according to the principle of subsidiarity, his share of the community's goods."[5] More succinctly still, Benedict states: "The just ordering of society and the State is a central responsibility of politics," since justice "is both the aim and the intrinsic criterion of all politics."[6]

The Church recognizes, respects, and supports this proper role of the state and has no wish to usurp its competencies. Contrary to the fears of some, Benedict asserted that Catholic social doctrine "has no intention of giving the Church power over the State." A moment later he repeats: "The Church cannot and must not take upon herself the political battle to bring about the most just society possible. She cannot and must not replace the State."[7] The Church gratefully recognizes the autonomy of the temporal sphere as well as her own inadequacy for assuring a just ordering of society.

The Church's Service to Society

Just as the state has a proper competency, so does the Church. In *Deus Caritas Est*, Benedict offers a historical analysis of the Church's institutional commitment to charity, tracing its origins to the apostolic period, as an essential characteristic of the Church's mission and self-identity. This institutional commitment is not only a historically verifiable practice, however, but also a necessary activity stemming from the Church's identity and willed by her Founder. "The Church cannot neglect the service of charity any more than she can neglect the Sacraments and the Word."[8]

The Church's practice of social charity preceded its theoretical exposition in modern Catholic social doctrine by many centuries, and constitutes one of her distinctive activities tied to her very identity and mission. Social charity was assimilated, lived, and institutionalized long before it became an object of systematic study. In the practice of Christian charity, Benedict recognizes a hierarchy, in that love of neighbor is "first and foremost a responsibility for each individual," and only secondarily a task for the entire ecclesial community. Yet this task is still essential. "As a community, the Church must practice love."[9] Moreover, this love is not merely a haphazard, spontaneous outpouring of beneficence, but an "ordered service" to the community—and thus Benedict can define the Church's "diakonia" as "the ministry of charity exercised in a communitarian, orderly way."[10]

The Church's dedication to service—*diakonia*—grew up alongside her dedication to proclaiming God's word (*kerygma-martyria*) and the celebration of the sacraments (*leitourgia*), such that the three form her "three-fold responsibility."[11] One can draw an interesting parallel here to Christ's *triplex munus* as priest, prophet and king—only here the *munus regale* becomes an office of service, rather than of rule, in line with Jesus' new teaching regarding the exercise of authority.[12] From the earliest days of Christianity the Church assumed this responsibility, and "love for widows and orphans, prisoners, and the sick and needy of every kind, is as essential to her as the ministry of the sacraments and preaching of the Gospel."[13] It was, according to Benedict, with the naming of the first seven deacons (Acts 6:5-6) that *diakonia* became "part of the fundamental structure of the Church."[14] Benedict traces the ecclesial institutionalization of her charitable outreach through the *diakonia* of each monastery in Egypt (middle of the fourth century) to its formal incorporation "with full juridical standing" by the sixth century.[15] As Church structures evolved, so did the centers of charitable activity. The office of *diakonia* was not solely a monastic institution but existed at the level of the individual dioceses as well. From this institution the present worldwide organization of *Caritas* evolved.

Benedict claims for the Church a right to practice charity and to do so on her own terms. "For the Church," Benedict insists, "charity is not a kind of welfare activity which could equally well be left to others, but is a part of her nature, an indispensable expression of her very being."[16] In other words, charitable outreach constitutes for the Church an *opus proprium*, "in which she does not cooperate collaterally, but acts as a subject with direct responsibility, doing what corresponds to her nature."[17] It is thus important not only for the sake of those served as a community service, but also for those serving, as a necessary expression of their Christian faith and of the nature of the Church. Freedom of religion also entails freedom for the exercise of charity rather than the usurpation of all service into the offices of the state. Moreover, the principle of subsidiarity itself calls for the state to allow for and encourage the subjectivity of society, an important part of which is the Church's activity. Benedict specifically rejects the notion of a state "which regulates and controls everything," and calls, rather, for a state "which, in accordance with the principle of subsidiarity, generously acknowledges and supports initiatives arising from the different social forces and combines spontaneity with closeness to those in need."[18]

Although this charitable activity is a necessity for the Church, it is also a necessity for society. It is a distinct service, with characteristics that cannot be found elsewhere, not in other volunteer activities and much less in State services. "There is no ordering of the State so just that it can eliminate the need for a service of love," and thus charity "will always prove necessary, even in the most just society."[19] The thought that if only social structures could be better ordered, charity would become superfluous manifests a subtle error, that of a materialist view of the human person, or, in Benedict's words, "the mistaken notion that man can live 'by bread alone.'"[20] By denying the person's deeper spiritual and emotional needs, this conviction "demeans man and ultimately disregards all that is specifically human."[21] According to Benedict, Christian charity distinguishes itself from social assistance in three key ways.

First, Christian charity must provide a "simple response to immediate needs," in a professionally competent manner but above all with "heartfelt concern," since human beings need more than technically proper care: "they need humanity."[22] This concern is fruit of a "formation of the heart" proper to Christians who have encountered God in Christ, "which awakens their love and opens their spirits to others."[23]

Second, Christian charitable activity must be distinguished by its independence from "parties and ideologies." Present needs are not ignored or sacrificed to future gains, since, as he writes in a passage we discussed in Chapter 6, "[o]ne does not make the world more human by refusing to act humanely here and now." The Christian's program is "a heart which sees" where love is needed and acts accordingly.[24] In short, personnel who carry out the Church's charitable activity "must not be inspired by ideologies aimed at improving the world, but should rather be guided by the faith which works through love."[25]

Third, and perhaps surprisingly, Benedict notes that Christian charity "cannot be used as a means of engaging in what is nowadays considered proselytism," since love is free and cannot be practiced as a means of achieving other ends. And yet while such charitable activity must reject aggressive proselytizing and cannot bind kindness to doctrinal prerequisites, Christians engaged in charitable outreach do not renounce their witness to Christ, since freely given love is itself the strongest testimony of God's presence. Thus Christians "realize that a pure and generous love is the best witness to the God in whom we believe and by whom we are driven to love."[26] It is their love itself that witnesses to Christ. God is love, and "God's presence is felt at the very time when the only thing we do is to love."[27]

The Church's Service to the State

Despite the distinct fields of activity proper to Church and state, they are not separate or unrelated. The Church, in fact, not only serves human society through her charitable activity; she also provides a specific service to the *state* in the latter's mission of procuring justice and the common good. While the Church is not responsible for this mission, she does offer a critical ancillary function. She does this, Benedict says, in a twofold way—one indirect, the other direct.

First, through her social teaching the Church serves the state indirectly by helping it answer the question: "What is justice?" The state is properly concerned with the common good, but it needs help in discerning the nature of this good and its concrete requirements. The Church, says Benedict, has an "indirect duty," in that "she is called to contribute to the purification of reason and to the reawakening of those moral forces without which just structures are neither established nor prove effective in the long run."[28] Practical reason needs purification, since political reason always risks ethical blindness because of the influence of power and special interests.[29] In this context, faith is "a purifying force for reason itself," since it "liberates reason from its blind spots and therefore helps it to be ever more fully itself."[30] Here Benedict presents a simple yet profound synthesis of Catholic social doctrine, whose aim "is simply to help purify reason and to contribute, here and now, to the acknowledgment and attainment of what is just."[31] For Benedict, Catholic social teaching is more than a discipline internal to theological studies; it is a gift to society. Through her social doctrine, the Church "wishes to help form consciences in political life and to stimulate greater insight into the authentic requirements of justice as well as greater readiness to act accordingly."[32]

Here we can discern the parallel service that exists among the three pairs of Church-state, faith-reason, and charity-justice. They complement and serve one another without wishing to assume the other's proper competencies. Just as charity completes justice, so faith is called to purify and perfect reason, so that reason can be truly itself and discover the objective demands of the just order. If, as the Second Vatican Council taught, Christ "fully reveals man to man himself and makes his supreme calling clear"—since "only in the mystery of the incarnate Word does the mystery of man take on light"[33]—then Christian anthropology provides an invaluable service to political authority in its quest to discover the requirements of true justice.

Though a branch of moral theology, Catholic social teaching does not press for the acceptance of revealed truth or confessional doctrine at the state level. Rather, Benedict asserts, the Church's social teaching "argues on the basis of reason and natural law, namely, on the basis of what is in accord with the nature of every human being."[34] In this way the Church addresses her social teaching to all men and women of good will and participates in civil discourse relying on the common tools of reason and human experience.

Along with this *indirect* duty, which the Church carries out through her social teaching, there is a *direct* service to the political task that the Church carries out through the political engagement of the lay faithful. As citizens of the state, the lay faithful "are called to take part in public life in a personal capacity."[35] The Church's direct engagement with the just ordering of society, then, is not carried out *institutionally* but *personally*.[36] Charity and justice converge in the hearts and souls of the lay faithful who, moved by love, work for justice.[37] Called to build up the social order according to the principles of the Gospel, the lay faithful take part fully in civil society and political life.

The Nature of Christian Charitable Service

A distinctive contribution of *Deus Caritas Est* is its extensive description of Christian charitable activity and how it is to be carried out. While this may seem only tangentially an aspect of the Church's social teaching, in reality it is central to Catholic teaching regarding a Christian's role in society. It is hinted at in earlier Magisterial texts, but never treated with the depth or breadth it finds in *Deus Caritas Est*.[38] In the first place, Benedict describes this charitable work as fruit of the love of Christ rather than mere philanthropic goodwill or sentimental compassion for the sufferings and needs of others. More than anything, he writes, "they must be persons moved by Christ's love, persons whose hearts Christ has conquered with his love, awakening within them a love of neighbour."[39] It is these Christian souls, touched and conquered by the love of Jesus, who carry out Christian charity in all its fullness.

Second, Benedict insists that true Christian charity can never be reduced to efficient, technical activity but must be moved by true love for the person. Taking his cue from Saint Paul's hymn to charity, which Benedict describes as "the *Magna Carta* of all ecclesial service," he notes that "[i]f I give away all I have, and if I deliver my body to be burned, but do not have love, I gain nothing" (1 Cor 13:3). Merely feeding the poor is never enough from a Christian perspective. "Practical activity will always be insufficient, unless it visibly expresses a love for man, a love nourished by an encounter with Christ."[40] Moreover, the gifts one gives of time and material goods must be an expression of personal self-donation, which lies at the heart of charity. "I must give to others not only something that is my own, but my very self; I must be personally present in my gift."[41]

This self-donation ties directly to Benedict's third consideration: that Christian charitable activity must be characterized by the virtue of *humility*. In philanthropic work there is always a danger that one may assume an attitude of superiority vis-à-vis the beneficiary of one's service, and in so doing, humiliate the one being served. Benedict notes that the way to overcome such an attitude is by realizing that when we serve others, we are the first beneficiaries. It is a gift to be able to help others. "Those who are in a position to help others will realize that in doing so they themselves receive help."[42] Further, this service leads us to discover our own neediness: "The more we do for others, the more we understand and can appropriate the words of Christ: 'We are useless servants.'"[43] The practice of humility enables the Christian to eschew ideological utopianism and vain activism. The knowledge that, in the end, we are only instruments in the Lord's hands "frees us from the presumption of thinking that we alone are personally responsible for building a better world."[44]

Such humility, coupled with an unswerving trust in God's providence, is also a safeguard against two contrasting temptations highlighted by Benedict. When we consider the situation of the world and the need for responsible activity, we can, on the one hand "be driven towards an ideology that would aim at doing what God's governance of the world apparently cannot: fully resolving every problem."[45] On the other hand, the prospect of the immensity of the task before us can also induce us to throw up our hands in desperation, convinced that our meager efforts cannot effect any real and meaningful good, since in Benedict's words, "it would seem that in any event nothing can be accomplished."[46] To overcome these two opposing temptations, more than human prudence and virtue are needed. The solution Benedict proposes is theological: "a living relationship with Christ is decisive."[47] This is not pietistic theory, but the lived experience of the Church, exemplified in her saints. "In the example of Blessed Teresa of Calcutta we have a clear illustration of the fact that time devoted to God in prayer not only does not detract from effective and loving service to our neighbour but is in fact the inexhaustible source of that service."[48] By its very nature as a theological virtue, charity is proper to believers who abide in Christ, as a branch abides in the vine and bears much fruit.[49]

Conclusion

Although Benedict never intended *Deus Caritas Est* to be a social encyclical per se, it contains an exceptional amount of material pertinent to the Church's ongoing social teaching. Making no pretensions to comprehensiveness, Benedict specifically delved into the question of the Church's commitment to ordered charitable activity, necessarily distinguishing it from the state's complementary effort to promote and defend justice and the common good. In so doing, he provided a fresh synthesis of the Church's understanding of Church-state relations and the competencies proper to each. He also showed, as no pope had done before, what the Church's specifically contributes to the social order and outlined the characteristics of Christian charity that both distinguish it from philanthropy and social assistance and define it as identifiably Christian.

Benedict also presented clear teaching regarding the service rendered by the Church to the state in its efforts to procure justice. Reiterating that the Church has neither the will nor the competence to replace the state in this important responsibility, she does however offer a twofold assistance. Through her social teaching, reasoning with principles of the natural law, she helps purify the state's understanding of social justice and its requirements.[50] As mother and teacher, the Church furnishes sound principles to form consciences and provoke discussion regarding the exigencies of the common good. Along with this *indirect* aid, the Church also offers *direct* assistance through the engagement of the lay faithful in the political process and in the different strata of social life.

Part of the beauty of this important encyclical—made possible, paradoxically, from the fact that it is not a social encyclical—is its extended theological treatment of the central virtue of charity in the Christian life. Benedict was able to seamlessly wed the Church's charitable activity to the inner life of the Trinity itself and the Christian vocation to image this life in the practice of love. Love of neighbor stands at the core of the Christian moral life and reveals itself particularly through the charitable activity of Christians in the social sphere—both institutionally and personally. Thus theology manifests its essential unity as a single science, with doctrine and morals nourishing one another in mutual implication. Though it will never be included in future catalogues of social encyclicals, the impact of *Deus Caritas Est* on the field of Catholic social doctrine will endure.

In our next and final chapter we will turn to another of Benedict's encyclicals, that which properly bears the name of social encyclical: *Caritas in Veritate*. Building on what he had laid out in *Deus Caritas Est*, Benedict offered in this encyclical a surprising and important contribution to the development of Catholic social thought, one which grants us an ever clearer vision of *the world as it could be*.

Chapter 12

A Paradigm Shift?
Caritas in Veritate and the
Future of Catholic Social
Thought

S aint Matthew relates Jesus' praise for a scribe who becomes a disciple, comparing him to "the master of a household who brings out of his treasure what is new and what is old."[1] This ability to keep up with a changing world, while holding on to what is perennially valid and useful, is particularly precious to Catholic social doctrine, a discipline that must constantly apply evergreen moral principles to fluctuating social realities.[2]

Striking this balance sometimes proves difficult and involves not only knowing what to throw out and what to keep but also sometimes what to fish out of the dustbin. Pope Paul VI's 1967 encyclical letter *Populorum Progressio* has often been dismissed as a rambling, incoherent document that uncritically embraced a typically 1960s *gauchiste* read of the economy and of the causes of wealth and poverty. As recently as 2009, Lord Brian Griffiths, vice-chairman of Goldman Sachs International, summarily described *Populorum Progressio* as "the encyclical published by Paul VI in 1967, at the height of anti-capitalism in Europe. It attacked liberal capitalism, was ambivalent about economic growth, recommended expropriation of landed estates if poorly used and enthused about economic planning."[3]

Pope John Paul II obviously didn't share this severe critique of the text and issued a commemorative encyclical in 1987, *Sollicitudo Rei Socialis*, in which he called *Populorum Progressio* a "distinguished encyclical" with "enduring relevance."[4] This was the first time that any social encyclical except *Rerum Novarum* had been commemorated in this fashion.

With the promulgation of *Caritas in Veritate*, however, Pope Benedict XVI arguably went one step further. Not content with merely producing a second encyclical in commemoration of *Populorum Progressio*, Benedict expresses his conviction "that *Populorum Progressio* deserves to be considered 'the *Rerum Novarum* of the present age.'"[5] This statement holds exceptional importance. For decades, as we discussed earlier, *Rerum Novarum* has been considered the most important document of Catholic social doctrine,[6] and Pope John Paul II wrote that through *Rerum Novarum* Pope Leo had "created a lasting paradigm for the Church."[7] In what will likely be the only social encyclical of his pontificate, Benedict modified this vision in no insignificant way. For this reason alone, *Caritas in Veritate* may very well be, as one commentator has observed, "more than just another social encyclical."[8]

The purpose of this final chapter will be to examine Benedict's re-evaluation of *Populorum Progressio*, discern what it means practically for the future of Catholic social doctrine, and explore Benedict's discussion of integral human development and its requirements for the world of today.

Populorum Progressio:
The "*Rerum Novarum* of the Present Age"?

In the rather brief history of formal Catholic social doctrine, popes have sought to continually update historical evaluations of social events and processes in an effort to keep social doctrine current and culturally relevant. In fact, since the vast majority of social encyclicals have been written to commemorate other social encyclicals (nearly always *Rerum Novarum*), each has sought to distill the perennial principles offered earlier (thus guaranteeing continuity) and to apply them to present circumstances (thus guaranteeing contemporary relevance). This has been, in practice, the standard methodology when popes have wished to contribute something to the ongoing corpus of social teaching.

Rerum Novarum has conveniently lent itself to this endeavor, in no small part through its title. Having treated the "new things" of his day, Leo XIII provided a perfect justification for his successors to continue applying the same dynamic. Thus he not only furnished a foundational document, but also provided a helpful model for what would become an important subset of papal teaching. Pope John Paul II, to take one example, in his encyclical commemorating the hundredth anniversary of *Rerum Novarum*, *Centesimus Annus*, proposed a re-reading of Leo's encyclical, which expressly included looking around "at the 'new things' which surround us and in which we find ourselves caught up, very different from the 'new things' which characterized the final decade of the last century."[9]

One of the side effects of this continual updating of papal social teaching has been a substantial amount of repetition of prior material. If one undertakes the sizable challenge of reading through the entire corpus of social encyclicals, one is necessarily struck by this phenomenon. The same ideas, principles and concepts are repeated over and over again, sometimes directly citing earlier encyclicals and sometimes simply reiterating the same reflections in slightly altered language. This is certainly true in the case of *Caritas in Veritate*, which restates ideas of traditional Catholic social teaching throughout.

In singling out *Populorum Progressio* as the new *Rerum Novarum*, Benedict in no way intended to break from the tradition of his predecessors. Rather he takes pains to stress the unity and continuity of all Catholic social doctrine and to place both *Populorum Progressio* and *Caritas in Veritate* squarely in the line of his predecessors' works. Benedict does not seek to place *Populorum Progressio* in a class by itself but rather notes that the Pauline encyclical "would be a document without roots" if viewed outside of tradition of the apostolic faith.[10]

To this end, Benedict locates *Populorum Progressio* in the context of Paul VI's entire magisterium (with intriguing reflections on encyclicals not normally associated with Paul's social teaching, such as *Humanae Vitae*) as well as in the still broader horizon of Catholic social doctrine generally. Benedict declares that Paul VI's social magisterium did not mark "a break with that of previous Popes" and warns against "certain abstract subdivisions of the Church's social doctrine," as if there were "two typologies of social doctrine, one pre-conciliar and one post-conciliar."

On the contrary, Benedict contends, "there is a single teaching, consistent and at the same time ever new."[11] This is especially noteworthy in Benedict's continuity with his immediate predecessor Pope John Paul II. In *Caritas in Veritate*, the most cited magisterial text after *Populorum Progressio* itself is John Paul's *Centesimus Annus*, the capstone of his social magisterium.

Yet clearly, by honoring *Populorum Progressio* with the title of "the *Rerum Novarum* of the present age," Benedict meant to elevate *Populorum Progressio*, conferring on it a paradigmatic status not dissimilar to that enjoyed by *Rerum Novarum* throughout the twentieth century. He didn't, after all, just state that *Populorum Progressio* was an important or useful encyclical—he called it "the *Rerum Novarum* of the present age." What specifically about *Populorum Progressio* provoked this important move by Benedict? In what way can *Populorum Progressio* assume a referential role for the present day like that played by *Rerum Novarum* for the past 120 years?

As I have argued earlier, *Rerum Novarum* was itself an unlikely candidate for the central place it was to assume in Catholic social thought. Leo XIII obviously had no idea that his letter on the "worker question" would generate an entirely new category of papal encyclicals and indeed a new theological discipline! Leo penned an incredible 87 encyclicals, several of which could be considered "social encyclicals," yet it was *Rerum Novarum* that was singled out for this exalted function. Why not, for instance, *Diuturnum* (June 29, 1881) on the origin of civil authority? Or *Immortale Dei* (Nov. 1, 1885) on the Christian constitution of states? Or *Graves de Communi Re* (Jan. 18, 1901) on Christian democracy? Or even *Inscrutabili Dei Consilio* (April 21, 1878) on the evils of modern society?

The prominence of *Rerum Novarum* grew out of its tremendous popularity, especially among workers, and the rise of real socialism, which had been condemned by the encyclical. It was, however, the decision of Pius XI to commemorate it in 1931 with *Quadragesimo Anno* that locked *Rerum Novarum* into its critical role. When introducing that encyclical, Pius wrote that it was *Rerum Novarum* out of all Leo's writings that had the special distinction of laying down for all mankind "the surest rules to solve aright that difficult problem of human relations called 'the social question.'"[12] Yet for all its importance and opportuneness, *Rerum Novarum* was, after all, a letter that addressed the worker question and the socialist response and was not a treatise on social morality.

Populorum Progressio, on the other hand, for all its real deficiencies, effected an important conceptual shift in Catholic social thinking, by moving from the worker question (with its attendant concerns of just wages, private property, working environment, and labor associations) to the broader and richer social benchmark of *integral human development*. As a touchstone for Catholic social thought, integral human development is unquestionably more central and encompassing than the labor question, and, in fact, comprises it.

In *Caritas in Veritate*, Benedict gives evidence that it was fundamentally this shift in focus—rather than Paul's analysis of concrete development issues or practical solutions to those problems—that led Benedict to hold up *Populorum Progressio* as especially apt for our age. In fact, regarding contingent judgments, Benedict notes that "an evaluation is needed of the different terms in which the problem of development is presented today, as compared with forty years ago."[13] On the contrary, Benedict summarizes the substantive and enduring contribution of *Populorum Progressio* as "two important truths" conveyed by Paul VI. The first is that the whole Church, in all her being and acting—when she proclaims, when she celebrates, when she performs works of charity—"is engaged in promoting integral human development."[14] In other words, human development (rightly understood) stands at the very center of the Church's mission, and everything the Church does can be seen as a service to this development.

The second "important truth" proposed in *Populorum Progressio*, according to Benedict, is that authentic human development "concerns the whole of the person in every single dimension."[15] The truth of development, Benedict insists, "consists in its completeness: if it does not involve the whole man and every man, it is not true development."[16] And the Pope importantly adds: "This is the central message of *Populorum Progressio*, valid for today and for all time."[17] Here Benedict underscores the nature of human development as going beyond the economic or merely material dimension and comprising every aspect of the person's good, including the spiritual. In fact, Benedict immediately invokes "the perspective of eternal life" as essential to human progress. To be true, "development requires a transcendent vision of the person, it needs God."[18]

Benedict's most lavish praise of *Populorum Progressio* is that Paul VI identified in the notion of integral development "the heart of the

Christian social message."[19] And Benedict concludes that Paul's vision of development at the core of *Populorum Progressio* is "*the principal reason why that Encyclical is still timely in our day.*"[20] To see *Populorum Progressio* as the *Rerum Novarum* of the present age, therefore, is to grasp its vision of integral development as the kernel of Catholic social thought.

"Charity in Truth" as the Core of Catholic Social Doctrine

Along with Benedict's significant statement concerning the enduring relevance of *Populorum Progressio*, he also offered another substantial contribution to the Church's social magisterium by introducing and developing the idea of "charity in truth" as the pivotal virtue underlying Catholic social thought. This, too, may represent a more important change than first meets the eye.

Ever since *Rerum Novarum*, the papal social magisterium has never accepted the notion that justice alone was sufficient as the ordering principle required to produce a truly human society. To those who would substitute a system of relief organized by the state, Leo XIII replied that "no human expedients will ever make up for the devotedness and self-sacrifice of Christian charity."[21] Yet although popes from Leo on had insisted that justice alone wasn't enough to rightly order human society and that charity was also essential, none had placed charity so squarely in the center of Catholic social doctrine as Benedict has.[22] "Charity," he writes, "is at the heart of the Church's social doctrine." Moreover, charity is the font from which the doctrine emerges. "Every responsibility and every commitment spelt out by that doctrine is derived from charity."[23] Benedict recognizes charity as the unique source of all of social doctrine, placing it even higher than the virtue of social justice, long considered the core virtue of Catholic social thought.

Yet to this idea of Christian charity Benedict importantly adds the complementary principle of *truth*. From his first encyclical, *Deus Caritas Est*, Pope Benedict acknowledged the ways that charity or love has become distorted in the modern mind, and the consequent need for a rehabilitation and purification of the term.[24] In *Caritas in Veritate* he returns to this ambiguity as a justification for tying charity closely to truth.

"I am aware of the ways in which charity has been and continues to be misconstrued and emptied of meaning," he writes, and it is precisely in the "social, juridical, cultural, political and economic fields"—the very areas dealt with by Catholic social doctrine—where charity is most exposed to this danger. "Hence the need to link charity with truth," Benedict concludes.[25] Charity and truth need each other; they complement and complete each other. "Deeds without knowledge are blind, and knowledge without love is sterile."[26] Moreover, "love is rich in intelligence and intelligence is full of love."[27] This leads to an altogether new definition of Catholic social doctrine as *"caritas in veritate in re sociali (charity in truth, in the social context)."*[28] *Caritas in veritate*, Benedict writes, "is the principle around which the Church's social doctrine turns."[29]

Witness to Truth as a Form of Charity

Benedict links charity to truth with a number of original considerations, of which we can distinguish five. He sees dedication to the truth, in the first place, to be a *form* of charity. To defend, articulate, or bear witness to the truth is an exalted expression of love for one's neighbor. Since knowledge of the truth is essential for true human development, the assistance we give others in this process of discovering and adhering to the truth aids them in their development and thus constitutes an act of love for them. "Each person finds his good by adherence to God's plan for him, in order to realize it fully: in this plan, he finds his truth, and through adherence to this truth he becomes free."[30] In other words, the human person is fulfilled through discovery of and adherence to the truth—and not just abstract, speculative truth, but the truth of his own existence and the divine plan for his life. His true good is tied directly to his knowledge and embracing of this truth. It is for this reason that "[t]o defend the truth, to articulate it with humility and conviction, and to bear witness to it in life are therefore exacting and indispensable forms of charity."[31] Without this witness to the truth, we fail to promote the true good of our neighbor; we fail to love fully.

Charity as Source of "Credibility" for Truth

Second, Benedict sees charity as giving "credibility" to truth. A self-assured possession of truth, devoid of charity, can easily be viewed as nothing more than hubris. Moreover, in this context the truth can be wielded as a weapon and rather than a liberating force, it appears as a hostile and even enslaving instrument to be feared rather than pursued and welcomed. Where truth is either feared in this way, or dismissed as irrelevant, charity serves to restore and showcase its value. When charity is "understood, confirmed and practised in the light of truth," we help "give credibility to truth, demonstrating its persuasive and authenticating power in the practical setting of social living."[32] One who claims to possess the truth but does not love impoverishes the truth and weakens its message. Charity, on the contrary, makes the truth believable, especially in a world where it has been discredited.

Truth Substantiates Charity

Third, according to Benedict, the truth performs a reciprocal service to charity. It enlightens, authenticates and gives meaning and value to charity. Under the light of truth—the truth of both reason and faith— charity shines as valuable and precious. The truth permits love to achieve its goal of truly serving the good of another, allowing charity "to be authentically lived."[33] Without truth, on the other hand, "charity degenerates into sentimentality," vague well-wishes with no objective content, and becomes "an empty shell, to be filled in an arbitrary way."[34] Without truth, social action carried out in the name of charity ends up "serving private interests and the logic of power."[35] The danger of a relativistic culture is that not only is the truth lost but that love is lost, too. Those who would sacrifice truth in favor of love find that they have forfeited both. When love loses its moorings to truth, it takes on a radical subjectivism where good intentions have no objective reference in action. Only the truth can preserve love and liberate it from emotionalism and fideism.

Dialogue in Truth Leads to Communion

A fourth important link between charity and truth can be found in Benedict's fascinating discussion of the role of truth in fostering communion. Because it is filled with truth, charity is intelligible and therefore also communicable. The truth serves charity directly, in that it "is lógos which creates diá-logos, and hence communication and communion."[36] Communication consists in making common what was particular. I take the truth I possess and offer it as a gift to another, without thereby ceasing to own it. It becomes a common possession, in which we both participate, and as a result a "common good" that creates communion between us. Historical and cultural prejudice and particularities that often separate human beings are overcome in a common search for the truth that underlies all things. The truth makes it possible for people "to come together in the assessment of the value and substance of things," and rescues the human person from isolation.[37] Love, then, becomes communion in the truth. Without this mutual search for truth, no deep or lasting communion is possible and neither is integral development of the person or society.

Jesus Christ as Truth and Love

A fifth and final consideration regarding the bond uniting charity with truth bears a more theological stamp. Benedict notes that God is "both Agápe and Lógos: Charity and Truth, Love and Word."[38] In his person Jesus Christ unites love and truth, perfectly revealing the love of the Father and the truth of both God and man. "In Christ, charity in truth becomes the Face of his Person, a vocation for us to love our brothers and sisters in the truth of his plan. Indeed, he himself is the Truth."[39] This theological consideration also makes evangelization possible and fruitful, since "practising charity in truth helps people to understand that adhering to the values of Christianity is not merely useful but essential for building a good society and for true integral human development."[40] A Christianity of charity without truth would be "more or less interchangeable with a pool of good sentiments, helpful for social cohesion, but of little relevance."[41]

Charity and Justice

Along with these five considerations, the intrinsic link between charity and truth sheds light on charity's close relation to justice as well. Far from abandoning the critical principle of justice for Catholic social doctrine, Benedict shows how the two are mutually implicative. Justice, writes Benedict, "is inseparable from charity, and intrinsic to it."[42] Justice is, moreover, "the primary way of charity." I cannot "give" what is mine to another, Benedict reasons, "without first giving him what pertains to him in justice."[43] If charity is *true*, it must therefore be *just*, since justice provides charity with its first essential content. "If we love others with charity, then first of all we are just towards them."[44] At the same time, Benedict will also insist throughout the encyclical that "charity transcends justice." We cannot attain authentic human development "merely by relationships of rights and duties" but must complement them "by relationships of gratuitousness, mercy and communion."[45]

Charity in Economic Life

Benedict's innovative reflections on the role of charity (as opposed to mere justice) in the field of economic life furnish another example of Benedict's original contribution to Catholic social thought. He dedicates the entire third chapter of the encyclical—titled "Fraternity, Economic Development and Civil Society"—to these considerations, as well as important sections of other chapters.[46] In a manner reminiscent of Pope John Paul II, Benedict suggests that the human person's essential vocation as being "made for gift" has concrete applications in the economic sphere. By its nature, Benedict reasons, gift "goes beyond merit, its rule is that of superabundance."[47] Merit, of course, is the language of justice, whereas superabundance is that of charity. For people accustomed to thinking of economic relationships merely in terms of justice, this language can prove unsettling. How, one may wonder, can such superabundance be applied in commercial affairs? Is this a case of theological idealism misapplied to human sciences?

Yet Benedict eschews such easy judgments, giving evidence of both moral realism and a surprising grasp of economic processes and systems. Regarding his realism, Benedict points immediately to man's fallen nature, noting (as John Paul had) that "Ignorance of the fact that man has a wounded nature inclined to evil gives rise to serious errors in the areas of education, politics, social action and morals."[48] He knows he is not counseling angels but fallen human beings. He also is fully aware that "attitudes of gratuitousness cannot be established by law."[49] The encyclical's grasp of the reality of economics, on the other hand, manifests itself throughout the text, in passages too numerous to mention. To his assertion that "in *commercial relationships* the *principle of gratuitousness* and the logic of gift as an expression of fraternity can and must *find their place within normal economic activity*," Benedict suggests that the market needs "commercial entities based on mutualist principles and pursuing social ends" alongside profit-oriented private enterprise, a reality which is in fact occurring in many parts of the world. It would seem that Benedict is asking for a twofold change: (1) a broadening of possibilities for real-world economic enterprises, and (2) a still more important broadening of mentality to transcend a minimalist, justice-based ethics in favor of a charity-based ethics.

The Requirements of Integral Human Development

When this charity is directed according to the truth of the human person, it necessarily contributes effectively to human development—both that of individuals and that of societies. In what does such development consist? In *Caritas in Veritate*, Benedict reiterates many of the components of genuine human development brought forward by Paul in *Populorum Progressio*. Benedict speaks of integral development as a "vocation," for instance, as Paul had.[50] Benedict underscores the spiritual dimension of development, as Paul had.[51] As we saw earlier, Benedict re-proposes the need for a global political authority (regulated by principles of solidarity and subsidiarity), as Paul had.[52] Benedict stresses the importance of basic education for development, as Paul had.[53] Benedict also decries the scandalous gap separating rich from poor as a dire threat to development, as Paul had.[54]

Significantly, however, he also adds some original requirements to the list and attributes special importance to them. Foremost among these issues are respect for human life, the right to religious freedom and concern for the environment. These are, if you will, some of the "new things" that Benedict discovered in his analysis of the contemporary world situation.

Life Issues

Bioethical concerns, and especially the scourge of abortion, do not appear as tangential issues in *Caritas in Veritate*. Not content with merely including life issues in his discussion, Benedict insists: "*Openness to life is at the centre of true development.*"[55] Benedict underscores the importance of life issues for human development in no uncertain terms and returns to the topic several times in the course of the encyclical. He calls respect for life one of the "most striking aspects of development in the present day," denouncing an "anti-birth mentality" and the added evil that it is often considered "a form of cultural progress."[56] This anti-birth mentality opposes true development because of the moral depravity it supposes but for other reasons as well. Benedict calls morally responsible openness to life "a rich social and economic resource."[57] He notes that population size has been a necessary component to the economic growth of populous nations, and that population decline has become "a crucial problem for highly affluent societies."[58] A decline in births (at times beneath the replacement level) "puts a strain on social welfare systems, increases their cost, eats into savings and hence the financial resources needed for investment, reduces the availability of qualified labourers, and narrows the 'brain pool' upon which nations can draw for their needs."[59] These situations are symptomatic—Benedict asserts—of "scant confidence in the future and moral weariness."[60]

In its link to integral human development, Benedict looks at a growing lack of respect for life as a new form of "poverty and underdevelopment," both where it is imposed as a method of demographic control and, especially in economically developed countries, where anti-life legislation "has already shaped moral attitudes and praxis."[61] Benedict ties bioethical questions to human development at the level of basic attitudes, where he sees them as necessarily related. "If personal and social sensitivity towards the acceptance of a new life is lost," Benedict reasons, "then other forms of acceptance that are valuable for society also wither away."[62] If a society ceases to value the life of its weakest and most vulnerable members, how can it find strength or motivation to assist other neighbors in their needs?[63] Where abortion and euthanasia are accepted, how can there be any true interest in the needs of the poor and underprivileged? And so Benedict cites John Paul II in saying that a society lacks solid foundations when, "on the one hand, it asserts values such as the dignity of the person, justice and peace, but then, on the other hand, radically acts to the contrary by allowing or tolerating a variety of ways in which human life is devalued and violated, especially where it is weak or marginalized."[64]

But the contrary is also true. By cultivating openness to life, Benedict adds, "wealthy peoples can better understand the needs of poor ones." The acceptance of life "strengthens moral fibre and makes people capable of mutual help."[65] In this light, a culture's basic attitudes toward human life can be seen as a thermometer of its ability and will to achieve true human development. But openness to life is also a door toward greater commitment to development generally.

In this same vein, Benedict discovers a relationship between the "culture of death" and "a materialistic and mechanistic understanding of human life." These are, in Benedict's words, signs of a "highly disillusioned culture, which believes it has mastered every mystery, because the origin of life is now within our grasp."[66] When this happens, Benedict suggests, it signals the supremacy of technology over true humanism, and in such a culture "the conscience is simply invited to take note of technological possibilities" rather than to guide the use of technologies so that they serve human development.[67] And so, Benedict notes, in our day the social question has become a radically anthropological question, "in the sense that it concerns not just how life is conceived but also how it is manipulated."[68] Once again the Pope asks how we can be surprised by the indifference shown towards situations of human degradation, when such indifference extends even to our attitude towards what is and is not human.[69]

Benedict concludes with an observation that mirrors many people's concerns in a politically correct world, where morality is detached from the truth of human nature. "What is astonishing," he states, "is the arbitrary and selective determination of what to put forward today as worthy of respect. Insignificant matters are considered shocking, yet unprecedented injustices seem to be widely tolerated."[70] And thus we commonly witness the shock and scandal of citizens over a person's choice to smoke a cigarette, go hunting, or fail to recycle, and the cavalier acceptance of the truly horrifying moral evils of abortion, human cloning, and euthanasia.

Religious Freedom

Ever since the promulgation of the Vatican II Decree on Religious Liberty, *Dignitatis Humanae*, the popes have not failed to hold up religious freedom as a fundamental human right. Pope John Paul II sought to connect this important Conciliar principle with the Church's entire social tradition, citing Leo's insistence on the right to discharge one's religious duties as a "springboard" for the principle of the right to religious freedom.[71] John Paul went so far as to call religious freedom "the source and synthesis" of human rights, understood as "the right to live in the truth of one's faith and in conformity with one's transcendent dignity as a person."[72]

In continuity with this tradition, in *Caritas in Veritate* Benedict highlights religious freedom as a core human right, but he does so with some surprising nuances. First, he puts forward religious freedom as a key component of human development.[73] True human development is impeded when religious freedom is obstructed or suppressed. Benedict notes that this happens in different ways and specifically mentions religious fanaticism (once more condemning killing "in the holy name of God"), as well as "the deliberate promotion of religious indifference or practical atheism," which ends up stifling spiritual and human resources.[74] In this way, the state can become an enemy of religious freedom (and thus of development) either by embracing a narrow-minded confessionalism that refuses to recognize the rights of those outside of it, or through implicit or explicit atheism.[75] Thus when "the State promotes, teaches, or actually imposes forms of practical atheism," it keeps citizens from moving forward in their human and spiritual development.[76]

Benedict insists that this religious freedom without which true development is impossible has a necessarily *public* dimension. Throughout the encyclical, the Pope emphasizes that religion has a social function and explicit recognition of God is integral to the growth of civilization. Religions can offer their contribution to development, Benedict states, "only if God has a place in the public realm," specifically in regard to the cultural, social, economic, and political dimensions of society.[77]

Second, as we have seen in chapter 10, Benedict contends that although religion deserves respect and reflects man's search for transcendence, this recognition does not imply that all religions are the same or that all religions promote the development of persons and societies. "Religious freedom," he wrote, "does not mean religious indifferentism, nor does it imply that all religions are equal"[78] The Pope notes that certain religions may end up "even obstructing authentic human development."[79] From this, Benedict concludes that society must engage in discernment among religions regarding their contribution to the common good, and that this discernment is necessary "especially on the part of those who wield political power"[80] and "based on the criterion of charity and truth."[81] It must be, in other words, a judgment based on universal principles of natural law and the common good, accessible to human reason.

The Environment

In chapter four of *Caritas in Veritate*, Benedict devotes extensive space (nos. 48-52) to the question of responsible stewardship for the environment, a topic he has addressed on numerous occasions elsewhere.[82] Not without reason has Benedict been called the "Green Pope."[83] Yet despite Benedict's undeniable environmentalism, it is a distinctly Catholic strain of environmentalism. His frequent calls for environmental responsibility bear none of the ideological tones common among more radical environmentalists but rather see man's relationship to the environment in theological terms.[84]

In the first place, Benedict's environmentalism is markedly *anthropocentric*. To the consternation of those who either view man as simply another piece in the cosmic puzzle or, worse still, a "cancer" for the environment, Benedict frames human environmental obligation in terms of our responsibility for one another. Thus the Holy Father notes that in our use of the environment, "we have a responsibility towards the poor, towards future generations and towards humanity as a whole."[85] In fact, the Pope sees our responsibility toward future generations as an expression of *"intergenerational justice."*[86] Nowhere does Benedict speak of the environment for its own sake but draws ethical conclusions from our responsibility toward other human beings. We are not responsible *to* the environment but rather *for* the environment *for the sake of one another*. Therefore, Benedict asserts, "it is contrary to authentic development to view nature as something more important than the human person," a position that can only lead to "attitudes of neo-paganism or a new pantheism."[87]

Man's relationship with creation reflects the way he views himself and his fellow man. Or in Benedict's words: "The way humanity treats the environment influences the way it treats itself, and vice versa."[88] Respect for one another necessarily generates respect for creation. The deterioration of nature, on the other hand, is "closely connected to the culture that shapes human coexistence: when 'human ecology' is respected within society, environmental ecology also benefits."[89] In his holistic view of human existence, Benedict sees a relationship between human attitudes toward the environment and attitudes to other critical aspects of human existence, such as respect for life, respect for marriage, and the common good. "Our duties towards the environment," Benedict states, "are linked to our duties towards the human person, considered in himself and in relation to others."[90]

At the same time, Benedict's vision is not only anthropocentric, it is also eminently *theological*—the environment is first and foremost "God's gift to everyone."[91] Even prior to our responsibility to one another, we have a duty toward our Creator. Benedict asserts that acknowledgement of God as Creator leads to environmental responsibility. True environmentalism cannot flourish outside of this theological horizon, but rather when nature, including human beings, "is viewed as the result of mere chance or evolutionary determinism, our sense of responsibility wanes."[92] On the other hand, nature itself "speaks to us of the Creator" and "expresses a design of love and truth."[93] In it we discover God's loving hand and the precious gift that serves as the setting for our earthly existence. And so respect for creation becomes a true "vocation," and human beings are called to care for it, "to till and to keep it" (Gen 2:15).[94] The vocation to development, including respect for creation, is therefore "not based simply on human choice, but is an intrinsic part of a plan that is prior to us and constitutes for all of us a duty to be freely accepted."[95] For this reason, man is called to avoid the two extremes of "reckless exploitation" on the one hand, and nature worship on the other, which would see in the environment an "untouchable taboo."[96]

Conclusion

Like so many of Pope Benedict's writings, both prior to and consequent to his election to the Chair of Peter, *Caritas in Veritate* does not lend itself to quick comprehension, and the summary judgments of the encyclical that emerged immediately after its promulgation—whether favorable or unfavorable—necessarily missed the mark in important ways. Its dense language, the complexity of its ideas and its interrelatedness with the entire corpus of Catholic social doctrine necessitates a slow, careful reading and re-reading of the letter so as not to miss the subtlety of the arguments Benedict puts forth.

With *Caritas in Veritate*, Benedict has left a substantial mark on Catholic social doctrine. He has laid out a series of priorities and offered points for reflection that will keep theologians and Catholic thinkers busy for years.

While much of the material contained in this lengthy encyclical reiterates the ideas and arguments of Benedict's predecessors, he adds a number of significant nuances to these ideas, as well as several important original reflections, as we have seen. His highlighting of integral human development as the central point of reference for Catholic social thought, his elevation of "charity in truth" as the core virtue for Christian social ethics, and his detailed and explicit inclusion of life issues, religious liberty and environmental responsibility as essential components of human development all affect Catholic social doctrine in substantial ways.

As did his predecessors before him, Benedict has added important building blocks to the ever growing corpus of Catholic social doctrine, drawing from his personal experience, particular theological perspective and original vision of evolving geo-political and economic realities. As Paul VI benefitted from his extensive dealings with the political theorists of his time, and John Paul II learned from his experience in a Poland dominated first by National Socialism and then by Soviet Communism, Benedict has brought his own experience as a German scholar and thoughtful interlocutor with some of the finest minds of his time. Both in *Deus Caritas Est* and *Caritas in Veritate* Benedict has offered the Church a refreshing reconsideration of how fundamental moral principles, and especially the commandment to love, must be applied in the social sphere. His unique theological vision, nourished by years of study, teaching and pastoral experience, has added important brush-strokes to the Church's challenging portrait of *The World as It Could Be*.

Notes

Abbreviations

1. Unless expressly stated otherwise, citations throughout the text will reference the version of these magisterial documents found on the Vatican's Web site (www.vatican.va).

Introduction / The Need for Development

1. John Henry Newman, *An Essay on the Development of Christian Doctrine* (New York: Longmans, Green, and Co., 1909), 51.

2. "As Newman himself intimated, doctrine of a social or political character does not follow exactly the same course of development as pure dogma. It is not simply spun out of the original deposit of faith, but emerges with a certain irregularity according to the vicissitudes of history" (Avery Dulles, "Religious Freedom: Innovation and Development," *First Things* (December 2001).

3. "The Church's social doctrine illuminates with an unchanging light the new problems that are constantly emerging" (CV, no.12).

4. In 1987, Pope John Paul II wrote that Catholic social doctrine, "beginning with the outstanding contribution of Leo XIII and enriched by the successive contributions of the Magisterium, has now become an updated doctrinal 'corpus' (SRS, no. 1).

Chapter 1 / Unity, Diversity, and the Common Good

1. Walter Kasper's essay, bearing the title "On the Church," was published in the April 23, 2001 issue of *America* magazine (Vol. 184 No. 14). Ratzinger's response, entitled "The Local Church and The Universal Church," appeared in the November 19, 2001, issue (Vol. 185 No. 16).

2. In its 1990 *Instruction on the Ecclesial Vocation of the Theologian* (May 24, 1990), the Congregation for the Doctrine of the Faith declared: "The freedom

proper to theological research is exercised within the Church's faith" (no. 11). Indeed, as *fides quaerens intellectum*, theology supposes as its point of departure the one faith of the Church, which sets very real bounds on the forays of theological speculation. The Congregation deemed it necessary to reiterate this point in its recent "Notification on the works of Father Jon Sobrino, SJ," (November 26, 2006), which noted that it is only in the ecclesial faith "that all other theological foundations find their correct epistemological setting." The notification goes on to say: "The theologian, in his particular vocation in the Church, must continually bear in mind that theology is the science of the faith. Other points of departure for theological work run the risk of arbitrariness and end in a misrepresentation of the same faith" (no. 2).

3. Congregation for the Doctrine of the Faith, Notification on the book *Toward a Christian Theology of Religious Pluralism,* Fr. Jacques Dupuis, S.J. (January 24, 2001).

4. "Majorities are products of chance and are too unstable to be the ultimate source of rights" (Joseph Ratzinger, *The Nature and Mission of Theology: Approaches to Understanding Its Role in the Light of Present Controversy* [San Francisco: Ignatius Press, 1995], 87).

5. Karol Wojtyla, "Thomistic Personalism," a paper presented at the Fourth Annual Philosophy Week, Catholic University of Lublin, February 17, 1961, trans. Theresa Sandok, in *Person and Community: Selected Essays,* vol. 4 of *Catholic Thought from Lublin,* ed. Andrew N. Woznicki (New York: Peter Lang, 1993), 174.

6. CA, no. 44.

7. Thus Joseph Ratzinger noted that "the democratic system of the limitation and division of power does not function on its own as a purely formal system. It cannot be applied in a complete absence of values, but presupposes and ethos which is jointly accepted and maintained, although its rational basis cannot be established absolutely conclusively" (Joseph Ratzinger, *Church, Ecumenism and Politics: New Essays in Ecclesiology* [Slough, UK: Saint Paul Publications, 1988], 188).

8. In his book, *Turning Point for Europe?* Ratzinger made a similar point. In commenting on Hobbes' saying *"Authoritas, non veritas facit legem,"* he notes that by this mindset: "The law is not based on the discernible reality of right and wrong but on the authority of the person with the power to enact it. It comes about through legislation, and in no other way. Its inner protection is thus the power to push it through, not the truth of being" (*Turning Point for Europe? The Church in the Modern World—Assessment and Forecast* [San Francisco: Ignatius Press, 1994], 50).

9. CA, no. 45.

10. CA, no. 44.

11. Thus Ratzinger observes: "A fundamental question for the democratic system is whether the will of the majority can and should do anything it likes. Can it declare anything it likes to be law that then is binding on everyone, or does reason stand above the majority so that something that is directed against reason cannot really become law?" (Joseph Ratzinger, *Church, Ecumenism and Politics: New Essays in Ecclesiology* [Slough, UK: Saint Paul Publications, 1988], 187).

12. CA, no. 46. Similarly, in *Veritatis Splendor* John Paul warned against "*the risk of an alliance between democracy and ethical relativism,* which would remove any sure moral reference point from political and social life, and on a deeper level make the acknowledgement of truth impossible" (VS, no. 101).

13. Again, Ratzinger writes: "Ultimately the democratic system can only function if certain fundamental values—let us call them human rights—are recognized as valid by everyone and are withdrawn from the competence of the majority" (Joseph Ratzinger, *Church, Ecumenism and Politics: New Essays in Ecclesiology* [Slough, UK: Saint Paul Publications, 1988], 188).

14. CA, no. 44.

15. EV, no. 20.

16. Ibid.

17. "It is the role of the state to defend and promote the common good of civil society, its citizens, and intermediate bodies" (CCC, no. 1910). "The attainment of the common good is the sole reason for the existence of civil authorities. In working for the common good, therefore, the authorities must obviously respect its nature, and at the same time adjust their legislation to meet the requirements of the given situation" (PT, no.54).

18. GS, no. 26, 1; cf. GS no. 74, 1.

19. See CCC, nos. 1907–1909.

20. EV, no. 71.

21. See, for example, Peter H. Schuck, *Diversity in America: Keeping Government at a Safe Distance* (Harvard University Press, 2003). Schuck makes the case that diversity, which is generally a good thing, is not a good in and of itself; it becomes valuable only when it contributes to other objectives.

22. In this regard, Ratzinger has observed: "In many cases, perhaps in virtually all cases, a majority decision is the 'most rational' way to achieve common solutions. But the majority cannot be the ultimate principle, since there are values that no majority is entitled to annul" (Joseph Ratzinger, *Values in a Time of Upheaval* [San Francisco: Ignatius Press, 2006], 27).

23. Ratzinger associates this tendency to the wonder of Pentecost, "in which there is not one single language (single civilization) prescribed for all the others, as in Babylon (the type of cultures of achievement and of power), but unity comes to pass in multiplicity" (Joseph Ratzinger, *Truth and Tolerance: Christian Belief and World Religions* [San Francisco: Ignatius Press, 2004], 82).

24. Pope Benedict has continued to build on essential elements of John Paul's personalism, and in *Caritas in Veritate,* he notes that reason finds inspiration in Christian revelation, "according to which the human community does not absorb the individual, annihilating his autonomy, as happens in the various forms of totalitarianism, but rather values him all the more because the relation between individual and community is a relation between one totality and another" (CV, no. 53).

25. Karol Wojtyla, "Thomistic Personalism," 174.

26. CCC, no. 1912.

27. CCC, no. 1907.

28. GS, 24.

29. Pope John Paul II, *Crossing the Threshold of Hope*, ed. Vittorio Messorio, trans. Jenny McPhee and Martha McPhee (New York: Alfred A. Knopf, 1994), 202–3; *emphasis* in original.

30. SRS, no. 38.

31. "Relationships between human beings throughout history cannot but be enriched by reference to this divine model. In particular, in the light of the revealed mystery of the Trinity, we understand that true openness does not mean loss of individual identity but profound interpenetration" (CV, no. 54).

32. See especially CCC, no. 1907.

33. Executive Board of the American Anthropological Association, "Statement on Human Rights," *American Anthropologist* 49/4 [October-December 1947]: 539.

34. Ibid.

Chapter 2 / Dignity and Its Discontents

1. See, as a sample, CCC 1930, 1935, 1944, 1945, 1956, 1978, 2203, 2407, 2414.

2. http://online.wsj.com/article/NA_WSJ_PUB:SB122359549477921201.html.

3. See http://www.scribd.com/doc/2931685/The-Dignity-of-Living-Beings-with-Regards-to-Plants.

4. See the Ecuadoran Constitution at http://issuu.com/restrella/docs/constitucion_del_ecuador, English translation: author.

5. Jacques Maritain, *Man and the State* (Chicago: University of Chicago Press, 1951), 76.

6. UN Universal Declaration of Human Rights, preamble, December 10, 1948 (www.un.org/Overview/rights.html).

7. "The dignity of the person constitutes the foundation of the equality of all people among themselves. As a result, all forms of discrimination are totally unacceptable, especially those forms which unfortunately continue to divide and degrade the human family, from those based on race or economics to those social

and cultural, from political to geographic, etc. Each discrimination constitutes an absolutely intolerable injustice, not so much for the tensions and the conflicts that can be generated in the social sphere, as much as for the dishonour inflicted on the dignity of the person" (CL, no. 37).

8. Peter Singer, *Rethinking Life and Death: The Collapse of Our Traditional Ethics* (Oxford: Oxford University Press, 1994), 180. See also Peter Singer, *Practical Ethics* (New York: Cambridge University Press, 1993), 110–11.

9. Singer, *Rethinking Life and Death*, 182.

10. Ibid., 183.

11. In the present work, all quotations from *A Theory of Justice* have been taken from the revised edition (J. Rawls, *A Theory of Justice*, Revised edition, Oxford: Oxford University Press, 1999).

12. *A Theory of Justice*, 442.

13. Ibid.

14. Ibid., 443. Rawls refrains from pronouncing on whether moral personality is necessary as well as sufficient for being entitled to equal justice, and recommends against denying justice to those persons who may lack it. On making it the fundamental criterion for entitlement to justice, however, Rawls unmistakably sets the groundwork for withholding justice from those who do not satisfy the condition.

15. Rawls offers a further explanation that would seem to provide for the possession of rights by children and some others who do not actually have a "rational plan of life," by distinguishing between capacity and exercise of powers, a distinction dear to the Christian moral tradition. "I have said that the minimal requirements defining moral personality refer to a capacity and not to the realization of it. A being that has this capacity, whether or not it is yet developed, is to receive the full protection of the principles of justice. Since infants and children are thought to have basic rights (normally exercised on their behalf by parents and guardians), this interpretation of the requisite conditions seems necessary to match our considered judgments" (Ibid., 445–6). Nonetheless, the allowance that some "scattered individuals" (443) of the human race do not possess this capacity opens the door to excluding some human beings from the principles of justice, based on the judgment that these human beings are somehow not moral persons.

16. John Finnis, "Abortion, Natural Law, and Public Reason," in R. P. George and C. Wolfe (eds.) *Natural Law and Public Reason*, (Washington, D.C.: Georgetown University Press, 2000), 91.

17. Wojtyla a writes that "a child, even an unborn child, cannot be denied personality in its most objective ontological sense, although it is true that it has yet to acquire, step by step, many of the traits which will make it psychologically and ethically a distinct personality" (Karol Wojtyla a, *Love and Responsibility*, 26).

18. "Certainly no experimental datum can be in itself sufficient to bring us to the recognition of a spiritual soul; nevertheless, the conclusions of science regarding the human embryo provide a valuable indication for discerning by the use of reason a personal presence at the moment of this first appearance of a human life: how could a human individual not be a human person? The Magisterium has not expressly committed itself to an affirmation of a philosophical nature, but it constantly reaffirms the moral condemnation of any kind of procured abortion. This teaching has not been changed and is unchangeable (Cf. Pope Paul VI, Discourse to participants in the Twenty-third National Congress of Italian Catholic Jurists, December 9, 1972: AAS 64 (1972), 777)" (DV, I, 1).

19. "Thus the fruit of human generation, from the first moment of its existence, that is to say from the moment the zygote has formed, demands the unconditional respect that is morally due to the human being in his bodily and spiritual totality. The human being is to be respected and treated as a person from the moment of conception; and therefore from that same moment his rights as a person must be recognized, among which in the first place is the inviolable right of every innocent human being to life" (Ibid.).

20. Mortimer Adler, *How to Think about the Great Ideas: From the Great Books of Western Civilization*, Ed. Max Weismann (Chicago: Open Court Publishing, 2000), 66.

21. Ibid., 66–67.

22. Joseph Ratzinger, *Values in a Time of Upheaval* (San Francisco: Ignatius Press, 2006), 66–67.

23. Ibid., 65.

24. John Locke, *A Letter Concerning Toleration*, Latin and English texts revised and edited with variants and an introduction (The Hague: Martinus Nijhoff, 1963), 89.

25. Joseph Ratzinger, *Values in a Time of Upheaval* (San Francisco: Ignatius Press, 2006), 65.

26. "The developments of the twentieth century have taught us that this evidential character—as the subsistent and reliable basis of all freedom—no longer exists. It is perfectly possible for reason to lose sight of essential values" (Joseph Ratzinger, *Values in a Time of Upheaval* [San Francisco: Ignatius Press, 2006], 50).

27. Jürgen Habermas, "A Time of Transition," cited in Christa Case, "Germans Reconsider Religion," *Christian Science Monitor*, September 15, 2006. See also "Europe's Faith Is Still Alive: Perhaps the Old World Is Not as Godless as Is Often Thought," *Atlantic Times* sec. 2, June 2005, 6.

28. GS, no. 21.

29. Kenneth L. Grasso, "Beyond Liberalism: Human Dignity, the Free Society, and the Second Vatican Council" in *Catholicism, Liberalism, & Communitarianism: The Catholic Intellectual Tradition and the Moral Foundations of Democracy*, eds. Kenneth L. Grasso, Gerard V. Bradley, and Robert P. Hunt (Lanham, MD: Rowman & Littlefield, 1995), 36.

30. Pope John Paul II, *Crossing the Threshold of Hope*, 197 (emphasis in original).

31. Joseph Ratzinger, *Values in a Time of Upheaval* (San Francisco: Ignatius Press, 2006), 52.

32. Thus, the *Catechism* states: "The precepts of natural law are not perceived by everyone clearly and immediately. In the present situation sinful man needs grace and revelation so moral and religious truths may be known 'by everyone with facility, with firm certainty and with no admixture of error'" (CCC, 1960).

33. See DF, IV: DS 3015.

34. See Thomas Aquinas, *Summa contra Gentiles*, I, 4. See also HG: nos. 2–4; DF, II (DS 3005).

35. Speaking of the difference between a purely natural ethics and Christian ethics, C. Henry Peschke asserts: "There is only a difference in the knowledge and understanding of human nature, of the ultimate end, and by that of the moral law; a difference, certainly, which is still important and which is not to be slighted. Christian faith imparts to man an insight into human nature, the final goal and the moral order which is much deeper, fuller, and more to the point than the insight gained by reason alone" (*Christian Ethics: A Presentation of General Moral Theology in the Light of Vatican II* [Dublin: C. Goodliffe Neale, 1977], 104).

36. Benedict M. Ashley, *Living the Truth in Love: A Biblical Introduction to Moral Theology* (Staten Island, NY: Alba House, 1996), 277.

37. FR, no. 16.

38. Pope John Paul II, *Crossing the Threshold of Hope*, 200–1; emphasis in original.

39. CL, no. 3.

40. See, for instance, John Paul II's forceful denunciation of the culture of death in EV, nos. 12, 19, 21, 24, 26, 28, 50, 64, 87, 95, 100.

Chapter 3 / Abortion as a Social Justice Issue

1. An earlier version of this paper was delivered in Rome at the Pontifical Council for Justice and Peace at a symposium entitled "The defense of life, the task of the social doctrine of the Church" on September 15, 2006.

2. EV, no. 5.

3. Ibid.

4. Pius broadcast his message "to call to the attention of the Catholic world a memory worthy of being written in letters of gold on the Church's Calendar: the fiftieth anniversary of the publication of the epoch-making social encyclical of Leo XIII, *Rerum Novarum*" (Cf. AAS 33 [1941], 196).

5. "It was at such a time and under pressure of such circumstances as these that Leo XIII wrote his social encyclical, *Rerum Novarum*, based on the needs of human nature itself and animated by the principles and spirit of the Gospel" (MM, no. 15).

6. "But first I wish to say a few words about the date of publication; the year 1967. The very fact that Pope Paul VI chose to publish a social Encyclical in that year invites us to consider the document in relationship to the Second Vatican Ecumenical Council, which had ended on December 8, 1965" (SRS, 5).

7. For example, in *Deus Caritas Est*, Pope Benedict offers his own catalog of social encyclicals, omitting both Pius XII's radio message of 1941 and John XXIII's encyclical *Pacem in Terris*, while including *Mater et Magistra* (no. 27). In *Populorum Progressio*, on the other hand, Paul VI includes both Pius's radio message and *Pacem in Terris* in his list of social encyclicals (no. 2). In *Laborem Exercens*, Pope John Paul II includes *Pacem in Terris*, and mentions the Conciliar document *Gaudium et Spes* as well, but omits Pius's radio message (no. 2). In *Sollicitudo Rei Socialis*, John Paul once again includes Pius's radio message (note 2).

8. DCE, no. 27.

9. For simplicity's sake, I am including Paul VI's *Octogesima Adveniens* in the list of social encyclicals, although technically it is an apostolic letter rather than an encyclical.

10. In his 1991 encyclical letter *Centesimus Annus*, Pope John Paul II specifically ties the Church's social doctrine with Leo's text and the papal documents that comment on it. "Although the commemoration at hand is meant to honour *Rerum novarum*, it also honours those Encyclicals and other documents of my Predecessors which have helped to make Pope Leo's Encyclical present and alive in history, thus constituting what would come to be called the Church's 'social doctrine', 'social teaching' or even 'social magisterium'" (no. 2).

11. QA, no. 39. This title was reiterated by John XXIII (MM, no. 26).

12. CA, no. 5.

13. Thus, in his 1981 encyclical, *Laborem Exercens*, Pope John Paul II wrote: 2.1 "It is certainly true that work, as a human issue, is at the very center of the "social question" to which, for almost a hundred years, since the publication of the above-mentioned Encyclical, the Church's teaching and the many undertakings connected with her apostolic mission have been especially directed" (LE, no. 2).

14. In *Sollicitudo Rei Socialis,* Pope John Paul II wrote that the Church's social doctrine belongs to the field "of theology and particularly of moral theology" (no. 41).

15. FR, no. 85. Pope Benedict XVI reiterated this point in *Caritas in Veritate* saying: "The excessive segmentation of knowledge, the rejection of metaphysics by the human sciences, the difficulties encountered by dialogue between science and theology are damaging not only to the development of knowledge, but also to the development of peoples, because these things make it harder to see the integral good of man in its various dimensions" (CV, no. 31).

16. Thus, in *Caritas in Veritate,* Pope Benedict notes that the unitive and the procreative meaning of sexuality treated by Paul VI in *Humanae Vitae* "is not a question of purely individual morality." Rather, Benedict continues, "*Humanae Vitae* indicates the strong links between life ethics and social ethics" (CV, no. 15).

17. In a commentary on the instruction of the Congregation for the Doctrine of the Faith *Dignitas Personae,* Archbishop Giampaolo Crepaldi, then secretary of the Pontifical Council for Justice and Peace, noted that the instruction "is not a document regarding bioethics alone, but also contains numerous considerations of a political and social nature." After John Paul II's *Evangelium Vitae,* "the theme of life has been tackled on a regular basis not only as a sectoral chapter of personal morals—a dimension it does have—but also as a fundamental dimension of public ethics" (www.zenit.org/article-25203?l=english).

18. In *Caritas in Veritate,* Benedict noted that "Charity... is the principle not only of micro-relationships (with friends, with family members or within small groups) but also of macro-relationships (social, economic and political ones)" (CV, no. 2).

19. See QA, nos. 58, 110.

20. CCC, no. 1943.

21. Memorandum of Cardinal Joseph Ratzinger titled "Worthiness to Receive Holy Communion. General Principles" sent to Cardinal Theodore McCarrick and Archbishop Wilton Gregory, and first made public by the Italian magazine *L'Espresso* in its online edition, July 3, 2004. The full text can be found at http://chiesa.espresso.repubblica.it/articolo/7055?eng=y.

22. The *Catechism of the Catholic Church* maintains this distinction, carefully including the adjective "innocent" in its sweeping prohibition: "The deliberate murder of an *innocent* person is gravely contrary to the dignity of the human being, to the golden rule, and to the holiness of the Creator" (no. 2261, emphasis added).

23. DV, Introduction, No. 5: AAS 80 (1988), 76–77, emphasis added.

24. EV, no. 17 (emphasis in original).

25. EV, no. 17 (emphasis in original).

26. EV, no. 11 (emphasis in original).

27. EV, no. 20.

28. "The Church's social teaching argues on the basis of reason and natural law, namely, on the basis of what is in accord with the nature of every human being. It recognizes that it is not the Church's responsibility to make this teaching prevail in political life. Rather, the Church wishes to help form consciences in political life and to stimulate greater insight into the authentic requirements of justice as well as greater readiness to act accordingly, even when this might involve conflict with situations of personal interest" (DCE, 28a).

29. GS, no. 26.

30. CCC, no. 1907.

31. EV, no. 101.

32. EV, no. 72.

33. See, for example, the excellent article by Jean-Marie Cardinal Lustiger "Liberty, Equality, Fraternity" (*First Things* 76 [October 1997]: 38–45).

34. SRS, no. 42.

35. CCC, 2448.

36. See Romans 13:1–3; Titus 3:1.

37. CCC, no. 1902, citing St. Thomas Aquinas, S.Th I-II.93.3, ad 2.

38. See CCC, no. 2242.

39. See CCC, no. 1903.

40. "Abortion and euthanasia are thus crimes which no human law can claim to legitimize. There is no obligation in conscience to obey such laws; instead there is a *grave and clear obligation to oppose them by conscientious objection*" (EV, no. 73).

41. "The attainment of the common good is the sole reason for the existence of civil authorities" (PT, no. 54).

42. EV, no. 70.

43. EV, no. 101.

44. See Thomas D. Williams, "On Refusing Holy Communion to Anti-Life Legislators: Canonical, Moral and Pastoral Considerations," *Alpha Omega* 7/3 (2004): 377–92.

45. Mario Cuomo, "Religious Belief and Public Morality," address delivered on September 13, 1984, at the University of Notre Dame, South Bend, IN (http://pewforum.org/docs/index.php?DocID=14).

46. See CV, no. 28.

Chapter 4 / A Presumption Against Violence?

1. An earlier version of this chapter was presented as a paper as part of the John Henry Cardinal Newman Lecture series entitled *Violence, Forgiveness and the Moral Order*, at the Cosmos Club, Washington, D.C., April 25, 2008.

2. CV, no. 29.

3. Georges Sorel, *Reflections on Violence*, "Introduction to the First Publication," (1908), (New York: Collier Books, 1972), 60.

4. Hannah Arendt, *On Violence* (New York and San Diego: Harcourt Brace & Company, 1969), 8.

5. The literature here is far too vast to enumerate, but by way of example some such studies include John Archer, "Sex Differences in Aggression in Real-World Settings: A Meta-Analytic Review," *Review of General Psychology* (2004), 8/4: 291–322; James Silverberg and J. Patrick Gray, *Aggression and Peacefulness in Humans and Other Primates* (Oxford: Oxford University Press, 1991); Richard E. Tremblay, "The Development of Aggressive Behaviour During Childhood: What Have We Learned in the Past Century?" *International Journal of Behavioral Development*, 24 (2000): 129–141; Charles W. Turner, John Layton, and Lynn S. Simons, "Naturalistic Studies of Aggressive Behavior: Aggressive Stimuli, Victim Visibility and Horn Honking," *Journal of Personality and Social Psychology* 31 (June, 1975): 1098–1107.

6. Here, too, the literature extensive, but a small simple could include Craig A. Anderson, and Karen E. Dill, "Video Games and Aggressive Thoughts, Feelings and Behavior in the Laboratory and in Life," *Journal of Personality and Social Psychology*, 78 (2000): 772–790; Jonathan L. Freedman, *Media Violence and Its Effect on Aggression: Assessing the Scientific Evidence*, (Toronto: University of Toronto Press, 2002); L. Rowell Huesmann, and Leonard D. Eron (eds.), *Television and the Aggressive Child: A Cross-National Comparison*, (Hillsdale, NJ: Lawrence Erlbaum Associates, 1986).

7. Steven Pinker, "A History of Violence," *The New Republic Online* (April 19, 2007), http://pinker.wjh.harvard.edu/articles/media/2007_03_19_New%20 Republic.pdf.

8. James Gilligan, MD, *Violence: Our Deadly Epidemic and Its Causes* (New York: G. P. Putnam's Sons, 1996), 5.

9. VS, no. 80.

10. For a fuller list, see GS, no. 27.

11. Aristotle, *Nichomachean Ethics* 2.6: 1107a9–16 (trans. Ross-Ackrill-Urmson).

12. John Hymers, "Regrounding the Just War's 'Presumption Against Violence' in George Weigel," *Ethical Perspectives* 11 (2004), 111.

13. Saint Thomas discusses this in several places: *In II Sent.*, d. 40, a. 5; *S. Th.*, I-II.18.9; *De Malo*, II.4.5.

14. Aquinas treats of these actions "indifferent in species" in *S. Th.*, I-II.18.8.

15. Though this language may sound similar to that employed by consequentialist and proportionalist authors, I wish to quickly point out some essential differences. In the first place, proportionalism makes a distinction between the area of "goodness" and that of "rightness." Good and evil would

be used only to describe persons according to their intentions, whereas "right" and "wrong" would properly describe actions in accord with their ability to promote greater pre-moral goods and reduce pre-moral evils. Second, as a consequence of this, one may not speak of actions as morally good or evil in themselves (intrinsically evil acts would not exist nor would absolute moral norms). Any types of action could become correct if in its concrete circumstances it was able to promote greater pre-moral goods or avoid pre-moral evils. One should not assume, however, that consequentialist authors promote a system of amorality. In general, they would agree that actions such as "enslavement" or "killing an innocent person" or "committing adultery" are wrong, since they would provoke grave pre-moral evils. Yet the possibility always remains open that in certain circumstances these actions could become right.

16. Thomas Aquinas, *S. Th.* II-II.120.1 resp.; II-II.62.5 ad 1.

17. Thomas Aquinas, *S. Th.* I-II.18.8 resp.

18. Or as Aquinas writes, citing pseudo-Dionysius, "Non tamen est actio bona simpliciter, nisi omnes bonitates concurrant, quia quilibet singularis defectus causat malum, bonum autem causatur ex integra causa, ut Dionysius dicit, IV cap. De div. Nom" (*S. Th.* I-II.18.4 ad 3).

19. Aquinas uses the example of theft from a generic place versus theft from a holy place, which by moral species becomes an act of sacrilege. "Consequently to steal from a holy place has an additional repugnance to the order of reason. And thus place, which was first of all considered as a circumstance, is considered here as the principal condition of the object, and as itself repugnant to reason" (*S. Th.*, I-II.18.10).

20. This ethical school grew around the book, *Situation Ethics: The New Morality* (Philadelphia: Westminster Press, 1966), by Episcopal priest Joseph Fletcher, a work that was in turn based on the theses of his 1959 lecture, "The New Look in Christian Ethics."

21. In the magnum opus once attributed to Hippocrates, *Epidemics* (Book I, Section XI), we read: "As to diseases, make a habit of two things: to help, or at least to do no harm." It was the Roman physician Galen who purportedly later translated the phrase into Latin as *Primum non nocere.*

22. We will examine this topic in greater detail in the following chapter.

23. EV, no. 56.

24. United Nations Convention Against Torture and Other Cruel, Inhuman, and Degrading Treatment or Punishment, Arts. 2.2, 2.3, adopted December 10, 1984 and entering into force on June 26, 1987 (G.A. Res. 39/46), http://daccessdds.un.org/doc/RESOLUTION/GEN/NR0/460/23/IMG/NR0 46023.pdf?OpenElement.

25. See CCC, no. 2297; GS, no. 27.

26. Thus, David Sussman writes that "there is something morally special about torture that distinguishes it from most other kinds of violence, cruelty, or degrading treatment." He goes on to deny that the wrongness of torture can be fully grasped by understanding it as just an extreme instance of more general moral categories. "I argue," he writes, "that there is a core concept of what constitutes torture that corresponds to a distinctive kind of wrong that is not characteristically found in other forms of extreme violence or coercion, a special type of wrong that may explain why we find torture to be more morally offensive than other ways of inflicting great physical or psychological harm" (David Sussman, "What's Wrong with Torture?" *Philosophy & Public Affairs* 33 [winter 2005]: 1–33, at 3).

27. See Seumas Millar, "Torture," *Stanford Encyclopedia of Philosophy* (entry first published Feb 7, 2006 with substantive revision Jan 5, 2008), http://plato.stanford.edu/entries/torture/#Bib.

28. See *Acta Apostolicae Sedis [AAS]* 44 [1952]:779–89, esp. 782). Under a different name, this same principle was discussed by Saint Thomas Aquinas regarding mutilation and amputation of members and cited by moralists with little modification of Aquinas' arguments. See *Summa Theologiae*, II-II.65.1.

29. J. J. Lynch, "mutilation," in *The New Catholic Encyclopedia*, Vol. X, p. 145.

30. See, for example, C.-R. Billuart, *Summa Sancti Thomae Hodiernis Academiarum Moribus Accomodata*, Paris, 1870, Vol. IV, dissert. X, art. IX, n. 1.

31. Pope Pius XII, *AAS* 44 (1952), 782.

32. CCC, no. 2296.

33. Thomas Aquinas, *S. Th.*, II-II.64.2, resp..

34. Pius XII, Address to the First International Congress of Histopathology of the Nervous System (14 September 1952), *AAS* 14 (1952): 786–7.

35. For the following synthesis, I rely on John Gallagher, CSB, in his essay "The Principle of Totality: Man's Stewardship of his Body," in *Moral Theology Today: Certitudes and Doubts* (Saint Louis: The Pope John Center, 1984): 217–42. Gallagher in turn refers to Bert J. Cunningham, *The Morality of Organ Transplantation*, (Washington D.C.: Catholic University of America Press, 1944).

36. *AAS* 50 (1958): 693–4.

37. HV, nos. 3, 14, 17.

38. CCC, no. 2297.

Chapter 5 / Capital Punishment and the Just Society

1. See M. Marazziti, "Perché non uccidere?" in *Non uccidere: Perché è necessario abolire la pena di morte* (Milan, Guerini e associati, 1998), 7.

2. David Gelertner, "What Do Murderers Deserve?" *Commentary Magazine* (April) 1998, available at http://www.utne.com/1999–03–01/WhatdoMurderers Deserve.aspx.

3. Deuteronomy similarly states: "Show no pity: life for life, eye for eye, tooth for tooth, hand for hand, foot for foot" (Deut 19:21), and Exodus specifies that for injury "you shall give life for life, eye for eye, tooth for tooth, hand for hand, foot for foot, burn for burn, wound for wound, stripe for stripe" (Exod 21:23–25).

4. See Saint Ambrose, *Epist. 25 ad Studium*, PL 16: 1083–1086.

5. CCC, no. 2266.

6. The *Catechism* condemns torture as a means to punish the guilty as "contrary to respect for the person and for human dignity" (CCC, 2297).

7. CCC, 2267.

8. GS, 26.

9. See CCC, 1930, 1935, 1944, 1945, 1956, 1978.

10. *Summa Theologiae*, II-II.64.2 ad 3.

11. Germain Grisez, *Living a Christian Life*, vol. 2 of the series *The Way of the Lord Jesus* (Quincy, IL, Franciscan Press, 1993), 893, footnote 107.

12. The *Catechism*, citing the declaration of the Congregation for the Doctrine of the Faith, *Donum Vitae*, speaks of the inalienable rights of the person which "belong to human nature and are inherent in the person by virtue of the creative act from which the person took his origin" and specifically mentions "every human being's right to life and physical integrity from the moment of conception until death" (CCC, 2273).

13. EV, no. 57.

14. Karol Wojtyla, *Love and Responsibility*, trans. H.T. Willetts (London: William Collins Sons & Co. Ltd, 1995), 41.

15. Ibid. 42.

16. DM, no. 12.

17. CV, no. 6.

18. Pius XII, Address to the Italian Association of Catholic Jurists (5 February 1955), *AAS* 47 (1955) 81, *Catholic Mind* 53 (June 1955), 381.

19. Lactantius, *Divinarum Institutionum*, V, 20, PL 6: 707–708.

20. Tertullian, *De Idolatria*, 17, PL 1: 763–764.

21. Cyprian, *Epist*. 56, 4, PL 4: 362.

22. Ambrose, *De Officiis*, 3, 4, PL 16: 161; *Epist. 25 ad Studium*, PL 16: 1083–1086.

23. Cyprian, *Epist. ad Donatum*, 4, PL 4: 208.

24. Augustine, *De Civitate Dei*, I, 21, PL 41: 35.

25. Thomas Aquinas, *S. Th.*, II-II.64.2. St. Thomas' approach based on the protection of the community from a dangerous member of society resembles the modern application of legitimate defense. His analogy of individual to community as part to whole, however, must be attenuated. In speaking of the limits of public authority over the physical being of citizens, Pope Pius XII distinguished between a physical organism, which "has a unity subsisting in itself," and whose members

have no sense or finality outside the whole organism, and the moral community which "is not a physical unity subsisting in itself and its individual members are not integral parts of it" (Pius XII, *Address to the First International Congress of Histopathology of the Nervous System* (14 September 1952), *AAS* 14 [1952], 786–7).

26. The first non-theological work was a small volume entitled *Dei delitti e delle pene*, written in 1764 by Cesare Beccaria. Among theologians the first to write against capital punishment was the abbot Cesare Malanima, who in 1786 published *Commento filosofico-critico sopra i delitti e le pene secondo il gius divino*.

27. See, for example, Giovanni Bucceroni, *Institutiones Theologiae Moralis* (Rome, 1898), 301.

28. Logically, if the preservation of public peace were an absolute value, not only the death penalty, but also torture and other "efficient" measures would be acceptable to achieve it. In focusing solely on ends, the consequentialist argument fails to take sufficiently into account the intrinsic moral quality of the means to be employed. This same defect can be found in arguments for the deterrent efficacy of capital punishment. Leaving aside the highly debated results of studies on the topic, pragmatic arguments based on deterrence beg the more fundamental question of the morality of executing criminals.

29. Innocent I, *Epist.* 6, c. 3. 8, *ad Exsuperium, Episcopum Tolosanum*, (405), PL 20, 495.

30. Nicholas I, *Epist.* 97, 25: *Responsa ad Consulta Bulgarorum*, PL 119, 991.

31. Some affirm that Nicholas did not intend to take a stand on the principle of the death penalty, but only the excessive facility with which recourse was had to such punishment. See, for example, Lino Ciccone, *«Non uccidere»: Questioni di morale della vita fisica* (Milan, Edizioni Ares, 1984), 79.

32. DS 795/425.

33. Leo XIII, PO, no. 2 (*ASS* 24 [1891–92], 203).

34. Pius XII, *To the San Luca Medical-Biological Union*, (12 November 1944), VI, 191.

35. Pius XII, *Address to the First International Congress of Histopathology of the Nervous System* (14 September 1952), XIV, 328. It should be borne in mind that in this address Pius was seeking to underscore the narrow limits of State sovereignty over the lives of citizens, and not to articulate a theory of justification of the death penalty.

36. A. Günthör, *Chiamata e risposta: Una nuova teologia morale*, Vol. III (Alba: Edizioni Paoline, 1979), 557–558.

37. LG, no. 25. This teaching was formally restated and explicated by the Congregation for the Doctrine of the Faith in its June 29, 1998 "Doctrinal Commentary on the Concluding Formula of the *Professio fidei*," issued as a companion to the *motu proprio* apostolic letter *Ad Tuendam Fidem*. The

Commentary reads: "As examples of *doctrines belonging to the third paragraph*, one can point in general to teachings set forth by the authentic ordinary Magisterium in a non-definitive way, which require degrees of adherence differentiated according to the mind and the will manifested; this is shown especially by the nature of the documents, by the frequent repetition of the same doctrine, or by the tenor of the verbal expression" (no. 11).

38. EV, no. 56.

39. Ibid.

40. CCC, no. 2267.

41. EV, no. 55.

42. The Pope intentionally uses the term *absolute* when describing the value and inviolability of innocent human life, a term he does not apply to the unjust aggressor. See EV, no. 57.

43. OT, no. 16.

44. EV, no. 56.

45. *ZENIT News Service*, September 15, 1997.

46. "The Church's wisdom has always pointed to the presence of original sin in social conditions and in the structure of society: 'Ignorance of the fact that man has a wounded nature inclined to evil gives rise to serious errors in the areas of education, politics, social action and morals'" (CV, no. 34, citing CCC, no. 407). See also CA, no. 25).

47. CL, no. 37.

48. National Conference of Catholic Bishops, "Statement on Capital Punishment" (November 1980), 2.10–13, in *Pastoral Letters*, ed. Nolan, 4:430–31.

Chapter 6 / The Church and Economic Development

1. An earlier version of this chapter was delivered as a paper at the Acton Institute international seminar, *Has International Development Failed the Poor? Populorum Progressio 40 Years Later*, at the Pontifical Athenaeum Regina Apostolorum in Rome on February 28, 2008.

2. Although progress and development are not exactly the same thing, here we will treat them as synonyms, following the practice of the papal magisterium. In its English translations of papal encyclicals, the Holy See interchangeably uses the terms "development" and "progress" for the Latin word "*progressio.*"

3. CV, no. 8.

4. This misconception was given scholarly justification by J. B. Bury's widely read book, *The Idea of Progress: An Inquiry into its Origin and Growth* (London: MacMillan, 1920).

5. See, for example, Robert Nisbet, *History of the Idea of Progress* (New York: Basic Books, 1980).

6. See Ludwig Edelstein, *The Idea of Progress in Antiquity* (Baltimore: The Johns Hopkins University Press, 1967).

7. Robert Nisbet, "Idea of Progress: A Bibliographical Essay," in *Literature of Liberty: A Review of Contemporary Liberal Thought*, II/1 (January/March 1979), 13.

8. Ibid.

9. Saint Augustine, *The City of God*, X, 14.

10. See Auguste Comte, *Positive Philosophy* (1830), tr. Harriet Martineau (New York: Calvin Blanchard, 1855).

11. In his book *Values in a Time of Upheaval*, Ratzinger asserted that progress "has always been a word with a mythical ring" and noted that progress, especially in a moral sense, can never definitively be achieved, since man, "precisely as man, remains the same in primitive and in technologically developed situations" (Joseph Ratzinger, *Values in a Time of Upheaval* [San Francisco: Ignatius Press, 2006], 25).

12. DCE, no. 31b.

13. Ibid.

14. Ibid.

15. SS, no. 22.

16. SS, no. 17.

17. SS, no. 23.

18. SS, no. 22. See also CV, nos. 14, 23.

19. This cautious judgment of human progress stands in stark contrast to John Paul's theological reading of progress *in Christ*, which follows the general lines of Augustine's pre-Enlightenment thesis. John Paul wrote that a part of this divine plan, which begins from eternity in Christ, "is our own history, marked by our personal and collective effort to raise up the human condition and to overcome the obstacles which are continually arising along our way." In Christ, "[t]he dream of 'unlimited progress' reappears, radically transformed by the new outlook created by Christian faith, assuring us that progress is possible only because God the Father has decided from the beginning to make man a sharer of his glory in Jesus Christ risen from the dead, in whom 'we have redemption through his blood...the forgiveness of our trespasses' (Eph 1:7)" (SRS, no. 31).

20. EV, no. 64.

21. EV, no. 17.

22. LW, no. 9

23. LF, no. 11.

24. LE, no. 26.

25. This comes across with exceptional clarity in a letter Paul wrote just four years after *Populorum*. "Since the nineteenth century, western societies and, as a result, many others have put their hopes in ceaselessly renewed and indefinite progress. They saw this progress as man's effort to free himself in face of the

demands of nature and of social constraints; progress was the condition for and the yardstick of human freedom. Progress, spread by the modern media of information and by the demand for wider knowledge and greater consumption, has become an omnipresent ideology. Yet a doubt arises today regarding both its value and its result. What is the meaning of this never-ending, breathless pursuit of a progress that always eludes one just when one believes one has conquered it sufficiently in order to enjoy it in peace?" (OA, no. 41).

26. PP, no. 19.

27. Ibid.

28. PP, no. 14.

29. See especially nos. 53–72.

30. PP, no. 14.

31. Ernest L. Fortin, "The Trouble with Catholic Social Thought," in *Human Rights, Virtue, and the Common Good: Untimely Meditations on Religion and Politics*, vol. 3 of *Ernest L. Fortin: Collected Essays*, ed. J. Brian Benestad (Lanham, MD: Rowman & Littlefield, 1996), 309.

32. This was manifestly the case with liberation theology. The Congregation for the Doctrine of the Faith felt obliged to correct this error with two consecutive documents: *Libertatis Nuntius* (1984) and *Libertatis Conscientia* (1986). The latter document notes that the evangelical poverty to be pursued consists especially in "detachment, trust in God, sobriety and a readiness to share." It is this poverty "that Jesus declared blessed" (no. 66).

33. Thus, the CDF document *Libertatis Conscientia* declares that poverty "is an evil from which human beings must be freed as completely as possible" (LC, no. 67).

34. Benedict XVI could affirm that emerging from economic backwardness, though insufficient to guarantee integral human development, is nonetheless "positive in itself" (CV, no. 23).

35. PP, no. 41.

36. Benedict XVI raises a similar point in *Caritas in Veritate*, where he notes: "The mere fact of emerging from economic backwardness, though positive in itself, does not resolve the complex issues of human advancement" (no. 23). Benedict notes the fundamentally positive quality of economic progress, while recognizing its insufficiency.

37. PP, no. 19.

38. PP, no. 18.

39. GS, no. 63.

40. GS, no. 64.

41. GS, no. 39.

42. GS, no. 72.

43. See CCC, no. 1906; GS, no. 26.

44. CCC, no. 1908.

45. PP, no. 14, citing L. J. Lebret, O.P., *Dynamique concrète du développement Paris: Economie et Humanisme* (Les editions ouvrieräs, 1961), 28.

46. PRM, no. 17 (my translation).

47. PP, no. 9.

48. PP, no. 8.

49. MM, no. 69.

50. GS, no. 63.

51. GS, no. 66.

52. SRS, no. 14.

53. See also *Libertatis Nuntius*: "The scandal of the shocking inequality between the rich and poor—whether between rich and poor countries, or between social classes in a single nation—is no longer tolerated. On one hand, people have attained an unheard of abundance which is given to waste, while on the other hand so many live in such poverty, deprived of the basic necessities, that one is hardly able even to count the victims of malnutrition" (LN, I, 6).

54. RN, no. 17.

55. Ibid.

56. CCC, no. 1936.

57. CCC, no. 1936.

58. CCC, no. 1937.

59. CCC, no. 1938.

60. The 2006 Nobel Laureate in Economics, Edmund Phelps, argues that there is little disagreement between those on the political left and those on the political right that such an arrangement is ethical. The prevailing view on the left, he asserts, "concedes that inequalities of income are tolerable, on condition that they benefit the lowest-paid workers" ("Economic Justice and the Spirit of Innovation," *First Things* 196 [October, 2009], 27). Phelps notes that few on the left complain about Bill Gates' wealth "precisely because the general perception is that everyone is better off as a result of inexpensive personal computers" (Ibid.).

61. Paul Collier, *The Bottom Billion: Why the Poorest Countries Are Failing and What Can Be Done About It* (Oxford: Oxford University Press, 2007).

62. PP, no. 48.

63. PP, no, 49.

64. PP, no. 48.

65. PP, no. 77.

66. PP, no. 15.

67. PP, no. 35.

68. PP, no. 65. These reflections are repeatedly echoed by Pope Benedict XVI in *Caritas in Veritate*. There he states: "*Integral human development presupposes the*

responsible freedom of the individual and of peoples: no structure can guarantee this development over and above human responsibility" (CV, no. 17).

69. Benedict XVI brings out a similar point in his reevaluation of *Populorum Progressio*. "For a long time," he observes, "it was thought that poor peoples should remain at a fixed stage of development, and should be content to receive assistance from the philanthropy of developed peoples. Paul VI strongly opposed this mentality in *Populorum Progressio*" (CV, no. 42).

70. In *Caritas in Veritate,* Benedict will return to this theme and reiterate this principle in striking terms. "At times it happens that those who receive aid become subordinate to the aid-givers, and the poor serve to perpetuate expensive bureaucracies which consume an excessively high percentage of funds intended for development" (CV, no. 47). Further, he notes that international development aid, "whatever the donors' intentions, can sometimes lock people into a state of dependence and even foster situations of localized oppression and exploitation in the receiving country" (CV, no. 58).

71. PP, no. 35.

72. PP, no. 35. The original encyclical adds, "[A]s We said in Our message to the UNESCO meeting at Teheran,"and the accompanying reference note cites *L'Osservatore Romano*, Sept. 11, 1965; *La Documentation Catholique*, 62 (1965), 1674–1675.

73. CA, no. 32.

74. Ibid.

75. PP, no. 25.

76. CA, no. 32.

77. Pope John Paul II pointed out some of these obstacles in *Centesimus Annus*, emphasizing the importance of the rule of law. There he states that economic activity "cannot be conducted in an institutional, juridical or political vacuum. On the contrary, it presupposes sure guarantees of individual freedom and private property, as well as a stable currency and efficient public services." He went on to say that "[t]he absence of stability, together with the corruption of public officials and the spread of improper sources of growing rich and of easy profits deriving from illegal or purely speculative activities, constitutes one of the chief obstacles to development and to the economic order" (CA, no. 48).

78. CA, no. 33.

79. CV, no. 58.

80. CV, no. 27.

81. CV, no. 41.

82. Ibid.

83. Ibid.

84. Here I refer to "aid" as a stable policy rather than a momentary remedy to immediate need. Some economic aid will always be necessary to assist people

afflicted by crises such as war and natural disasters. Since the human person is an end and never a mere means, the Church would never advocate the suppression of emergency aid—sacrificing those in present need—in favor of a long-term goal of economic development.

85. PP, no. 57.

86. PP, no. 54.

87. We will return to an analysis of the enduring value of *Populorum Progressio* in our final chapter, where we examine in greater depth the meaning of Benedict's statement that *Populorum Progressio* deserves to be considered "the *Rerum Novarum* of the present age" (CV, no. 8).

Chapter 7 / Beyond Distributive Justice

1. An earlier version of this chapter appeared in the journal *Logos* (8/1 [Winter 2005]: 90–101) and is reprinted here with permission.

2. Saint Thomas Aquinas, S.Th. I.21.1.

3. Aristotle, *Nichomachean Ethics*, 1131b.13, tr. H. Rackham (Cambridge, MA: Harvard University Press, 1982), 273. See also 1131a.24.

4. MM, no. 115.

5. CA, no. 32.

6. In fact, in *Caritas in Veritate* Benedict observed the opposite: "If we look closely at other kinds of poverty, including material forms, we see that they are born from isolation" (CV, no. 53).

7. And so Benedict has also stated his conviction that "in the economic sphere, the principal form of assistance needed by developing countries is that of allowing and encouraging the gradual penetration of their products into international markets, thus making it possible for these countries to participate fully in international economic life" (CV, no. 58).

8. Thomas L. Friedman, *The Lexus and the Olive Tree: Understanding Globalization* (New York: Farrar, Strauss and Giroux, 1999).

9. CV, no. 37. See also CV, no. 39, where Benedict states that the civil order, for its self-regulation, requires "intervention from the State for purposes of redistribution."

10. CV, no. 60.

11. CV, no. 60.

12. CV, no. 65, *emphasis* in original.

13. CV, no. 42.

14. CV, no. 42.

15. CV, no. 36.

16. SRS, no. 38.

17. See S.Th. II-II.58.5. See also I-II.60.3 obj. 2; I-II.61.5 obj. 4; I-II.113.1; II-II.58.6; II-II.58.12.

18. CV, no. 38.
19. GS, no. 69.
20. Ibid.
21. RN, no. 8.
22. Ibid.
23. LE, no. 14.
24. GS, no. 69.

Chapter 8 / Global Governance and the Universal Common Good

1. As just a sampling of this consternation, Douglas Farrow wrote: "The frequent rhetoric about human solidarity, embodied in institutions with global reach and authority, for example, left some wondering whether they had picked up the latest white paper from the United Nations" (Douglas Farrow, "Charity and Unity," *First Things* 196 [October 2009], 37). Or as George Weigel wrote, more pointedly still: "And another Justice and Peace favorite—the creation of a 'world political authority' to ensure integral human development—is revisited, with no more insight into how such an authority would operate than is typically found in such curial fideism about the inherent superiority of transnational governance" (George Weigel, "*Caritas in Veritate* in Gold and Red," *National Review Online*, July 7, 2009).

2. Actually, the official Latin text was more subdued than the "real teeth" translation, expressing desire only that "*familiae Nationum notio re efficiatur*," or that the concept of the family of nations might become more real or effective.

3. As Held and McGrew have stated, the achievements of global governance "appear decidedly thin" (David Held and Anthony G. McGrew, *Governing Globalization: Power, Authority and Global Governance* [Malden, MA: Blackwell, 2002], xi).

4. Thus, Stutzer and Frey of the University of Zurich have noted: "It is argued that, rather than reflecting 'world opinion,' [international organizations] represent the specific interests of the donors who fund NGO activities" (Alois Stutzer and Bruno S. Frey, "Making International Organizations More Democratic," *Review of Law and Economics* 1/3 [2005], 306).

5. The distancing of government from the governed means that "taxpayers of the nations funding the international organizations... do not effectively and sufficiently control the behavior of bureaucrats in international organizations" and that the delegation of competencies to international organizations and their policy-making "do not meet adequate procedural conditions to ensure that people in member countries feel like empowered citizens with autonomy and influence"

(Alois Stutzer and Bruno S. Frey, "Making International Organizations More Democratic," *Review of Law and Economics* 1/3 [2005], 306).

6. Aquinas states that "the end of law is the common good" (S.Th. I-II.96.1, resp.).

7. Aquinas later adds: "And as the care of the common weal is committed to those who are in authority, it is their business to watch over the common weal of the city, kingdom or province subject to them" (S.Th. II-II.40.1, resp.). Elsewhere he writes that "in every community, he who governs the community, cares, first of all, for the common good" (Ibid. I-II.21.4).

8. The role of public authority is "to ensure as far as possible the common good of the society" (CCC, no. 1898). Leo similarly noted that "civil power ... was established for the common good of all" (ID, no. 5).

9. CCC, no. 1906; GS, no. 26; cf. GS, no. 74.

10. cf. CCC, nos. 1907–1909.

11. "Each human community possesses a common good which permits it to be recognized as such" (CCC, no. 1910).

12. "In view of the increasingly close ties of mutual dependence today between all the inhabitants and peoples of the earth, the apt pursuit and efficacious attainment of the universal common good now require of the community of nations that it organize itself in a manner suited to its present responsibilities, especially toward the many parts of the world which are still suffering from unbearable want" (GS, no. 84).

13. "Thanks to increased opportunities for many kinds of social contact among nations, a human family is gradually recognizing that it comprises a single world community and is making itself so" (GS, no. 33). "The risk for our time is that the de facto interdependence of people and nations is not matched by ethical interaction of consciences and minds that would give rise to truly human development" (CV, no. 9).

14. CV, no. 33.

15. Ibid.

16. SRS, no. 38. Despite the novelty of the term, John Paul's definition sounds remarkably similar to a much older virtue which Thomas Aquinas called "legal justice." Aquinas, again following Aristotle, wrote that legal (or general) justice is that virtue "which directs human actions to the common good." (See S.Th., I-II.60.3 obj. 3 and ad 3).

17. CV, no. 53.

18. Regarding the moral duty of solidarity in the economic sphere, Pope John Paul wrote: "Therefore political leaders, and citizens of rich countries considered as individuals, especially if they are Christians, have the moral obligation, according to the degree of each one's responsibility, to take into consideration, in personal decisions and decisions of government, this relationship of universality,

this interdependence which exists between their conduct and the poverty and underdevelopment of so many millions of people" (SRS, no. 9).

19. "The ordering of the degrees of attention, the distinction between justified and unjustified neglect of consequences, the boundaries between what we will as the means and what we ought to accept as the secondary consequences, this is all the affair of that *ordo amoris* which sketches out the structure of moral responsibility" (Robert Spaemann, *Happiness and Benevolence*, [Notre Dame, IN: University of Notre Dame Press, 2000], 146). Elsewhere Spaemann notes that "there may be good grounds to give prior attention to self and near neighbours in many cases, since that is what is implied in the realization of our nature, which we grant to others as to ourselves on the basis of the *ordo amoris*" (Robert Spaemann, *Persons: The Difference Between 'Someone' and 'Something'*, [Oxford: Oxford University Press, 2006], 217).

20. CCC, no. 1941.

21. "Solidarity... presupposes the effort for a more just social order where tensions are better able to be reduced and conflicts more readily settled by negotiation" (CCC, no. 1940).

22. "Human society can be neither well-ordered nor prosperous unless it has some people invested with legitimate authority to preserve its institutions and to devote themselves as far as is necessary to work and care for the good of all" (PT, no. 46) . See also CCC, no. 1898.

23. ID, no. 3.

24. "By 'authority' one means the quality by virtue of which persons or institutions make laws and give orders to men and expect obedience from them" (CCC, no. 1897).

25. "Therefore, under the present circumstances of human society both the structure and form of governments as well as the power which public authority wields in all the nations of the world, must be considered inadequate to promote the universal common good" (PT, no. 135).

26. PT, no. 137.

27. David Held and Anthony G. McGrew, *Governing Globalization: Power, Authority and Global Governance* (Malden, MA: Blackwell, 2002), 8.

28. See Ibid., 9.

29. CA, no. 48. See also QA, no. 79, CCC, no. 1885.

30. PT, no. 137.

31. PT, no. 140.

32. PP, no. 78.

33. CV, no. 67. In his speech to the United Nations assembly in 2008, Benedict had underscored more forcefully still the importance of subsidiarity in international relations, noting that the United Nations embodies the aspiration

for a greater degree of international ordering "inspired and governed by the principle of subsidiarity" (Benedict XVI, speech to United Nations General Assembly, New York, April 18, 2008).

34. CV, no. 57.

35. CV, no. 41.

36. CV, no. 57.

37. CV, no. 57.

38. CV, no. 41.

39. CV, no. 24.

40. GS, no. 80.

41. Ibid..

42. And so the Council expressly stated: "Any act of war aimed indiscriminately at the destruction of entire cities of extensive areas along with their population is a crime against God and man himself... The unique hazard of modern warfare consists in this: it provides those who possess modern scientific weapons with a kind of occasion for perpetrating just such abominations" (GS, no. 80).

43. Ibid.

44. Ibid.

45. *Acta Apostolica Sedis* 55 (1963), p. 291.

46. GS, no. 81.

47. CA, no. 51.

48. CA, no. 52.

49. CA, no. 27.

50. CV, no. 67.

51. Joseph Ratzinger, *Values in a Time of Upheaval* (San Francisco: Ignatius Press, 2006), 35.

52. Ibid.

53. GS, no. 84.

54. GS, no. 65.

55. CA, no. 52.

56. Ibid.

57. CA, no. 58.

58. Ibid..

59. CV, no. 53, emphasis in original.

60. CV, no. 34.

61. CV, no. 38, referencing CA, no. 35, emphasis in original.

62. CV, no. 38.

63. CV, no. 22.

64. CV, no. 22.

65. CV, no. 23.
66. See CV, no. 24.
67. See CV, nos. 37, 39.
68. CV, no. 38.
69. CV, no. 27.
70. CV, no. 41.
71. CV, no. 41.
72. CV, no. 42.

Chapter 9 / "Tolerance" and Religious Liberty

1. An earlier version of this chapter was delivered as a paper at the international conference, *Religious Liberty and Relativism,* organized by The Becket Fund for Religious Liberty to commemorate the 40th anniversary of the Vatican II Declaration on Religious Liberty *Dignitatis Humanae* at the Gregorian University (Rome, December 10, 2005).

For an excellent synopsis of the Church's historical development in the area of religious liberty, see Avery Dulles, "Religious Freedom: Innovation and Development," *First Things* (December 2001).

2. The General Assembly of the United Nations proclaimed 1995 the Year for Tolerance on December 20, 1993 (resolution 48/126).

3. Archbishop Fulton Sheen remarks in his waggish style, "The good is never to be tolerated; rather it is to be approved; aye! it is to be loved. You never say, 'I'll tolerate a beefsteak dinner.' Do you tolerate patriotism? Do you tolerate science? . . . Can you imagine a love song in which one changes the word 'love' to tolerate? 'I tolerate you in June, under the moon.' How absurd it is!" (Fulton J. Sheen, *Life is Worth Living* [Image Books, Garden City, NY, 1954], 100).

4. Voltaire did not formally lump superstition and religion together. In fact, he went so far as to state: "Superstition is to religion what astrology is to astronomy: the foolish daughter of a very wise mother" (Voltaire, *A Treatise on Toleration and Other Essays,* tr. Joseph McCabe [Amherst NY: Prometheus Books, 1994], 207). On the other hand, his understanding of superstition includes many aspects of religious faith.

5. Ibid., 161.
6. Ibid., 209.

7. John Locke, for instance, in his *Letter Concerning Toleration,* in no way advocates a universal tolerance but specifically writes on "my Thoughts about the mutual Toleration of Christians in their different Professions of Religion" (John Locke, *A Letter Concerning Toleration* [hereafter *Letter*], edited and introduced by James Tully, [Indianapolis: Hackett Publishing Company, 1983], 23). Concretely that meant, toleration on the part of a confessional Christian state—Anglican— toward other Christians (excepting Catholics).

8. DH, no. 3.

9. "Declaration of Principles on Tolerance," proclaimed and signed by the Member States of UNESCO on 16 November 1995, 1.1.

10. Shaw wrote: "We must face the fact that society is founded on intolerance. There are glaring cases of the abuse of intolerance; but they are quite as characteristic of our own age as of the Middle Ages... we may prate of toleration as we will; but society must always draw a line somewhere between allowable conduct and insanity or crime" (George Bernard Shaw, *Saint Joan*, in "Great Books of the Western World," Vol. 59, 56).

11. "We are obliged to recognize that they themselves were intolerant"(Voltaire, *A Treatise on Toleration*, tr. Joseph McCabe [Amherst NY: Prometheus Books, 1994], 177.

12. "Declaration of Principles on Tolerance," proclaimed and signed by the Member States of UNESCO on 16 November 1995, 2.4.

13. H. R. Fox Bourne, *Life of John Locke*, 2 vols., (London: 1876), I, p. 187. In this regard the political theorist John Dunn reflects that "almost any form of overt religious behavior could under some circumstances constitute a threat to public order" (John Dunn, *The Political Thought of John Locke*, [Cambridge: Cambridge University Press], 1990, 32).

14. cf. Voltaire, *Traité sur la Tolérance, à l'occasion de la mort de Jean Calas*, in vol. II of "Nouveaux Mélanges philosophiques, historiques, critiques" (Paris, 1772), 64.

15. *Letter*, 23.

16. Fox Bourne, *John Locke*, I, 33.

17. *Letter*, 23.

18. "Declaration of Principles on Tolerance," proclaimed and signed by the Member States of UNESCO on 16 November 1995, 1.3.

19. EV, no. 70.

20. DH, no. 2.

21. Ibid.

22. CCC, nos. 1737, 2279.

23. CCC, nos. 2338, 2383, 2391.

24. For a concise statement of the Catholic position regarding the uniqueness of Christ's salvific mission, see DI.

25. Desmond Doig, *Mother Teresa: Her People and Her Work* (Glasgow: William Collins Sons & Co. Ltd., 1976), 137.

26. "If all religions are in principle equal, then mission can only be a kind of religious imperialism, which must be resisted. But if in Christ a new gift, the essential gift—truth—is being granted us, then it is our duty to offer this to others—freely, of course, for truth cannot operate otherwise, nor can love exist" (Joseph Ratzinger, *Truth and Tolerance: Christian Belief and World Religions* [San Francisco: Ignatius Press, 2004], 105).

27. "Or la doctrine catholique nous enseigne que le premier devoir de la charité n'est pas dans la tolérance des convictions erronées, quelque sincères qu'elles soient, ni dans l'indifférence théorique ou pratique pour l'erreur où le vice oó nous voyons plongés nos frères, mais dans le zèle pour leur amélioration intellectuelle et morale non moins que pour leur bien être matériel" (St. Pius X, letter *Notre charge apostolique*, August 25, 1910: AAS 2 [1910], 619).

28. RM, no. 39.

29. Pope John Paul II, *Crossing the Threshold of Hope* (New York: Alfred A. Knopf, 1994), 115.

30. DH, no. 3.

Chapter 10 / A Case for Religious Discrimination?

1. In this encyclical Benedict adds a parallel discussion of the relationship between charity and justice, as we will examine in greater depth in a later chapter.

2. CV, no. 55.

3. CV, no. 55. Recourse to the official Latin text of the encyclical does nothing to mitigate the force of this passage: "*Iudicium de culturarum religionumque opera necessarium fit ad socialem communitatem aedificandam, servato bono communi praesertim ab eo qui politicam gerit potestatem.*"

4. CV, no. 54.

5. CV, no. 55.

6. DH, no. 2.

7. John Locke, *A Letter Concerning Toleration*, Latin and English texts revised and edited with variants and an introduction (The Hague: Martinus Nijhoff, 1963), 49.

8. Esther 3:8–9.

9. DH, no. 6.

10. "The Church and the political community in their own fields are autonomous and independent from each other. Yet both, under different titles, are devoted to the personal and social vocation of the same men" (GS, no. 76).

11. "Fundamental to Christianity is the distinction between what belongs to Caesar and what belongs to God (cf. Mt 22:21), in other words, the distinction between Church and State, or, as the Second Vatican Council puts it, the autonomy of the temporal sphere" (DCE, no. 28a). See also Mt 22:21; Mk 12:17; Lk 20:25.

12. Joseph Ratzinger, *Salt of the Earth: The Church at the End of the Millennium*, an interview with Peter Seewald (San Francisco: Ignatius Press, 1997), 239.

13. Ibid., 240.

14. Ibid., 155.

15. DCE, no. 28a.

16. Thus the Second Vatican Council taught that both Church and State, "under different titles, are devoted to the personal and social vocation of the same men. The more that both foster sounder cooperation between themselves with due consideration for the circumstances of time and place, the more effective will their service be exercised for the good of all" (GS, no. 76).

17. Therefore Ratzinger could write: "It has always been the case in history that not even the Church has had the capacity to reject earthly possession on her own; rather, her possessions have had to be taken away from her again and again, and this forcible removal then turned out to be for her salvation" (*Salt of the Earth: The Church at the End of the Millennium*, an interview with Peter Seewald (San Francisco: Ignatius Press, 1997), 173).

18. GS, no. 76.

19. Joseph Ratzinger, *Salt of the Earth: The Church at the End of the Millennium*, an interview with Peter Seewald (San Francisco: Ignatius Press, 1997), 132.

20. In this regard, the Church's overriding concern reflects Jesus emphatic question: "For what will it profit a man if he gain the whole world but forfeits his life?" (Mt 16:26; see also Mk 8:36; Lk 9:25).

21. CV, no. 11; original *emphasis*.

22. Joseph Ratzinger, *Salt of the Earth: The Church at the End of the Millennium*, an interview with Peter Seewald (San Francisco: Ignatius Press, 1997), 240; *emphasis* added. Thus Benedict also writes: "Denying the right to profess one's religion in public and the right to bring the truths of faith to bear upon public life has negative consequences for true development" (CV, no. 56).

23. Benedict writes that "the Church wishes... to stimulate greater insight into the authentic requirements of justice as well as greater readiness to act accordingly" (DCE, no. 28a).

24. DCE, nos. 29, 28a.

25. "The political community exists, consequently, for the sake of the common good, in which it finds its full justification and significance, and the source of its inherent legitimacy" (GS, no. 74). "The public good is the rule and measure of all law-making" (John Locke, *A Letter Concerning Toleration*, Latin and English texts revised and edited with variants and an introduction [The Hague: Martinus Nijhoff, 1963], 59).

26. Ratzinger declares that "the goal of the state, and hence the ultimate goal of all politics, has a moral nature, namely peace and justice" (Joseph Ratzinger, *Values in a Time of Upheaval* [San Francisco: Ignatius Press, 2006], 24).

27. Ibid., 20.

28. Ibid., 22.

29. Ibid.

30. Ibid., 59.

31. Joseph Ratzinger, *Truth and Tolerance: Christian Belief and World Religions* (San Francisco: Ignatius Press, 2004), 116.

32. "But this means that one is no longer in the business of protecting those things that enjoy legal protection but is merely concerned to prevent opposing interests clashing with each other. This is admittedly logical if morality as such is no longer recognized as something deserving the protection of the law because it is seen as a matter of subjective preference which can only become a matter for legal action if the public peace is in danger" (Joseph Ratzinger, *Church, Ecumenism and Politics: New Essays in Ecclesiology* [Slough, UK: Saint Paul Publications, 1988], 210).

33. CCC, no. 1907.

34. CCC, nos. 1908, 1909.

35. See CCC, no. 1906.

36. Joseph Ratzinger, *Truth and Tolerance: Christian Belief and World Religions* (San Francisco: Ignatius Press, 2004), 142.

37. This idea of the churches is more typical of the liberal tradition. Locke, for instance, wrote: "A church, then, I take to be a voluntary society of men, joining themselves together of their own accord in order to the public worshipping of God in such manner as they judge acceptable to Him" (John Locke, *A Letter Concerning Toleration*, [The Hague: Martinus Nijhoff, 1963], 23). He adds that these churches "the magistrate ought to tolerate, for the business of these assemblies of the people is nothing but what is lawful for every man in particular to take care of" (ibid., 57).

38. DH, no. 3; *emphasis* added.

39. DH, no. 2.

40. DH, no. 4.

41. Joseph Ratzinger, *Truth and Tolerance: Christian Belief and World Religions* (San Francisco: Ignatius Press, 2004), 248–49.

42. Christopher Hitchens, *God Is Not Great: How Religion Poisons Everything* (New York: Hachette, 2007).

43. Ibid., 56.

44. Richard Dawkins, *The God Delusion* (London: Bantam Press, 2006), 36.

45. Joseph Ratzinger, *Truth and Tolerance: Christian Belief and World Religions* (San Francisco: Ignatius Press, 2004), 105.

46. See, for example, Thomas Aquinas, *Summa Theologiae* II-II.81.2.

47. Joseph Ratzinger, *Salt of the Earth: The Church at the End of the Millennium* (San Francisco: Ignatius Press, 1997), 22.

48. Joseph Ratzinger, *Truth and Tolerance: Christian Belief and World Religions* (San Francisco: Ignatius Press, 2004), 65–66.

49. Ibid., 204.

50. Joseph Ratzinger, *God and the World: Believing and Living in Our Time*, a conversation with Peter Seewald (San Francisco: Ignatius Press, 2002), 28.

51. He thus writes that "there exist highly dangerous *pathologies in religion* that make it necessary to regard the divine light of reason as a kind of controlling authority. Religion must continually accept the purification and regulation that reason carries out" (Joseph Ratzinger, *Values in a Time of Upheaval* [San Francisco: Ignatius Press, 2006], 42); *emphasis* in original.

52. Joseph Ratzinger, *Salt of the Earth: The Church at the End of the Millennium* (San Francisco: Ignatius Press, 1997), 22.

53. Joseph Ratzinger, *Truth and Tolerance: Christian Belief and World Religions* (San Francisco: Ignatius Press, 2004), 158.

54. Joseph Ratzinger, *Salt of the Earth: The Church at the End of the Millennium* (San Francisco: Ignatius Press, 1997), 23.

55. Ibid.

56. Ibid., 24.

57. *Manuel II Paléologue, Entretiens avec un Musulman*, ed. Theodore Khoury, « 7e Controverse, », 2 c (Sources Chrétiennes n. 115, Paris 1966), 142–143.

58. See, for example, DCE, no. 1; or CV, no. 29, where Benedict writes that today "people frequently kill in the holy name of God, as both my predecessor John Paul II and I myself have often publicly acknowledged and lamented."

59. Joseph Ratzinger, *Truth and Tolerance: Christian Belief and World Religions* (San Francisco: Ignatius Press, 2004), 144.

60. Joseph Ratzinger, *Salt of the Earth: The Church at the End of the Millennium* (San Francisco: Ignatius Press, 1997), 244.

61. Ibid.

62. Ibid., 244–45.

63. Ibid., 245.

64. Leonardo Boff, "I Cinquecento anni della conquista dell'America Latina: Un 'venerdi Santo' che dura ancora oggi" [The five hundredth anniversary of the conquest of America: A "Good Friday" that is still continuing today], quoted after the Italian version of the text, circulated by the Adista news agency on January 25, 1992 and cited in Joseph Ratzinger, *Truth and Tolerance: Christian Belief and World Religions* (San Francisco: Ignatius Press, 2004), 56.

65. Joseph Ratzinger, *Truth and Tolerance: Christian Belief and World Religions* (San Francisco: Ignatius Press, 2004), 74.

66. Ibid., 74–75.

67. CV, no. 54.

68. CV, no. 55.

69. Joseph Ratzinger, *Salt of the Earth: The Church at the End of the Millennium*, an interview with Peter Seewald (San Francisco: Ignatius Press, 1997), 134.

70. Ibid.

71. See Joseph Ratzinger, *Truth and Tolerance: Christian Belief and World Religions* (San Francisco: Ignatius Press, 2004), 126–29. Though he speaks of the New Age movement as a phenomenon of the 1990s, Ratzinger recognizes that the concept of "New Age," or "Age of Aquarius" was introduced toward the middle of the twentieth century by Raul Le Cour and by Alice Bailey and that the Esalen Institute was set up in California between 1960 and 1970. (See Ibid., 127, n. 11)

72. Ibid., 127.

73. Ibid., 128–29.

74. Ibid., 129.

75. Joseph Ratzinger, *Truth and Tolerance: Christian Belief and World Religions* (San Francisco: Ignatius Press, 2004), 204.

76. See CV, no. 55.

77. Joseph Ratzinger, *Salt of the Earth: The Church at the End of the Millennium*, an interview with Peter Seewald (San Francisco: Ignatius Press, 1997), 23.

78. Joseph Ratzinger, *The Ratzinger Report: An Exclusive Interview on the State of the Church*, with Vittorio Messori (San Francisco: Ignatius Press, 1985), 138.

79. Joseph Ratzinger, *Salt of the Earth: The Church at the End of the Millennium*, an interview with Peter Seewald (San Francisco: Ignatius Press, 1997), 23.

80. Ibid.

81. See CV, no. 55.

82. Joseph Ratzinger, *Values in a Time of Upheaval* (San Francisco: Ignatius Press, 2006), 69.

83. Ibid.

84. Here Ratzinger is referring to Vittorio Possenti, *Le società liberali al bivio: Lineamenti di filosofia della società* (Genoa: Marietti, 1991), 308ff.

85. Joseph Ratzinger, *Salt of the Earth: The Church at the End of the Millennium*, an interview with Peter Seewald (San Francisco: Ignatius Press, 1997), 24.

86. Ibid.

87. Joseph Ratzinger, *Truth and Tolerance: Christian Belief and World Religions* (San Francisco: Ignatius Press, 2004), 204.

88. Ibid., 258.

89. Ibid.

90. Locke writes that "those are not at all to be tolerated who deny the being of a God. Promises, covenants, and oaths, which are the bonds of human society, can have no hold upon an atheist. The taking away of God, though but even in

thought, dissolves all" (John Locke, *A Letter Concerning Toleration*, Latin and English texts revised and edited with variants and an introduction [The Hague: Martinus Nijhoff, 1963], 84).

91. Joseph Ratzinger, *Truth and Tolerance: Christian Belief and World Religions* (San Francisco: Ignatius Press, 2004), 258.

92. Ibid., 180.

93. Ibid., 182.

94. Richard Dawkins, "Let's all stop beating Basil's car," *Edge: The World Question Center* (2006); see www.edge.org/q2006/q06_9.html.

95. One example is the case of terrorism carried out in the name of religion. Since religious fanaticism is one of the sources on which terrorism draws, Ratzinger writes, "*can it be correct to call religion a healing and saving force? Is it not rather an archaic and dangerous force that constructs false universalisms*, thereby leading to intolerance and terror?" (Joseph Ratzinger, *Values in a Time of Upheaval* [San Francisco: Ignatius Press, 2006], 36; *emphasis* in original).

96. The document continues: "However, government is not to act in an arbitrary fashion or in an unfair spirit of partisanship. Its action is to be controlled by juridical norms which are in conformity with the objective moral order" (DH, no. 7).

97. In this instance, the Catholic position would parallel that of the liberal tradition (except for the thorny issue of conscientious objection). Locke, for instance, wrote that nothing illegal should be permitted in the name of religion: "You will say, by this rule, if some congregations should have a mind to sacrifice infants, or (as the primitive Christians were falsely accused) lustfully pollute themselves in promiscuous uncleanness, or practise any other such heinous enormities, is the magistrate obliged to tolerate them, because they are committed in a religious assembly? I answer: No. These things are not lawful in the ordinary course of life, nor in any private house; and therefore neither are they so in the worship of God, or in any religious meeting" (John Locke, *A Letter Concerning Toleration*, Latin and English texts revised and edited with variants and an introduction [The Hague: Martinus Nijhoff, 1963], 65).

98. Joseph Ratzinger, *Truth and Tolerance: Christian Belief and World Religions* (San Francisco: Ignatius Press, 2004), 59.

99. "Cultures are not therefore fixed once and for all in one single form; they have the inherent capacity for progression and metamorphosis, though also of course the risk of decadence" (Joseph Ratzinger, *Truth and Tolerance: Christian Belief and World Religions* [San Francisco: Ignatius Press, 2004], 195)

100. Joseph Ratzinger, *Church, Ecumenism and Politics: New Essays in Ecclesiology* (Slough, UK: Saint Paul Publications, 1988), 188.

101. Joseph Ratzinger, *Turning Point for Europe? The Church in the Modern World—Assessment and Forecast* [San Francisco: Ignatius Press, 1994], 139.

102. Ibid., 56.

103. Joseph Ratzinger, *Truth and Tolerance: Christian Belief and World Religions* (San Francisco: Ignatius Press, 2004), 251.

Chapter 11 /*Deus Caritas Est and Catholic Social Thought*

1. The establishment of a semi-official canon of social encyclicals has been chiefly the work of the popes themselves, who in their own social teaching often make explicit reference to the social documents that have preceded them. This custom grew out of the commemorative encyclicals celebrating different anniversaries of Leo XIII's *Rerum Novarum*, beginning with Pius XI's 1931 encyclical *Quadragesimo Anno*.

2. In his inaugural homily, Pope Benedict expressly eschewed the question of a "program" for his pontificate. "At this moment there is no need for me to present a programme of governance. I was able to give an indication of what I see as my task in my Message of Wednesday 20 April, and there will be other opportunities to do so. My real programme of governance is not to do my own will, not to pursue my own ideas, but to listen, together with the whole Church, to the word and the will of the Lord, to be guided by Him, so that He himself will lead the Church at this hour of our history" (Homily of Pope Benedict XVI at the Mass for the inauguration of his pontificate, St. Peter's Square, April 24, 2005).

3. DCE, no. 28a.

4. Cf. DCE, no. 26.

5. DCE, no. 26.

6. DCE, no. 28a. In this, Benedict is simply restating settled Catholic teaching regarding the nature and role of the State. Thus John XXIII wrote that the whole raison d'être of the State "is the realization of the common good in the temporal order" (MM, no. 20) and "the justification of all government action is the common good" (MM, no. 151), and finally: "The attainment of the common good is the sole reason for the existence of civil authorities" (PT, no. 54). See also: RN, nos. 32, 35, 51; QA, nos. 25, 110; GS, no. 74; OA, no. 46; LE, no. 20; CL, no.42; CA, nos. 11, 40.

7. DCE, no. 28a.

8. DCE, no. 22.

9. DCE, no. 20.

10. DCE, no. 21.

11. DCE, no. 25a.

12. See Matt 20:25–28.

13. DCE, no. 22.

14. DCE, no. 21.

15. See DCE, no. 23.

16. DCE, no. 25a.

17. DCE, no. 29.

18. DCE, no. 28b.

19. DCE, no. 28b. See parallels in earlier Magisterial texts. In *Rerum Novarum*, Leo wrote: "At the present day many there are who, like the heathen of old, seek to blame and condemn the Church for such eminent charity. They would substitute in its stead a system of relief organized by the State. But no human expedients will ever make up for the devotedness and self sacrifice of Christian charity" (no. 30). Similarly, Pius XI wrote in *Quadragesimo Anno*: "How completely deceived, therefore, are those rash reformers who concern themselves with the enforcement of justice alone—and this, commutative justice—and in their pride reject the assistance of charity! Admittedly, no vicarious charity can substitute for justice which is due as an obligation and is wrongfully denied. Yet even supposing that everyone should finally receive all that is due him, the widest field for charity will always remain open. For justice alone can, if faithfully observed, remove the causes of social conflict but can never bring about union of minds and hearts" (no. 137).

20. DCE, no. 28b.

21. Ibid.

22. DCE, no. 31a.

23. Ibid.

24. DCE, no. 31b.

25. DCE, no. 33.

26. DCE, no. 31c.

27. Ibid.

28. DCE, no. 29.

29. See DCE, no. 28a.

30. DCE, no. 28a.

31. DCE, no. 28a.

32. Ibid.

33. GS, no. 22.

34. DCE, no. 28a.

35. DCE, no. 29.

36. See also GS, no. 76: "It is very important, especially where a pluralistic society prevails, that there be a correct notion of the relationship between the political community and the Church, and a clear distinction between the tasks which Christians undertake, individually or as a group, on their own responsibility as citizens guided by the dictates of a Christian conscience, and the activities which, in union with their pastors, they carry out in the name of the Church."

37. See DCE, no. 29.

38. See, *inter alia*, RN, no. 63; QA, no. 137; MM, no. 6; GS, nos. 21, 88; SRS, no. 40; CA, nos. 11, 49.

39. DCE, no. 33.

40. DCE, no. 34.

41. Ibid.

42. DCE, no. 35.

43. Ibid.

44. Ibid.

45. DCE, no. 36.

46. Ibid.

47. Ibid.

48. Ibid.

49. See John 15:4–5.

50. Ratzinger has noted that "in view of the fact that existing law ('positive law') may in fact be unjust, there must be a law that derives from nature, from the very existence of man" (Joseph Ratzinger, *Values in a Time of Upheaval* [San Francisco: Ignatius Press, 2006], 37).

Chapter 12 / A Paradigm Shift? Caritas in Veritate and the Future of Catholic Social Thought

1. Matt. 13:52.

2. "This twofold dimension is typical of her teaching in the social sphere. On the one hand it is constant, for it remains identical in its fundamental inspiration, in its 'principles of reflection,' in its 'criteria of judgment,' in its basic 'directives for action,' and above all in its vital link with the Gospel of the Lord. On the other hand, it is ever new, because it is subject to the necessary and opportune adaptations suggested by the changes in historical conditions and by the unceasing flow of the events which are the setting of the life of people and society" (SRS, no. 3).

3. Lord Brian Griffiths, *London Times*, July 13, 2009.

4. SRS, no. 2.

5. CV, no. 8.

6. QA, no. 39; MM, no. 26.

7. CA, no. 5.

8. Scott P. Richert, "First Thoughts on *Caritas in Veritate*," July 7, 2009 (http://catholicism.about.com/b/2009/07/07/first-thoughts-on-caritas-in-veritate.htm).

9. CA, no. 3.

10. See CV, no. 10.

11. See CV, no. 12.

12. QA, no. 2.

13. CV, no. 10.

14. CV, no. 11.

15. CV, no. 11, referencing PP, no. 14.

16. CV, no. 18.

17. CV, no. 18.

18. CV, no. 11.

19. CV, no. 13.

20. CV, no. 16, emphasis added.

21. RN, no. 30. Pius XI similarly decried "rash reformers" who would concern themselves with justice alone while rejecting the assistance of charity. Even supposing that everyone should finally receive all that is due him, Pius reasoned, "the widest field for charity will always remain open. For justice alone can, if faithfully observed, remove the causes of social conflict but can never bring about union of minds and hearts" (QA, no. 137, *AAS* 23 [1931], 223).

22. It would be mistaken to suppose that Benedict's special emphasis on charity represents a departure from past social teaching. John XXIII, for instance, taught that charity "summarizes the whole of the Church's social teaching and activity" (MM, no. 6). It is rather the case that Benedict wishes to underscore this element of Catholic social doctrine and hold it up for particular consideration.

23. CV, no. 2. In this Benedict echoes the Catechism, which states: "Charity is the greatest social commandment. It respects others and their rights. It requires the practice of justice, and it alone makes us capable of it" (CCC, no 1889)

24. See especially DCE, no. 2, where Benedict writes that "the term 'love' has become one of the most frequently used and misused of words."

25. CV, no. 2.

26. CV, no. 30

27. CV, no. 30.

28. CV, no. 5.

29. CV, no. 6.

30. CV, no. 1.

31. CV, no. 1; "Now it is an outstanding manifestation of charity toward souls to omit nothing from the saving doctrine of Christ" (HV, no. 29).

32. CV, no. 2.

33. CV, no. 3.

34. CV, no. 3.

35. CV, no. 5.

36. CV, no. 4.

37. CV, no. 4.

38. CV, no. 3.

39. CV, no. 1.

40. CV, no. 4.

41. CV, no. 4.

42. CV, no. 6.

43. CV, no. 6.

44. CV, no. 6.

45. CV, no. 6.

46. See, for example, CV, nos. 45–47.

47. CV, no. 34.

48. CV, no. 34.

49. CV, no. 39.

50. See CV, nos. 11, 16–19; PP, nos. 15–16.

51. See CV, nos. 76–77, 79; PP, no. 16.

52. See CV, nos. 41, 57, 67; PP, no. 78.

53. See CV, no. 61; PP, no. 35.

54. See CV, no. 22; PP, nos. 8–9, 29, 57.

55. CV, no. 28, emphasis in original.

56. CV, no. 28.

57. CV, no. 44.

58. CV, no. 44.

59. CV, no. 44.

60. CV, no. 44.

61. CV, no. 28.

62. CV, no. 28.

63. See also EV, no. 20.

64. CV, no. 15; see also EV, no. 101.

65. CV, no. 28.

66. CV, no. 75.

67. CV, no. 75.

68. CV, no.75.

69. CV, no. 75.

70. CV, no. 75.

71. See CA, no. 9.

72. CA, no. 47.

73. See CV, no. 29.

74. See CV, no. 29.

75. "The exclusion of religion from the public square—and, at the other extreme, religious fundamentalism—hinders an encounter between persons and their collaboration for the progress of humanity" (CV, no. 56).

76. CV, no. 29.

77. See CV, no. 56.

78. CV, no. 55.

79. CV, no. 54.

80. CV, no. 55.

81. CV, no. 55.

82. Among the many possible references, the Pope's 2010 message for the 43rd World Day of Peace, *If You Want to Cultivate Peace, Protect Creation*, stands out. See also CV, nos. 27, 67, 69.

83. "Pope Benedict XVI's track record on the environment already has been robust enough to justify a book-length treatment, *Ten Commandments for the Environment* by Woodeene Koenig-Bricker, in which he's proclaimed the greenest pope in history" (John L. Allen, Jr., "Benedict XVI's very own shade of green," *All Things Catholic*, http://ncronline.org/blogs/all-things-catholic/benedictxvi%E2% 80%99s-very-own-shade-green).

84. In *Salt of the Earth*, Ratzinger had noted the essential difference between a Christian ecology "which sets limits to man's caprice, which places normative criteria before freedom" and an anti-Christian ecology, with a New Age inspiration, which "spawned a kind of embarrassment about humanity, about man who, as it were, sucks creation dry" and questions "what man is, after all, and whether he shouldn't take his place once more among the other animals" (Joseph Ratzinger, *Salt of the Earth: The Church at the End of the Millennium*, an interview with Peter Seewald [San Francisco: Ignatius Press, 1997], 134).

85. CV, no. 48.

86. CV, no. 48. He further affirms that "we must recognize our grave duty to hand the earth on to future generations in such a condition that they too can worthily inhabit it and continue to cultivate it" (CV, no. 50).

87. CV, no. 48.

88. CV, no. 51.

89. CV, no. 51.

90. CV, no. 51.

91. CV, no. 48.

92. CV, no. 48.

93. CV, no. 48. Benedict's vision mirrors that of Saint Augustine, from whom he draws inspiration. Compare, for example, the following. "And what is this? I asked the earth, and it said, 'I am not he.' And all things in it confessed the same. I asked the sea and the deeps, and among living animals the things that creep, and they answered, 'We are not your God! Seek you higher than us!' I asked the winds that blow: and all the air with the dwellers therein said, '... I am not God!' I asked the heavens, the sun, the moon, and the stars: 'We are not the God whom you seek,' said they. To all the things that stand around the doors of my flesh I said,

'Tell me of my God! Although you are not he, tell me something of him!' With a mighty voice they cried out, 'He made us!' My question was the gaze I turned on them; the answer was their beauty" (St. Augustine, *Confessions*, Book X, ch. 6).

94. CV, no. 48.

95. CV, no. 51.

96. CV, no. 48.

Index to CST Documents Cited in the Text

Herder & Herder is proud to present books that celebrate what is distinctive about Catholic theology. Each of these books offers a greater appreciation for the enduring value and urgency of Catholic intellectual life in our new millennium.

Grant Kaplan
ANSWERING THE ENLIGHTENMENT
The Catholic Recovery of Historical Revelation

Revelation is one of the most important concepts in Western religious thought. Since the Enlightenment, however, traditional notions of revelation have come under critique, even to the pointof being wholly abandoned. In this book Grant Kaplan examines some of the well-known and lesser-known figures in the Enlightenment and post-Enlightenment, showing that a Catholic retrieval of revelation is possible and even preferable to alternative paths.

Major figures and topics include: Lessing • Kant • Fichte • Schelling • Johannes Kuhn • The philosophy of history • German idealism • The Catholic Tübingen School • The genealogy of modernity • Faith and reason

978-0-8245-2364-0 (pbk.)

Francis Cardinal George, OMI
THE DIFFERENCE GOD MAKES
A Catholic Vision of Faith, Communion, and Culture

"A scholarly and spiritual collection of essays on the role of the Catholic faith in the modern world, from one of the most thoughtful men in the American hierarchy."—*Publishers Weekly*

In contemporary American society, it can seem as though there is little room left for religious faith. Is there any need for belief today? Does God make any difference in our lives? In this wide-ranging vision of Catholic faith, Cardinal George, Archbishop of Chicago, calls us to reflect on how God, revealed in Jesus Christ, makes a difference in everything we do and all that we are. In the light of the risen Christ, Catholics are united to each other, to other Christians, and to people of other religions and no religion at all. By recognizing our identity in communion, we learn that we are not individuals—we can discover our identities only in and through others. Our relations, whether personal or public, make us who are.

To invite use to enter more deeply into this vision, Cardinal George draws from the great voices of Catholic faith, from Cyril of Alexandria, Maxim us the Confessor, and St. Francis of Assisito Popes John Paul II and Benedict XVI. He also weaves in his own experiences of faith—from a moving encounter with a non-Christian in Zambia to the remarkable pilgrimage of young people who observed Pope John Paul II's visit to Mexico City.

978-0-8245-2627-6 (paper)

About the Author

Fr. Thomas D. Williams, LC, Th.D. (www.thomasdwilliams.com) is one of the world's best-known Catholic teachers and apologists. Known to millions as the Vatican analyst for major network news programs, Fr. Williams is a Catholic ethicist who teaches at the Regina Apostolorum Pontifical University in Rome. His previous works include the national bestseller *Spiritual Progress* and *Knowing Right from Wrong*.